ACCLAIM FOR *FIXING FAILED STATES*

"Ashraf Ghani is a practitioner turned theoretician. Drawing on his background at the World Bank and as the first post-Taliban finance minister of Afghanistan, he together with Clare Lockhart develops a comprehensive framework for understanding the problem of state-building. He argues persuasively that this will be the central challenge underpinning world order in our globalized age, and offers practical solutions for meeting it."—Francis Fukuyama, author of *State-Building: Governance and World Order in the 21st Century*

"This book is an important and timely alarm bell for the world's next crisis—and proves that no one knows more about how states function (and don't) than Ghani and Lockhart. We ignore their remedies at our peril."—Hernando de Soto, author of *The Mystery of Capital: Why Capitalism Triumphs in the West and Fails Everywhere Else*

"*Fixing Failed States* provides a brilliantly crafted and extraordinarily valuable analysis of what makes states fail and what makes them succeed. Everyone concerned about improved governance—and particularly public officials at all levels in industrialized, emerging and developing nations alike—will benefit enormously from reading this and studying the great insights it provides."—Robert Hormats, Vice Chairman of Goldman Sachs (International)

"Ashraf Ghani and Clare Lockhart have filled a critical gap in our understanding of development, security and state-building. By combining an insightful analysis of weak and failed states with a clear-eyed proposal rooted in practical experience, the authors provide the international community with both a better understanding of the challenges we face and a solution."—Gayle Smith, Senior Fellow at the Center for American Progress and former Senior Director for African Affairs at the National Security Council

"Ashraf Ghani has held one of the toughest jobs on earth: the Finance Minister responsible for the reconstruction of Afghanistan. This experience grounds the analysis of failed states in a rare sense of realism. Here, he and Clare Lockhart cover the full array of problems that beset failed states, which range far beyond the conventional remit of development agencies."—Paul Collier, author of *The Bottom Billion*

ASHRAF GHANI

CLARE LOCKHART

FIXING FAILED STATES

*A Framework for Rebuilding
a Fractured World*

OXFORD
UNIVERSITY PRESS

OXFORD

UNIVERSITY PRESS

Oxford University Press, Inc., publishes works that further
Oxford University's objective of excellence
in research, scholarship, and education.

Oxford   New York
Auckland   Cape Town   Dar es Salaam   Hong Kong   Karachi
Kuala Lumpur   Madrid   Melbourne   Mexico City   Nairobi
New Delhi   Shanghai   Taipei   Toronto

With offices in
Argentina   Austria   Brazil   Chile   Czech Republic   France   Greece
Guatemala   Hungary   Italy   Japan   Poland   Portugal   Singapore
South Korea   Switzerland   Thailand   Turkey   Ukraine   Vietnam

Copyright © 2008, 2009 by Ashraf Ghani and Clare Lockhart

Published by Oxford University Press, Inc.
198 Madison Avenue, New York, NY 10016

www.oup.com

First issued as an Oxford University Press paperback, 2009

Oxford is a registered trademark of Oxford University Press

Library of Congress Cataloging-in-Publication Data
Ghani, Ashraf, 1949–
Fixing failed states / Ashraf Ghani and Clare Lockhart.
p. cm.
ISBN 978-0-19-539861-8 (pbk.)
1. Failed states.   I. Lockhart, Clare.   II. Title.
JC328.7.G43 2008
341.5'84—dc22   2007038638

1 3 5 7 9 8 6 4 2

Printed in the United States of America
on acid-free paper

Preface

WHEN *FIXING FAILED STATES* was first published, articulating a framework of core state functions for the twenty-first century, there were three types of reaction. Citizens of developing countries and practitioners seeking to assist them thought it was tailor-made for places ranging from Haiti and Kosovo to Somalia and Sri Lanka. Discussions with a wider group of colleagues, however, revealed that the framework had relevance to a much broader range of countries struggling with crafting a pathway forward and finding the right balance between state, market, and civil society in the particular conditions of twenty-first-century globalization, from Mexico and Malaysia to Ghana and Indonesia. Finally, the current global financial crisis has indicated the need for a framework that clearly and broadly describes the core state functions and the rebalancing needed between the state, the market, and civil society across the developed world. It is now clear that at this critical juncture in world history, we need a framework for state functions that can preserve the gains of globalization but also ensure that the social contract of the twentieth century is not lost, for all parts of the world.

THE IMPACT OF THE 2009 ECONOMIC CRISIS

The state took center stage at the Davos meetings in January 2009. The Swiss village has now become synonymous with the power and resilience of the corporate sector. In 2009, however, the who's who of the private sector had only one theme in mind: how state intervention was going to salvage and shape the economy. There was consensus that rescuing globalization would require the state to exercise some of its core functions in more assertive or new ways and that actions would have to be coordinated among states at the global level. Yet it was clear that politicians were improvising in reaction to the events and had not yet mastered a story line to guide the process of global recovery and reconstruction.

Since Thatcher and Reagan's advocacy of the spontaneity of the market, there has been a high degree of trust that the market can correct itself. Alan Greenspan long personified this view, repeatedly arguing that markets should be left to regulate themselves, but in the wake of the crisis testified to Congress that "I made a mistake...something which looked to be a very solid edifice and indeed a critical pillar to market competition and free markets did break down....Yes, I've found a flaw. I don't know how significant or permanent it is. But I've been very distressed by that fact." The issue was to address the question of design of the balance between state and market. With the failure of regulation emerging as one of the key explanations for the current crisis, it is clear that failure is built in to the dynamics of markets and that the state is the only organization capable of orchestrating collective political and social responses at times of market failure. While there is an emerging consensus on the need to rebuild the capability of the state for regulation of the market, the appropriate balance between regulation and private and corporate initiative has yet to be worked out.

Risk taking is inherent to entrepreneurship. A key accomplishment of the twentieth century was to identify and group risks into categories and devise systems of risk management to reduce the risks and increase predictability for entrepreneurs. The instruments ranged from insurance to credit and risk guarantees. However, in the early years of the twenty-first century, prudent management of risk was abandoned. As both the assessment and the management of risk were privatized, the checks and balances between the market and the state were distorted. The net result has been that no one has had a full view of the extent of the crisis or the amount of funds required to rescue the system. All that is required to illustrate this fact is a glance at the ratings of key financial institutions by the major risk assessment groups at the end of 2007 and then the summer and fall of 2008. A corporate or individual investor whose decisions were made on the basis of trust in these ratings will have suffered losses that would have seemed incommensurate with the perceived risk.

THE BALANCE BETWEEN THE STATE AND THE MARKET IN THE DEVELOPED WORLD

The confidence of the state sector in the approaches and practices required to appropriately regulate the current economic system has been deeply shaken by the current crisis. The issue is no longer whether there should be regulation but how, when, and where the state should regulate the market. This is first a question of knowledge. In the short term, the people who are to perform the regulatory function are very likely to be recruited from the ranks of those who were in the corporate financial sector and steeped in business mental models and assumptions. Therefore, in the medium to long term, a renewed spirit of public service will be required through intensive training in think-tanks and research institutions to broaden the perspective of the regulator. Related to knowledge is the issue of rules. Recovery requires speed, but public sector rules generally lack flexibility to allow for the exercise of power by officials. As the legislative branches of governments are going to require increased accountability, state officials will constantly be forced to balance speed and accountability. The third question is the design and implementation of the right instruments. As the experience of AIG shows, the dependence of the private sector on the state has not yet translated into the need for examination of sinecures and privileges acquired during the boom days.

While the first priority will be the restoration of confidence in the global economic system, designing ways to harness globalization is going to be critical. The test here will be creating sufficient state capacity to preempt market failures of the current magnitude while reenergizing the entrepreneurial spirit that permits the dynamic of the market economy. Achieving this dual objective is likely to require an overhaul of current national regulatory systems in OECD countries and emerging economies. It will also require agreement on more standardized mechanisms for data sharing and regulatory responses. In other ways, the regulatory function of the state will have to become the focus of a disciplined approach in practice. The level of knowledge required across the system to understand patterns and react to them transparently will be critical, and this requires harmonizing and standardizing data. Finding new checks and balances between risk assessment and risk management instruments will be a critical part of this equation.

The role of public finance will loom in public policy discussions for decades. Massive stimulus packages will require replenishing the reserves that made the intervention possible. Until new reserves are built, it is likely that difficult trade-offs will have to be made among priorities in public expenditure, and social policy will face particular challenges. The rights of citizenship that have been taken for granted will need to be reconciled with relatively scarce resources. At a time when the savings and retirement accounts of tens of millions of people are decimated by market failures, the state's willingness, capacity, and ability to maintain or expand social policy coverage is reduced. Vulnerable citizens will test the limits of the social contract. Public debate is likely to generate a reversion to the politics of division of a fixed pie, which OECD countries have not witnessed for decades. Management of social conflict will require the renewal and expansion of state capabilities in developed countries that previously considered these to be problems of developing countries. Managing a way out of the crisis is going to require medium- to long-term horizons from politicians, not short-term electoral considerations. Under such circumstances, making the case for aid to developing countries will become increasingly difficult. This makes finding alternative pathways to stability and sound management for all contexts even more urgent.

THE EXPENDITURE CONSTRAINT

"More is better" has been the slogan of the aid lobby. This position, however, ignores the reality of the expenditure constraint. Many developing countries are unable to spend either their own domestic revenues or the aid they receive from abroad. Iraq has spent just 12 percent ($2 billion) of the $17.2 billion allocated since 2005 for the reconstruction of oil, electricity, and water sectors. Of the nation's total revenues from 2005 to 2008 ($116.5 billion), only 71 percent has been spent.[1] Our discussions with the World Bank and other international agencies reveal that this is a general pattern. When examined from a comparative perspective, the surprise is not the expenditure constraint per se but the inability of the aid system to focus systematically on removing that constraint. Ireland, Spain, Singapore—once developing countries—owe their transformations to overcoming this problem through building their own core state functions and being prudent about the type of money they accepted. Development of National Accountability Systems on the one hand and development of a competitive domestic construction industry on the other were the critical ingredients to overcoming the expenditure constraint. The persistent failure of the aid system to harmonize its myriad of rules and regulations around an agenda of building the National Accountability Systems of developing countries, and the insistence of the aid system to implement projects through a largely unregulated contracting system, continue to undermine rule of law, accountability, and transparency. As commitment to aid is likely to be severely tested by public opinion in OECD countries, it is essential that aid become more effective. The key to making a global partnership effective is going to lie in framing the way forward as a state-building agenda.

PROGRESS ON AN INTERNATIONAL STATE-BUILDING AGENDA

There has been increasing recognition by, and convergence among, world leaders on an agenda for state building in recent months. Robert Zoellick, President of the World Bank, has called fragile states "the toughest development challenge of our era." Like Zoellick, the U.S. Army Stability Operations Manual of October 2008 emphasizes the constellation of problems generated by fragile and conflict-affected countries and is designed "to reduce the drivers of conflict and instability and build local institutional capacity to forge sustainable peace, security, and economic growth." As Robert Cooper observed, "there is no substitute for a functioning state." The difficulty has been in moving from the acknowledgment of the problem by leaders to reorganizing the bureaucratic cultures of the organizations that are charged with administering aid. One of the best illustrations is provided by Haiti, where in one report the need "to resolve issues of governance and political instability" headed a long list of failures in the instruments of foreign aid.[2] Despite the acknowledgement of parallel organizations in Haiti and elsewhere, business is continuing as usual at the country level.

The ongoing challenges in countries ranging from Afghanistan, Haiti, Iraq, and Kosovo to Somalia, Sudan, and Zimbabwe make it abundantly clear at the conceptual level that state building—that is, the creation of appropriate systems of governance within a particular society—must be the central objective. However, at the level of implementation, failures continue. Our experience and research indicate that the high level ministerial agreements concluded in recent years in large meetings in Paris and Accra which promised better aid cannot be implemented without building National Accountability Systems and National Programs on the ground. A recent Center for American Progress simulation exercise, testing the tools available to the United States in stabilizing Afghanistan, found that even the "maximalist" tools now available did not go far enough: "Additional tools would be required to achieve fundamentally different development outcomes."

National Accountability Systems move the discussion of governance from the desirable and abstract to the realm of feasible, concrete, and pragmatic actions based in the rule of law. The more the space of accountability is unified around a national system, the easier it is for stakeholders to cohere around a national project and vision and to intensify their loyalty through repeated transactions. When combined with National Programs, coherence can be introduced into developmental planning and implementation. National Programs become mechanisms for accountability and transparent delivery to citizens and have the potential dual virtue of simplifying tasks and allowing priorities to be addressed in sequence while harnessing the energies of the citizens through their participation. Despite the deterioration of the quality of governance in Afghanistan since 2005, most of the successes that have been seen are results of the application of a National Programmatic model. These outcomes range from the Afghan National Army to the health and education system, the National Solidarity Program, the exchange in currency and creation of a public finance system, and the telecoms system.

THE POLITICS OF STATE BUILDING

State building is inherently a political process. The central point that John Dewey made, and as we emphasize in this book, is that politics acquires shape, direction, and meaning through public discussion. The current state of public discourse on the financial crisis leaves little doubt that political discussion finds a concrete anchor in the degree of importance of a core state function or of the state's relation to the market and civil society. The very space for a technical discussion of a core state function requires a prior political agreement and a political settlement that establishes a leadership and management team with the capability to gain and maintain the trust of the citizens. Transparency, accountability, and public voice are therefore not just technical domains but also symbolic expressions of public desire or public frustration. To frame a core state function from a systemic perspective is to call for a politics of strategic, rather than tactical, engagement. Politics then reconnects to moral purpose and becomes a calling rather than a quest for personal power or prestige. Our call for a double compact is therefore a call for a politics of double limitation on abuse of power. Citizen mobilization is essential to challenging corruption and bad governance. Kleptocratic governments, however, consider themselves immune from pressures of civil society and politics of civic engagement and accountability. Changing the behavior of such regimes requires sustained engagement and coherent responses from the international community, rather than looking the other way or ceding to the inevitability of poor management and leadership. Hence the need for a compact between the citizens and the state, on the hand, and between the state and the international community on the other.

ONGOING LESSONS FROM THE FIELD

Our own understanding of statecraft has deepened since the first publication of *Fixing Failed States*, through intensive discussions and facilitations on the ground. We have been honored to have continued to learn from those countries that have successfully transformed and to have been called upon through the Institute for State Effectiveness to help frame the challenge and way ahead for leaders of countries facing transitions. Our continuous engagement both in the front lines of fragile states and with the experience of countries undergoing transformation converge on a single point: statecraft is never complete. As the state has no essence but is a mechanism for the realization of collective goals, it will constantly change. History, however, matters. Understanding patterns of transformation through both the political lens of vision and leadership and the technical lens of management and resource mobilization can make the task of state-builders easier. As we have recently argued, we need to recover capacities that have been lost and, as well, create a new set of instruments to serve the goal of state building in the twenty-first century. In particular we must gain greater command of the art of statecraft, increasing our knowledge and learning to design to context without failing to recognize the importance of vision. Mastering statecraft at these levels requires us to rescue political and social sciences from the abstractions of the ivory tower and to connect them with the lives that we live in the villages, neighborhoods, and workplaces that are the arenas of our interactions and the spaces for the definition of our identities.

As we have studied transitions in more detail from across the world, six factors that drive successful transitions have become clear. The first is the essential factor of a leadership and management team committed to a goal of transforming their country or region. History often speaks of a great man, but careful investigation usually reveals a team of individuals who were committed to being founding fathers and mothers, working across ethnic, religious, or political boundaries. The second factor is a relentless focus on accountability in the management of public finances, often accompanied by a "zero tolerance" attitude to corruption in the public purse; the third, privileging of investment in the human capital of the country, with a long-term plan for establishing capability in the skills necessary to drive the economy and staff the civil service, from accountants and engineers through to plumbers, stonemasons, and agronomists. The fourth factor is channeling the aid money available through their own budget systems to drive the creation of a domestic construction industry, through carefully crafted public–private partnerships, often starting with housing projects. The fifth factor is understanding the need to broaden from a narrow elite to a growing middle class, and the sixth, commitment to transform individuals from subjects to citizens. While often the leadership's early focus lay on establishing basic security, their vision was to win the trust of citizens through social policies.

All our readings make crystal clear that a state-building agenda can only be driven from the country's society and leadership, when different stakeholder groups cohere around a national agenda. While each case often made good use of funding available from external sources, the institution-building process by definition is an endogenous process. Those who assume that state building is a process that can be driven by capital cities miles away from the territory in question are fundamentally misreading history.

BALANCING STATE, MARKET, AND CIVIL SOCIETY

Our identities are shaped and reshaped by the temporal and spatial rhythms of the twenty-first century. The market and civil society had already been globalized in the last decades of the twentieth century. Deferring to the creative market forces, the state had retreated to the background in the Anglo-Saxon world. The financial crisis, however, has brought the state to the center stage. While the state's role is likely to loom large in the next decade, the central question for sustainable development is going to be in finding the balance between the state, the market, and civil society. The massive failure of the financial markets should neither hide the successes of the trading system nor ignore the comparative advantage of the market as an instrument for delivery of goods and services. In the developing countries, suffering from politicization of the market and criminalization of the economy, it is not less but more market that is required.

The point to grasp is that the market is not the product of the invisible hand but an institution created and nurtured by a visible hand under the rule of law. Neither value chains nor supply chains have lost their relevance or their efficacy for alleviating poverty and creating wealth. Redistribution is important in taking care of the vulnerable and needy, but the lives of the poor who constitute the majority of the inhabitants of our planet are not going to be changed without providing them with the instruments to produce wealth. If left to their own devices, neither the market nor the state will be inherently accountable. Civil society is going to be vital not only for harnessing the spirit of volunteerism and civic engagement but also for keeping both the state and the market in check. Our challenge, therefore, is to find a new balance between these three dominant institutions of our time that can align them around the goal of global stability and prosperity.

The very occurrence of the financial crisis at the heart of the developed world is an illustration of our collective vulnerability and the need for fundamental rethinking at the global level. States are going to retain the responsibilities they have to their nations. Resorting to economic nationalism, however, will produce a lose–lose proposition in the medium term, and statesmen need to practice and preach the type of statecraft that can bring about coordinated actions in our interdependent world. As our future depends on it, we must rise to the challenge.

NOTES

1. "Iraq and Afghanistan: Security, Economic and Governance Challenges to Rebuilding Efforts Should Be Addressed in US Strategies," U.S. Government Accountability Office, Testimony Before the Committee on Armed Services, House of Representatives, March 25, 2009; www.gao.gov/new.items/d09476t.pdf.
2. T. Buss and A. Gardner, *Why Foreign Aid to Haiti Failed: A Summary Report of the National Academy of Public Administration* (Washington, D.C.: National Academy of Public Administration, 2006).

Acknowledgments

W̲E̲ ̲W̲O̲U̲L̲D̲ ̲L̲I̲K̲E̲ to thank a number of individuals for their support, advice, and comments over the last several years. They are too numerous to list in full, but for their close readings of different versions of papers and support for the ideas and establishment of the Institute for State Effectiveness we extend special thanks to Chris Anderson, Jack Bell, Lakhdar Brahimi, Michael Carnahan, Robert Cooper, Anis Dani, Ishac Diwan, Lyse Doucet, Karl Eikenberry, James Elles, Rula and Tarek Ghani, Robert Greenhill, Scott Guggenheim, Vivien Haig, Rick Hillier, Marty Hoffman, Lou Hughes, Hilde Johnson, Fred Kempe, Nick and Samantha Leader, Alexander Lennon, Amory Lovins, Simon Maxwell, Bill Neukom, Dick and Deborah O'Neill, Ken Ohashi, Ted Okada, Carlos Pascual, Praful Patel, Eric and Demi Rasmussen, Gabrielle Rifkind, Mitch Shivers, Hernando de Soto, Marin Strmecki, David Thorpe, Ed Tivnan, and Lin Wells.

We are grateful to the citizens and leaders across business, civil society and governments, in countries across the world, including Sudan, Nepal, Lebanon, Kosovo, Kenya, Russia, China, Singapore, Indonesia, and India, who took time to explain patiently their perspectives on the questions this book addresses.

Between 2001 and 2005 Afghanistan was the site where we developed and implemented many of the ideas contained in this book. In particular, the framework we describe informed our work on the design of the Bonn Agreement, the National Development Framework, Securing Afghanistan's Future, the budget of Afghanistan, the national programs, and the outline of the Afghan Compact. Numerous individuals contributed to these programs and made them work. Several took a gamble on new plans such as the National Solidarity Program when they were just an idea, and for this we owe them our thanks.

In January 2005 we made our first full presentation of the set of ideas contained herein at the Lancaster House meeting on fragile states, convened by the United Nations, World Bank, Department for International Development (DFID), and Organisation for Economic Cooperation and Development (OECD), and we have continued to refine them since then. Many of the concepts were improved through a program we led at the World Bank in the late 1990s on institutions and organizations; our thanks go to Jonathan Maack, Pascaline Cure, and Sabine Beddies for their work on this program. In September 2005 the United Nations and the World Bank convened a conference of leaders of postconflict transitions to meet with us at the Greentree Estates to consider the framework that we present here, and the valuable feedback these leaders provided considerably enriched it. Additional opportunities to debate these ideas have arisen during presentations to the UN General Assembly, workshops and retreats at the World Bank, the African Development Bank, discussions with the governments of Norway, Canada, Japan, and the United Kingdom, and meetings with various members of the U.S. government. Conferences and brainstorming meetings became forums in which to present, test, and polish the book's ideas; these took place at Fortune Brainstorm; Technology, Entertainment, Design (TED); the Aspen Ideas Festival; Wilton Park; Ditchley Park; Bellagio; the European Ideas Network; the Rocky Mountain Institute; the Institute for Liberty and Democracy; bar associations; the Trans-Atlantic Policy Network; Highlands; Operation Strong Angel; and the Atlantic Council.

Very special thanks go to Tina Bennett; no one could have asked for a better agent, and she has been a true partner in bringing this material to the public domain. Dave McBride, our editor at Oxford University Press, has provided excellent comments, and the whole team at OUP has been enthusiastic, dedicated, and professional.

Philip Munger shepherded the book into the realm of the possible with dedication and wisdom. Blair Glencorse and Sam Vincent worked with immense skill and commitment to improve the text. The Smith Richardson Institute, DFID, the World Bank, and the Rockefeller Brothers Fund provided timely support.

Ashraf would like to acknowledge his indebtedness to the American University of Beirut, the University of California at Berkeley, Johns

Hopkins University, Kabul University, Brookings, the World Bank, the United Nations, and his colleagues in Afghanistan, as well as international interlocutors during his service in Afghanistan. He would like to express his appreciation to those who nominated him for the UN candidacy, and he is grateful for the opportunity to put forward and discuss a set of ideas and programs for global stability in the context of setting an agenda for the United Nations for the twenty-first century. In particular, he wishes to thank his family in Afghanistan, Lebanon, and the United States, as well as Rula, Mariam, and Tarek for their loving patience and support and for enduring the long absences. He dedicates this book to his wife, Rula.

Clare would like to acknowledge her thanks to Oxford University, the Kennedy School at Harvard University, and law schools in England; these same institutions, as well as the Inner Temple and the Kennedy Memorial Trust, also provided generous stipends and scholarship funds. She is grateful for her experiences at the World Bank, the United Nations, and ISAF-NATO. Lectures and seminars at the NATO Defense College, Shrivenham, Wilton Park, Operation Strong Angel III, the Rocky Mountain Institute, Bellagio, Oxford University, a number of Foundations and other venues have provided indispensable questioning and feedback. Colleagues and friends in Afghanistan particularly made the work possible and enjoyable. She would like to thank the many friends and family who have tolerated and supported the book-writing process, with special appreciation to her parents, Christopher and Rosamund, and to Alice and Edward, and Mary-Ellen. Clare dedicates the book to her grandmother Diana Elles, who has been an inspiration all her life.

Contents

FIXING FAILED STATES

Introduction

W E HAVE A collective problem: Forty to sixty states, home
to nearly two billion people, are either sliding backward
and teetering on the brink of implosion or have already
collapsed. While one half of the globe has created an almost seamless
web of political, financial and technological connections that underpin democratic states and market-based economies, the other half
is blocked from political stability and participation in global wealth.
Within these countries, vicious networks of criminality, violence and
drugs feed on disenfranchised populations and uncontrolled territory.
In a period of unprecedented wealth and invention, people throughout
Africa, Central Asia, Latin America, and the Middle East are locked
into lives of misery, without a stake in their countries or any certainty
about or control over their own futures.

The hundreds of millions of people who are not currently enfran-
chised by the economic and political system want in, not out. The globalized media beam the benefits of the good life into their homes daily.
They see a world on the move and full of opportunity, innovation, and
prosperity, and this defines their expectations. They simply want their
states, economies, and societies to function. But their daily encounters
with the state produce frustration and humiliation. They know that it
is the dysfunctional state that stands between them and a better life.
The yearning for civil order and enfranchisement in the system is the
overwhelming desire of ordinary men and women around the world.

A glaring gap—what we call the sovereignty gap—exists between
the de jure sovereignty that the international system affords such
states and their de facto capabilities to serve their populations and act

as responsible members of the international community. The ground reality is that many states have collapsed and are unable to provide even the most basic services for their citizens. The failure to maintain basic order not only makes fear a constant of daily life but also provides a breeding ground for a small minority to perpetuate criminality and terror. As 9/11 and subsequent attacks showed, people in prosperous countries can no longer take the security of their daily lives for granted. This problem—the failed state—is at the heart of a worldwide systemic crisis that constitutes the most serious challenge to global stability in the new millennium.

Slowly but surely, politicians, generals and business leaders are beginning to realize that we must arrest and reverse state failure. Politicians now understand that issues such as refugee flows and humanitarian action have their root in the failure of states to provide basic opportunities for their citizens. Security organizations recognize that crumbling states are at the root of ongoing conflicts, terrorism, and expanding networks of criminality that traffic in drugs, arms and people. Developmental institutions are beginning to discover that an effective state is the necessary condition for eradicating poverty. And corporations have come to comprehend that market stability and growth stem from strong institutions everywhere, not just in the countries where they do business. A consensus is now emerging that only sovereign states—by which we mean states that actually perform the functions that make them sovereign—will allow human progress to continue.

Moreover, in the twenty-first century, illegitimate networks will not be conquered except through hierarchical organizations that have legitimacy and are rethought in terms of orientation to both citizenship and the flows of globalization. The virtuous, legitimate networks needed to enfranchise populations—through flows of human, financial, and informational capital—cannot thrive in areas of the world that suffer from chronic misgovernance. Groups involved with terrorism, criminality, arms, and narcotics thrive and fester in areas of misrule. The vicious networks they spawn can be controlled only if the state functions and allows society to narrow their space of operation through expansion of a sense of citizenship. Accordingly, solutions to our current problems of insecurity, poverty, and lack of growth all converge on the need for a state-building project. Just as the firm is the most effective unit of organization in the economy, the state is the most effective form of organization of the polity. Only the state can organize power so as to harness flows of information, people, money, force, and decisions necessary to regulate human behavior.

Despite this emerging consensus in the top echelons of the world's wealthy capitals, at the front lines in failed states the current international responses are often counterproductive. People in prosperous countries realize they can no longer ignore these issues but do not know how to react to them. Taken by surprise, we have rushed to address each problem without understanding the whole, using atavistic, haphazard, fragmented, and short-term responses that sometimes exacerbate the collection of problems we set out to fix. Our first impulse has been to use force. (This is nowhere more clearly manifested than in declaring a "war on terror.") But we have reached the limits to the use of force, and neither a war of necessity in Afghanistan nor a war of choice in Iraq has yet succeeded. Despite the presence of NATO and coalition forces, as well as massive infusions of aid, Afghanistan has become the largest producer of heroin in the world. Daily life in Iraq has become a perpetual nightmare of violence and criminality.

While we all agree that global poverty is intolerable, we attempt to deal with it by using mechanisms developed fifty years ago. From Sudan and Somalia to Nepal, East Timor, and Kosovo, the expenditure of tens of billions of dollars over half a century has resulted only in disenchantment and mutual recrimination without many significant breakthroughs in wealth creation. Rather than allowing those we are trying to help to drive the process forward themselves, we insist on imposing our own outdated solutions. As a result of these attempts, many aid practitioners and observers are in despair that the solutions lie beyond our reach and that we are marching toward global disorder.

We argue that there are several problems inherent in current international responses to state failure. First, there is little understanding of what a state needs to do in the modern world to serve its citizens and connect to global flows. Second, there is consequently insufficient understanding of how the international community can help a government acquire the capacity to serve its citizens; rather, we see a random series of efforts to "win hearts and minds" through projects that instead cause frustration and resentment. Third, there is little understanding of the kind of timeline that is required or of the interdependencies between functions that would determine sequences of intervention: rather, projects tend to be confined within the annual budget cycle of whichever capital originated their planning. Fourth, the solutions applied tend to be one size fits all, thereby ignoring the demands of a state's particular context or the new global context—and have proved time and again to be self-defeating. Finally, there is no understanding of shared responsibility, a vision for a coproduced outcome, or an international role that does not involve, at one extreme, imposed solutions that amount to viceregal hubris or, at the other extreme, a type of benign neglect that consigns the international community to the role of interested observers.

Despite the enormity of the task, we believe that the world has the resources and imagination to arrive at solutions to this problem if a different approach is adopted. Failure on the ground has been the result of the inability of the international community to agree on what states actually do and how they can perform these functions. This book attempts to fill this gap. If we look in the right places, the building blocks of an approach to state building materialize. The key lies in examining what successful states actually did in practice. Practice has outstripped theory, and the world is rich in examples of countries that have transitioned from poverty and instability to prosperity and security. Because the change has been gradual, it has not yet been framed. If viewed through the right lens, however, a new paradigm for state building emerges.

Our optimism is based on three arguments. First, the world has generated prosperity on an unprecedented scale. To put it simply, more money than the world has ever known is now in circulation, with trillions of dollars daily on the move, looking for outlets. Second, global knowledge and information technology are expanding at a rapid pace, making it possible for people to communicate with each other more quickly and more affordably than ever before. The world is experiencing an explosion in knowledge, yet the approaches that are being applied to developing countries are dominated either by abstract ideas, which rarely move beyond first principles, or by improvisation in the field. Web-based communities of learning and solution finding are proving that collective problem solving is a much greater asset than the old-fashioned individualized forms of knowledge. Both the young and the old who want to contribute actively to a more secure and prosperous world are exhibiting a new spirit of problem solving. However, the creative power of networks has yet to be fully mobilized in this field.

Third, and most important, there is now a stock of experience in transforming states; practice has been far richer than theories of politics and power. The last sixty years have witnessed enormous progress in innovation in governance, particularly in the relationship between the state, the market, and civil society. As a result, the scale of the challenge is much more manageable than it was in 1945: Europe and East Asia, the two magnets of growth and prosperity today, had then endured cataclysmic wars, and parts of East Asia were to be engulfed in war for another four decades. Nonetheless, clarity of purpose, persistence, and bold commitments paid off handsomely and have left us with a useful stock of knowledge. This knowledge is enhanced by the development of multistakeholder relations and processes that herald the power of networks to support state functionality and create webs of trust.

This book argues for a reorientation in the international response to create capable states. The key to state building is first to agree on a goal and the functions of the state to support this objective and then to follow up with a pragmatic search for means of implementation. Therefore, the book proposes a strategic framework for defining the functions of the state, designing the organizational structure necessary for the performance of those functions, and aligning actors to the goal of state building. It presents ideas for reorganizing international security so that political and economic organizations can serve the purpose of creating and sustaining effective states. When applied to a specific context, our framework translates into a strategic map for understanding the strengths and weaknesses of individual functions. On this basis, specific strategies can then be devised that are tailored to context and deal with the issue of sequencing in a systematic way. Strategies would be cemented through "double compacts" between country leadership and the international community on the one hand and the citizenry on the other. Finally, the book proposes methods for comparative reporting on state capacity in the form of a "sovereignty index" that would be presented each year to the General Assembly of the United Nations and to the annual meetings of the World Bank.

This framework argues for a citizen-based approach to state building: a new legal compact between citizen, state and the market, not a top-down imposition of the state. The forty to sixty states now in crisis cannot follow Europe's path to state formation from the sixteenth to the twentieth century. While the legitimate use of force is an important criterion in defining states, it is no longer the sole criterion. Our task is to establish legitimate states at a time when the use of force has reached its limit. States now derive their legitimacy from performing specific functions in the economic, social and political domains. Even if it were desirable, it is neither credible nor feasible to impose order from the top down. Rather, the solution must come through establishing legitimacy in the eyes of the international community and a country's citizens. It does not make sense to conceive of sovereignty as an untrammeled right, divorced from obligations both to the population governed and to the international community of states. This principle—that the rights of sovereignty also entail obligations—is fundamental to the legitimacy of states and therefore to their ability to close the de facto gap in their sovereign capacities.

We conceptualize the underlying process—the network of rights and obligations underpinning the state's claim to sovereignty—in terms of a double compact. The first—and most critical—compact is between a state and its citizens, providing and enforcing citizenship rights, embedded in a coherent set of rules that do not remain on paper but become the actual rules of the game. The second compact is between a state and the international community to ensure adherence to international norms and standards of accountability and transparency. The measure of the state is the citizens' judgment of the performance of these functions. As we can better value what we measure, we are offering a framework of state functions and mechanisms for enhancing their performance as a way of building effective states. We now have access to a previously unimaginable range of information that is interlinked with and informed by communities on the Web and expanding educational opportunities. The public can now truly become principals in state-building processes by making an agenda of accountability and transparency concrete.

In our view, strategies of state building are inherently about "coproduction" because internal and external actors have to agree on rules, a division of labor and a sequence of activities. Until now the pendulum has swung between imposition of international preferences on the one hand, where decisions are appropriated and prescribed, and neglect on the other, where ambassadors and representatives merely observe and report, while venal government officials and rulers systematically destroy institutions. In contrast, our framework provides for an assessment whereby outsiders might be asked to perform a specific function for a limited time and then, through a clear process of handover, see national actors take on that function. In this situation, members of the public are not just passive recipients or observers of "service delivery." It is critical to devise ways to empower and enfranchise citizens in decision making with regard to resources to ensure that they become coproducers of public value.

In our view, legitimacy is not a one-time event conferred through an election or the establishment of a charismatic authority but a continuous process of deepening and broadening the rights and obligations of citizenship. For the state to perform its multifunctional role there must be a virtuous circle in which authority translates into collective power that is kept accountable to the citizenry. While a view of legitimacy that rests purely on electoral validation is based on a zero sum game with clear winners who rule over the losers, a conception of collective power requires cooperation and constant innovation through public discussions of the new institutional means to deal with critical tasks that a public agrees upon.

While the international organizations were set up after World War II, state building must now take place against the backdrop of a radically changed context in which flows have globalized and intensified. Whereas in 1945, polities, economies, and civil societies were defined predominantly in national terms, today's global networks and actors are wielding powers that had been held for generations by states. The weight and combination of these forces have overwhelmed our traditional frameworks of understanding. And, because we have been taken by surprise, our response to these challenges has been deeply atavistic.

Those who control hedge funds, private equity funds and sovereign wealth funds, including those of newly emerging powers, are making decisions that shape global economic policy. A network of instantaneous communications has redefined work, space, and time at a global level. The advent of new information technology has overcome one of the greatest constraints in human history—the ability to process large amounts of information and identify patterns. This has brought about a geometric decline in the cost of information for societies active in the digital age. New communities of trust have emerged and are now transacting billions online and collaborating in social networks. Technology has become a mediator for a huge range of human relationships by creating new forms of organization for society and businesses. However, globalization and technological change also mean that instability, insecurity, and terror are now more easily exported than previously.

The fates of billions of people are now tied to each other as never before. Unlike the first, empire-centered wave of globalization a century ago, this wave is truly global: Decisions on these flows are not being made only in New York and London but also in Beijing, Dubai, Johannesburg, Mumbai, Moscow, São Paulo, Singapore and Tokyo. Markets, states, and networks are interacting under conditions of radical uncertainty, improvising the rules of the game as they go. Civil society lobbies are setting agendas on human rights and the environment.

The market has revealed both its potential for creating prosperity and also its vulnerability and blindness in mitigating the social debris it creates. Along with newfound freedom and opportunity, the rapid changes brought about by globalization have also generated multiple uncertainties. The middle classes of wealthy countries are increasingly nervous as to whether they will have health care and their children will continue to have the opportunities they enjoyed in their youth.

In Europe, the social model is under question. In the United States, job insecurity has translated into a fear of outsourcing. On both sides of the Atlantic, India and China are seen as threats to competitiveness and the very survival of current social models. Simultaneously, China, India, Russia, Brazil, and other large economies fear a backlash from Europe and the United States and the internal instability that a slow-down of their economies would bring.

More broadly, we frame our responses at the nation-state level rather than harnessing our collective energies and readjusting to emerging patterns. Because globalization is a mostly spontaneous process, strategies are not yet in place that would enable the poorest to benefit from it. As a result, the common thread that can bring these challenges together and provide a coherent frame of reference has escaped us. Moreover, the actors that could play the greatest role, especially centers of learning in businesses and universities, are not yet actively included in the search for solutions.

As a result, international organizations as currently constituted are an obstacle to state building. The new international order that emerged after 1945 assumed that its constituent parts would be sovereign states that enjoyed popular legitimacy at home and behaved as responsible members of the international order. It vested each unit with authority—and latitude—to behave with unaccountable power vis-à-vis its citizens. This order continued an older notion of sovereignty that prioritized state control and freedom from interference rather than accountability: a license for arbitrary power.

Assuming the role of the state as a given, international organizations did not invest much in trying to understand it. Their organizational structures consider political, economic, and security areas as distinctive domains, and they themselves are organized into separate "silos"—or organizational buckets—along similar lines. In conflict or postconflict, these organizations, more or less isolated from each other, often end up only reproducing the hidebound bureaucratic practices of the past. Their lack of coordination is usually the largest obstacle to achieving coherence of purpose or efficient resource use.

The issue is neither less nor more aid but the design of the aid system. The current design is geared toward micromanagement and microaccountabilities without connecting to an overall goal of global stability and prosperity. It does not have to be this way, however. The architects of the Marshall Plan considered six alternatives before agreeing to make Europe a more or less equal partner in the transatlantic relationship. Had the Marshall planners adopted the approach of scrutinizing the financing of every project proposed for Europe—the approach now in use in other parts of the world—the consequences would have been very different. Multilateral approaches have never been needed more, but the practices of our multilateral organizations now stand in the way: The next step is to reach agreement on the ways and means for such policies. When effective states confront a changed reality, they are quick to adjust their methods and shed or acquire functions. The same pragmatism is required of multilateral organizations.

In our opinion, such an approach would be more effective in military, political, and economic terms. Rather than focusing on financial resources alone, it would mobilize strategy and rules differently and more sustainably. Constant humanitarian interventions cost billions of dollars to maintain yet do not prevent conflict from reemerging and do not leave capable states in their wake. A state-building path would enable both humanitarian actors and international military forces to exit more quickly once deployed. Moreover, by creating more stable and effective states, this approach reduces the likelihood of state collapse and therefore military deployment in the first place.

The framework has been refined and tested through four lenses. The first is an analytic perspective that builds on the disciplines of sociology, anthropology, business literature, systems theory, law, and political science. The second has involved practical experience and a mapping of the aid system from work within the World Bank, NATO, and the United Nations and by close observation of the processes and interactions of a wide range of bilateral organizations, nongovernmental organizations (NGOs), and UN agencies. The third has been through acting as both participant and adviser within the state-building process, working at the forefront of the effort in Afghanistan from 2001 to 2005 and subsequently in a range of other contexts. In recent years various leaders and stakeholders have called on us to analyze and enter into dialogue on framing the context and designing a pathway to follow in southern Sudan, Nepal, Lebanon, and Kosovo, which has added a comparative perspective on the limits—and possibilities—of the current international system. Finally, our approach has been refined through a viewpoint informed by the successes and failures of different state-building trajectories throughout history. Our discussions with leaders and citizens in Singapore, China, Russia, India, Spain, Vietnam, Kenya, Peru, Ethiopia, and Afghanistan have also helped shape our vision.

This book is not about Afghanistan, but that country has formed a backdrop for our understanding of the challenges involved in state building, the global assets that one can draw upon for this task, and the obstacles that the current form of international organizations presents. It has also made us keenly aware that legitimacy flows from citizens. The creative energies of ordinary men and women and their eagerness to participate in inclusive orders have been an inspiration that has guided our labor. Understanding the significance of what we call an "open moment" in Afghanistan, we framed the deep desire of the Afghan citizens for a functioning state in the strategies of development we shared with the international community; these policies then guided Afghanistan's path between 2001 and the end of 2004. At that time the international community was resistant to the concept of state building. Now, old approaches have been wrapped in the language of state building without fundamental changes in designs, skills, or practices.

This initial resistance and the persistence of disjointed and wasteful practices are contributing factors to the current crisis and loss of momentum in Afghanistan. At the same time, Afghan leaders had a chance to become the founding fathers and mothers of a new statebuilding project in Afghanistan. Some chose this option, whereas others opted for personal gain and compromise. The consequences of those choices have helped foster the widespread perception that the state is corrupt and ineffective. Neither the international community nor the Afghan government has succeeded in responding to and harnessing the energies of ordinary Afghans for building a state that would have legitimacy at home and internationally. We hope that this will change. Ordinary Afghans, like citizens around the world, have a deep desire to be participants in an inclusive international order. We hope that the Afghan leaders and their international partners can learn from the past and act with wisdom and determination to respond to the people's noble aspirations. This book has been written in large part to both explain the dominant process today and suggest a different repertoire not only for Afghanistan but also for many other nations mired in political crisis.

The goals of this book are fourfold. The first is to serve as a catalyst for a new understanding of the state as a dynamic, citizen-oriented mechanism that is necessary for the constitution of a legitimate economic, social, and political order. The second is to inspire those constituencies who have often regarded the state as unimportant or even irrelevant (including corporations and advocates of "civil society"). This book emphasizes that a functioning state is a necessary condition for the ability of business and civil society, in turn, to function. In turn, they themselves are necessary components of a new conception of the state that balances global and local networks of rights and obligations.

Cooperation and understanding between these actors are therefore key elements of positive change.

The third objective is to seek the engagement of the global public in an agenda of state building. If accountability of state institutions is to become real, it will require the full participation of domestic stakeholders and the international public. The fourth is to suggest the contours of a pragmatic agenda of action. It is not our intention to produce the definitive work on the subject of state building or to write an academic reference book, but rather to contribute to public discussion and action on a vital issue. If we stimulate a general discussion, we will have succeeded in our purpose. If a larger community of practice develops in this field, our collective wisdom will be enhanced.

Part I of the book describes our understanding of the distinctiveness of the present world: the gaps, stocks, and flows of a world on the move. Chapter 1 outlines the critical problem in the forty to sixty states that suffer from a sovereignty gap between the functions desired by the population and the day to day reality of mismanagement, corruption, and disorder. Chapter 2 outlines the way in which certain regions and countries—from Singapore to the American South to Ireland—have "reversed history" and created effective states despite facing significant problems. Chapter 3 describes our networked world—a "world of flows" in which those countries that have reversed history have solidified the relationships between the state, market, and citizens and now mutually reinforce economic prosperity, whereas countries that are outside the realm of networked governance continue to backslide into deeper poverty and institutional degradation. Chapter 4 further depicts life in that half of the world that is excluded from the opportunities and economic and political relationships that people in the West take for granted. Chapter 5 explains how foreign aid has created an "aid complex" that exacerbates the very problems that the international community hopes to solve.

Part II of the book (chapters 6 and 7) presents a multifunctional framework for understanding state practices and delineates the performance of ten core functions that states must perform. We outline the development of state functionality and the emergence of the budget as the central instrument of policy. This conceptual structure can enable citizens and officials to measure the sovereignty gap reliably. Once a more quantitative framework is in place, we can assess proposed interventions and make an overall judgment of whether international statebuilding practice is actually helping to close this gap or widening it instead.

Part III of the book lays out a range of pragmatic mechanisms that will make a state-building agenda practicable. Chapter 8 outlines a sovereignty strategy based on long-term compacts that integrate the current raft of interventions in the economic, political, security, judicial, administrative, and social domains into a single, long-term approach that is tailored to a specific context and designed to reach the goal of a fully functioning state. Chapter 9 explains the key modality for implementing this strategy: national programs that enable a government to perform a state function throughout its territory in an effective and transparent manner through the mobilization of relevant actors—government, the private sector, and/or civil society—to perform critical tasks. This process delivers results and builds domestic capability for the performance of each function in the medium-to-long term.

Global security cannot be ensured so long as large regions of the globe are mired in violence, poverty, and illegitimacy. Disenfranchised populations of the world must be transformed into stakeholders in our expanding global prosperity. Despite the giant steps forward that have been taken in many places, there is still no global project that gives these marginalized billions a sense of hope or belonging. In the past, nationalism, socialism, secularism, or feminism might have provided a rallying cry, but today the silence is deafening. Global stability will lie in the creation of a global middle class of citizens who can see paths of upward social and economic mobility, and trust in their institutions. Hope will emerge only when their governments are able and determined to perform the full range of functions of a modern state. The more able the state is to perform these functions, the less required will be the use of force.

Each time the world has confronted a problem it has managed to find an institutional solution—such is the ingenuity of the human race. The conditions are now ripe for devising a new approach to generating worldwide stability and prosperity. However, we must summon our imagination to design a new, effective global system. Our hope is that we can combine the collective knowledge, wisdom, and imagination that already exist with the right type of focus and mobilization and then apply them to the task of making our divided world whole.

PART ONE

DEFINING THE CONTEXT

ONE

The Creeping "Sovereignty Gap"

T O FIND A hotel room in New York City in September, you need to be at least the chancellor, vice president, or foreign minister of a sovereign state, if not the president. We advise you to take the subway or, better still, walk because all around the city, taxi passengers are stuck in gridlock, cursing the day the United Nations was born. For as soon as the New York summer is over and the kids are back in school, heads of state from around the world put on their best Italian suits for their annual visit to Manhattan. They are accompanied by their entourages, limousines, police escorts, and other heavy security measures, all making their way from their embassies, consuls, legations, and deluxe hotel rooms uptown, downtown, and across town to the UN headquarters. There on the East River they will attend the annual opening of the General Assembly. No sooner has the Big Apple recovered from the weeklong marathon of speeches and cocktail parties at the United Nations than the circus—and traffic—switches to Washington, D.C., where the world's finance ministers, governors of central banks, and their associates gather for the annual meetings of the International Monetary Fund (IMF) and the World Bank, both headquartered in the U.S. capital.

Many U.S. commentators consider these get-togethers to be empty rituals, a waste of the U.S. taxpayers' hard-earned money—not to mention the public resources of many small and debt-ridden states, where the funds spent on limousines and lavish entertainment could be put to better use improving the lives of the people, most of whom are desperately poor. Yet leaders from the developing world will not boycott these meetings any time soon. In fact, the smaller or more distressed their state is, the more they need the bright TV lights of New York and Washington to broadcast, via satellite, the video highlights of these meetings to local news studios in Central America and the Caribbean, Africa, Asia, and the former Soviet Union so as to prove that these weaker states have a place on the world stage along with the big powers: the United States, Great Britain, France, China, and Russia.

These are the rituals of sovereignty. The rites of September bestow legitimacy and authority on these leaders, at least in principle, to the extent that the United Nations, IMF, and World Bank treat the national government of every state in the world as the sovereign representative of its people. In fact, these global organizations need these states as much as the states themselves need the support of the United Nations, the IMF, and the World Bank, for the international community is by definition made up of its constituent sovereign units. Membership in this community, however tenuous, thus gives state leaders the crucial power to enter into agreements, receive funding for development projects, borrow money from private banks and public institutions to finance other projects, grant to other nations concessions to their natural resources (often in a way that benefits those who are already rich), or enter into treaties that commit their people to legally binding obligations, such as setting borders.

When these elites return to their capitals at the end of the month, the ceremonies in America will seem like a distant mirage. Many of them are forced to live in virtual fortresses, surrounded day and night by armed men. Rumors run through the streets as to how much of the country's patrimony has been deposited abroad in secret personal bank accounts and how many concessions have been granted to members of the leader's family. Local and international contractors are already lined up and ready to grease the palms of those who can smooth the way toward their companies' share of big infrastructure projects, which offer endless possibilities and speedy paths to personal profit. Thanks to the very doctrine of "noninterference in the internal affairs" of sovereign states, governments have great latitude to plunder the national coffers and turn their nation's resources into privately held assets.

The states in question tend to be deep in debt to the IMF and big banks in Europe, Asia, and the United States (the open secret is that these debts are likely never to be discharged, at least by the current leaders). Meanwhile, those civil servants who are honest and dedicated to the welfare of their nation, have to operate in the shadow of international organizations and NGOs, often working two or three jobs to supplement salaries that are one-tenth or even one-twentieth of the average pay received by a chauffeur working for these same NGOs. According to the report of the Commission for Africa, in 2005, $3.2 billion was paid to one hundred thousand "experts" to provide technical assistance to Africa.

The offices of international organizations and NGOs are networked by means of huge satellite dishes atop new concrete buildings, with security guards and strict rules of access, all signs that mark them as places of privilege. Although physically present in Africa, Latin America, or Asia, mentally most of the bureaucrats working in these buildings remain firmly back in the developed world. They are preoccupied with the latest intellectual fashions and initiatives at their faraway headquarters. Their time is spent managing hundreds of disparate projects that can never compose an organized developmental vision. Though living in the same country, the two bureaucracies—one international and well-funded from abroad, one national and almost always starved for funds—are conceptually (and in terms of available resources) miles apart and therefore rarely interact meaningfully. Foreign officials gravitate toward each other socially as well through their clubs and other groups, thus creating segregated spaces of interaction. Their understanding of the people they serve and the dynamics of the national polity, economy and society, especially outside the capital city, tends to be limited, thus limiting the relevance of their recommendations. While these foreigners despair of seeing movement toward their declared policy goals, the national officials end up blaming the foreigners for giving wrong or at least patently useless advice. And most of the time they are right.

The contrast between the two bureaucracies is not only financial but also evident in the physical appearance and even in the mood of the bureaucracies. Most government buildings lack sanitation, heating, and cooling and suffer frequent power cuts. Often they are without the most basic supplies: pens, paper, official forms. Communication is by handwritten correspondence, which is carried physically from office to office, since officials rarely have phones or computers. But the worst problem is that native civil servants are so continuously berated by foreign "experts" as incompetent that the officials come to believe this censure. Having struggled hard to win a place in the bureaucracy, they find themselves maligned by the very citizenry they hope to serve as a result of the government's failure to provide even the most elementary means of survival, such as clean water, primary education, and support of home-grown food (by means of irrigation, flood walls, and so forth), let alone the tools that would really give a path to advancement, such as higher education. The civil servants who are responsible for making and implementing major policy decisions are discouraged: They are neither motivated nor educated to carry out the tasks appointed to them.

Why can't the civil service of distressed nations be adequately funded? After all, many countries which receive aid have extensive natural resources. The answer is that these valuable commodities tend to be contracted out to extractive industries, often foreign; this creates another layer of relationships between a section of the local elite and these companies. Contracts for the extraction of resources such as petroleum or minerals are not disclosed to the public, so the industries and their procedures remain highly opaque. Most frequently, rents from these resources go to offshore accounts to which only a privileged few in the country have access. Government officials who are responsible for this domain work in gleaming offices and live a lifestyle of conspicuous consumption. This massive diversion of funds means that usable domestic revenue on the books is a fraction of its potential. Many developing countries have also been hurt by frequent banking crises, where powerful interests have defaulted on hundreds of millions of dollars. Astonishing amounts of cash suddenly disappear. It is this wealth that could have been used instead to invest in the people of the country, through creating a set of *functioning* institutions, governed by the citizens themselves.

For their part, ordinary citizens simply give up expecting to receive even basic health, education, and security services from either their governments or the international aid projects. Most people keep their heads down, avoid taking sides, try not to get pressed into joining the militia, and scratch together a living if they can. Despite generally heavy expenditures on the military in afflicted countries, citizens are deeply anxious about their personal safety.[1] In these countries, many of which have sunk into conflict on average twice a decade, millions of people have experienced internal displacement and exile, and millions more are threatened by it. Their lives are marked by continuous interruptions: They are forced to make repeated new beginnings, never knowing whether or when conflict will break out again.

Hundreds of millions of people have been on the move from the countryside to the cities, where the speed of urbanization, particularly in capital cities, outpaces job creation. Many of these millions have put all of their savings into buildings to which they do not have legal title. And although they have valuable assets—in the form of property and businesses—they must generally hold them outside the law; this illegality means that even successful businesses remain "dead capital" from the point of view of lenders, and are therefore useless as collateral for securing loans to generate the kind of minimal wealth required to climb out of poverty.[2]

Even those persistent or lucky enough to enter the legal system run into obstacles, such as unpredictable regulations that lack logic but are always costly: Making headway most often requires a bribe. In Afghanistan in 2002 a citizen had to pay $8 in bribes, almost half the monthly wage, to obtain the twenty signatures required from functionaries spread out across the city and to fill out twenty-four pages of documentation, consuming as much as a week of that person's life—all for the "pleasure" of paying a $2 customs fee. In Sierra Leone, the national identity card—the basic device to demonstrate citizenship—has to be renewed every three months. Unimaginable hardships for poor and displaced people are required just to demonstrate that they exist. Indeed, tens of millions of people in impoverished countries lack access to an identity or an address; the high costs of dealing with the government have forced them into a legal limbo. Billions are trapped in poverty and informality without access to the legal tools that would give them the formal rights necessary to buy or sell property, divide labor among themselves, or gain access to the expanded markets that most entrepreneurs in the developed world take for granted.

The people thus rendered powerless are victims of what we call the sovereignty gap—the disjunction between the de jure assumption that all states are "sovereign" regardless of their performance in practice—and the de facto reality that many are malfunctioning or collapsed states, incapable of providing their citizens with even the most basic services, and where the reciprocal set of rights and obligations are not a reality. In Washington, D.C., and New York, these states may be treated as sovereign, as autonomous units in the international system of nations, but in reality many developing and post-Soviet states are sites of bad governance, misrule and corruption. In the forty to sixty countries that constitute an "arc of crisis" that extends from Africa through the Middle East and Central and East Asia, the crucial, mutual relationship between citizens and their governments is missing. Governance entails an orderly process for arriving at and implementing decisions regarding collective goods. But in these countries, the missing element is a process for connecting citizens' voices to government and making government accountable to citizens for its decisions. Instead, the prevailing elements are disorder and an almost total disjunction between rulers and ruled. What is needed is not a new idea of sovereignty in theory, but an analysis of the necessary functions of the state in relation to the people, such that, empirically speaking, the missing element we described begins to take formation. The facts, namely whether citizens begin to rise from voicelessness to acquire real decision-making power, from a dead-end life to one that has a hopeful future, are what interest us. The true legitimacy of the sovereign government, which arises from the empowering of the populace, is not a matter of an "ought"; it is a matter of an "is."

Unfortunately, the gap between what might be called de jure, versus de facto sovereignty is growing, rather than receding. As time goes on, conditions continue to deteriorate. We need an answer to the question of how to bridge this widening gap. How does the international community face up to the realities that the system is only as strong as its weakest link and that as many as sixty states are either on their way to ruin or have already collapsed? What can be done that has not already been tried, unsuccessfully, to rescue and rebuild failing states in Haiti, East Timor, Bosnia, Somalia, Afghanistan, Iraq, Sudan, Nepal, and so many other struggling nations? Empirical studies are depressing: Nearly 50 percent of countries that emerge from conflict revert to hostilities within ten years.[3] Nevertheless, the international system has failed to devise mechanisms to arrest these reversions successfully. In the past twenty years, for example, $300 billion has been spent in Africa alone, yet the continent is still rife with weak and collapsed regimes—two million people a year are dying of AIDS, three thousand children die every day of malaria, and forty million receive no schooling at all.[4] How do we redefine a sovereign state in such a way that we can objectively measure its functionality and success? By what practicable and empirically successful method can we help struggling states get back on their feet on a sustainable basis?

Our international system is premised upon states that are capable of fulfilling a range of international and domestic responsibilities. As the locus of political authority in a country, the state's decisions are simply assumed to be legitimate and representative of its citizens' wishes and aspirations. The state is also assumed to have the capability to implement these decisions, project its authority throughout the territory, possess a domestic resource base to meet its spending obligations, and have a legitimate monopoly on the physical means by which it can guarantee its citizens' security. Membership in the international system affords to governments a range of rights—namely to enter into treaties, borrow money from public and private institutions against the sovereign guarantee, regulate their borders, represent their country abroad, and participate in the governance of international organizations.

The concept of noninterference in internal affairs, together with the sovereign guarantee, has given governments carte blanche with regard to the assets of their countries at will. There is little or no accountability. As might be expected, arbitrary power is abused: Financial resources are squandered or diverted, natural resources are wasted through corruption, and profits are mismanaged. It would be bad enough if the wealth of the country were simply stolen. But where countries have been enduring sporadic civil wars, or wars with neighboring countries, public resources are devoted to the pursuit of means of destruction and to arming youths against civilians. Families are forced to flee. The tens of millions of lives lost during the second half of the twentieth century to the present, and the millions of refugees and internally displaced people—the carriers of their country's capabilities—are a sad testimony to both the failure of public authority and the state's weak institutional structures. This gap between de jure and de facto notions of sovereignty, we argue, lies at the heart of the worldwide predicament of developing nations.

This predicament has consequences we can no longer ignore. A number of contemporary global crises have their roots in forty to sixty fragile countries. As these states have experienced prolonged conflict or misrule, networks of criminality, violence, and terror have solidified, providing an ever expanding platform that threatens the entire globe. State failures that the rich countries used to be able to ignore can thus no longer be overlooked. Intrastate and interstate conflict, drug rings, and the smuggling of arms, timber, antiquities, and precious stones—combined with money laundering and the large-scale, speedy financial transactions made possible by globalization—are resulting in an agile and flexible complex of networks that mostly thwart any attempt to create order. No international police or army can substitute for a combination of well-ordered markets and states that have legitimized themselves in the eyes of their populaces. Criminal networks are making their way into the first world, with consequences of increased violence, human trafficking, and, at worst, the threat of terrorism.

Estimates indicate that the volume of illegal financial flows through many countries is several times larger than their annual government budgets. This huge imbalance between funds available to criminal networks and those at the disposal of the state reinforces a culture of corruption. Concessions to natural resources are granted for a fraction of their real value in the global market, in return for secret transfers to private bank accounts; owners rely on their own security firms and militias to guard their shady and highly profitable operations. Conversely, the positive, networked, noncriminal global flows of international capital, information, knowledge and people cannot thrive in these areas. The rules of the game in failing states—the parameters that people impose upon themselves to shape their interactions—are poor governance and rampant corruption. The very means that could bring prosperity to billions—global capital—cannot find a home in such countries.

These large-scale criminal actions erode both nature and historical memory in the countries of concern. Exactly where global environmental issues such as the destruction of forests, overuse of delicate ecosystems, pollution, and coastal and soil erosion are prevalent, the institutions needed to address them are absent. At the same time, the cultural heritage that could provide a basis for a revived, positive national identity disappears as thieves loot and destroy archaeological sites and museums. Some of these criminals are sophisticated and smuggle for large profits in the black market, but many articles are pilfered and sold into illegal antiquities' markets for small change.

We can conceptualize this culture of systematic corruption in another way: The common people of failing states have no real stake in the success or failure of their countries. They are not "stakeholders" in that they have no legal title to whatever they possess, no guarantees against its expropriation at any time, and no real belief that the conditions they face will ever improve. In other words, they have no stake in the present since they are totally disenfranchised; they have no stake in the past since it is being stolen from them, as their heritage is destroyed, and the needs of subsistence and lack of education prevent appreciation for it; finally, they have no stake in the future since they see no evidence that the state is bettering their lot. There is nothing to motivate them except the imperatives of simple survival. That citizens feel and recognize that they have a stake in their country is another goal that can only be reached by conceptualizing, and putting into practice, empirically tested methods of increasing the proper functioning of the state apparatus and the civil service, with full and public accountability.

Facing constant deprivation, millions of people are willing to give up entirely on their own countries and to pay high prices to human traffickers to move them illegally to Organization for Economic Cooperation and Development (OECD) countries, often risking their freedom or their lives in the process. On arrival, they try to find new lives, either by seeking asylum or by disappearing underground. Despite increasing investment in border controls, it is clear that an impermeable barrier around OECD countries cannot be constructed, as the combined impact of the push-and-pull factors on potential migrants is too strong.

Back in the home country, a powder keg is being formed. Those who are left behind resent the organization of power and wealth, in which internal elites block the paths to influence that at one time may have been clearly delineated and accessible and where promises of the realization of human rights—and the expenditure of billions of dollars in aid—have resulted only in a half-finished, poorly constructed infrastructure. This resentment manifests itself in the swing to populist movements evident in both Latin America and South Asia. These movements have proved incapable of solving problems in the past, but the citizenry's support for them points to extreme dissatisfaction with fickle democracies and crooked civil and economic playing fields.

To OECD countries, someone like Venezuela's Chavez, an icon for this sort of populism, seems like an anomaly. In the past he might have been ignored. But no more. Despite the increasing importance of information technology to the global economy, both as a means of capital transfers, and as an industry in its own right, the underlying basis of that economy is still raw materials, specifically petroleum and natural gas. Since the conversion of these natural assets to commodities depends on security of the sites of production, pipelines, and transportation routes, any disruption can have unsettling consequences for the entire world economy. With the rapid economic development of China, India, and Brazil, the demand for oil and metals is on the rise, and the competition for supplies of basic ores such as iron, copper, and zinc can only increase.

Although the September 11 attacks might be the most vivid in our memories, numerous other events in the 1990s, not to mention the first, unsuccessful World Trade Center attack, have indicated that neglect of fragile states is not an option. The international community has been forced to intervene on a number of occasions—Bosnia and Afghanistan are two prominent examples—to prevent state collapse. The global trend in peacekeeping is quite clear: Between the founding of the United Nations in 1945 and 1990, there were sixteen peacekeeping interventions. In the seventeen years since 1990 the Security Council has authorized forty-eight peacekeeping operations. The cost of deploying these multilateral forces is immense; the security costs of the coalition and North Atlantic Treaty Organization (NATO) in Afghanistan are likely to exceed $15 billion a year for the foreseeable future. The cost of Balkan operations has been similarly vast. For the

United Nations, the bill for humanitarian interventions (a large portion of which supports people adversely affected by civil wars and interstate conflicts) is running into tens of billions a year. Counting the support from bilateral, multilateral, and nongovernmental organizations probably doubles the initial estimate of the cost. Hundreds of thousands of projects have been put into place to patch up these devastated polities, but since they are not designed to serve a systematic agenda, they amount to less than the sum of their parts. And the cost of failed peacekeeping missions is not only in money but also in the lives of tens of millions of civilians and thousands of peacekeepers.

These issues, each of worldwide scope, have become divided into areas of concern to particular stakeholders. Aiding collapsed and incapable states could previously be seen as an altruistic, idealistic, indeed perhaps a personal, "optional" matter of concern. Those who adopted poverty-reduction as an agenda could find their place in the international aid bureaucracy. But in the post–9/11 world, this has become a global issue: Like it or not, we are moving toward a common security-development paradigm. It is increasingly clear that one key phenomenon—the failed state, or the sovereignty gap—connects the entire complex of these problems. An effective state is necessary for the solution of both local and global problems. Just as a business firm, when it acts in a transparent manner and is responsible to its stockholders, is the most effective unit of organization for the market economy, so a stable international order depends on its constituent unit—the state—to perform its functions effectively, transparently, and responsibly for the benefit of its stakeholders: its citizens.

Academic attention on the significance of the state has tended to wax and wane. During periods of stability, the state as a political and economic construct has receded to the background, which has in turn given rise to counter-trends such as "bringing the state back in," the title of a collection of academic articles.[5] During other periods, including the present day, the state has been the focus of critical attention and conceptualization. Several different developments that took place during the 1990s and the first few years of the 21st century account for the renewed recognition of the state's contemporary centrality. As the Soviet Union disintegrated, the end of the Cold War brought about a substantial increase in the number of states. Meanwhile, a series of political conflicts in the Balkans, Africa, and Asia resulted in the collapse of many nations. East Asia's rise further contributed to the focus on the state, particularly in terms of its role in creating the enabling conditions for economic growth. At the same time, difficulties in implementing "second generation" reforms have led to acknowledgement of the importance of effective state institutions. The final factor highlighting the critical relevance of weak or failed states—and their potential threat to the international system—has been the global focus on security in the wake of September 11.

A number of recent international commissions have now given their stamp of authority to the state as the essential locus of contemporary international efforts. The Commission for Africa concludes that "One thing underlies all the difficulties caused by the interactions of Africa's history over the past 40 years. It is the weakness of governance and the absence of an effective state."[6] The report of Kofi Annan's High-level Panel on Threats, Challenges, and Change reinforces this view: "States are still the front-line responders to today's threats," and states are "necessary to achieve the dignity, justice, worth and safety of their citizens."[7] The World Bank's anticorruption strategy of 2006 puts effective states at its center. There is finally global recognition both of the centrality of effective states for global peace, stability, and prosperity and of the immense shortfall in the capability of the governments in the "arc of crisis" to meet the challenges. The question is no longer whether to bring the state back in, but how to do so.[8]

We maintain that the creation of effective states is not achievable by means of the old (but still almost universally utilized) methods, since almost all of these derive from an experience of the world as it was in the years directly following World War II, of a world that no longer exists. To act effectively, we need a new conceptualization of how states function, how they fit in the contemporary globalized world, and how the international community should use its vast resources to help the recovery of failed or failing states. First, the use of force is inherently limited in a project of state building. For example, the $300 billion in expenditures, the deaths of thousands of military personnel, the wounds of thousands more, the millions in refuge and the massive loss of Iraqi civilian life (with no appreciable results in the political settlement) clearly underline the limitations of imposed authority. Sending in contractors hot on the heels of use of force, without an approach to state building may not lead to the desired results. As the U.S. Inspector General has pointed out, the creation of a massive network of bribery in international projects, involving both Iraqis and foreigners, also makes evident the limitations of aid expenditure in conditions of insecurity. Where projects do get built, they are usually of shoddy quality or unfit for purpose, and thus stand empty, thousands of lifeless hulks pointing to the futility of the ongoing endeavor. The *how* of international help turns out to be much more important than the *how much*. The use of violence, or expenditure of funds, unless carefully thought out, far from producing order, will cause further loss of control and descent into chaos. Contrast this example of force in state building with the near absence of the use of violence by police forces and armies in OECD countries. The injury of one citizen by state authorities causes not only civil action but also public outcries, as attested by the killing of Jean Charles de Menezes (a Brazilian national) by the police in London, even in the wake of the bombings of July 7, 2005. General Rupert Smith, in his book, *Utility of Force*, has clearly indicated not only the limits of the use of force (especially where it is not exercised within a framework of legal status) but also the inherent inability of the armies and accompanying doctrines of the industrial war paradigm to face the challenges of war amongst the people.[9]

It should be equally clear that the model of charity does not work. Ceding what should be functions of the state to outside aid agencies, private companies, and NGOs is not sustainable precisely because it undermines the corresponding branches of the state, whose legitimacy is crucial to its functioning. Whether it is in East Timor or Cambodia, where the UN system was given direct administrative authority, or in Sudan and Afghanistan, where social programs have been entrusted to NGOs and contractors, the provision of services to the general population has not been able to proceed on a cost-effective or sustainable basis, especially where the goal of the international presence is eventual exit. Ceding state functions to outside agencies severs the critical link of accountability between the state and citizens. And once ceded, even if on a temporary basis, entrenched interests develop, which means that the NGO, contractor or agency will lobby for funds to keep performing that function. In Bosnia and Kosovo, the international community has yet to determine such an exit strategy—i.e., one that will not precipitate a new round of chaos and violence, thereby undoing all their previous work—despite years of effort. Only by closing the sovereignty gap and using a tested model in which the state becomes self-sufficient can permanent occupation be avoided.

Although there is increasing consensus on the goal of state building, the ineffectiveness of existing models, the limits to the use of force, and the danger of allowing foreign bureaucracies to substitute for state functions, agreement has not been reached on a positive strategy for building effective states. Citizens of OECD countries, while pressing for more aid (an aid, trade, and debt campaign resulted in calls for 0.7

percent of the gross domestic product [GDP] of rich countries to be earmarked for aid to developing countries), are increasingly questioning the efficacy of the aid system. The generosity of the world's peoples in the aftermath of the tsunami in Indonesia was overwhelming, but the mismanagement and failure in the administration of this bounty was shocking. The UN agencies responsible for coordinating the disaster response have yet, almost three years later, to provide a full accounting of the funds. Just as failing states do not consider themselves obligated to publish regular internal audits, neither do most international organizations. In 2006 in the residents of Banda Aceh had significant questions about the quality of construction, delivery of services, lack of town planning, and the transparency of NGOs and UN agencies regarding expenditures of money and whether these expenditures had achieved their objectives. Scandals are now besetting much of the aid community who participated in the disaster relief effort. Until we have a clear vision of how to orient policy and utilize donor and taxpayer money more effectively, there is a clear risk that good will could turn into disaffection and isolationism.

Although terrible poverty exists in most of these countries, to call them "poor countries" is inappropriate in many cases. Many have vast natural resources—oil, natural gas, valuable industrial metals, minerals, and fertile soil. They have the capacity to manufacture goods, grow fruits and vegetables, generate exports, and provide services. But because most citizens are forced to operate outside the legal system (or indeed any system of agreed-upon conventions) due to burdensome, costly, and corrupt bureaucratic procedures, the governments in question are able to tap into the incomes of only a fraction of the potential taxpayers. After massive diversions of funds from mining operations and customs procedures, domestic revenue on the books will appear minimal. The frequent banking crises that have buffeted developing countries, have often been caused by exactly this sort of off-balance transaction, where powerful interests have defaulted on hundreds of millions of dollars. Often there is either no accounting at all or a sort of pseudo-accounting that hides all of the key transfers and expenditures.

What is needed is a homegrown capital and economic growth that builds on the existing and potential human, financial, natural and institutional capital of the country to enable the provision of the services and opportunities the people want and deserve. The missing link is the functioning state itself. Even when revenues are generated, they generally leave the state rather than remaining at the local level, where they could be reinvested and foster the growth of capital. Only in this way can we end the cycle of poverty.

The experience of nation building in post–World War II Europe and Japan—in contrast to that of the Soviet Union and Central Europe—shows that a state based on the consent of citizens and legitimacy of rules is likely to be more enduring than one imposed by force or whose civil structures are simply bypassed and weakened by duplicative aid efforts. Further confirmation has come recently with the consolidation of market economies and democracies in southern and Central Europe through European Union (EU) membership and the EU's process of accession. The systematic institutional reengineering and constant monitoring of actual and would-be members have proved much more sustainable than any measures provided by the international aid system. While accession to Europe is not an option in the near future for most of the states trapped in the sovereignty gap, we can learn a great deal from the way in which the EU has devised alternative approaches to state building in recent years.

The accession process, for example, has many attributes that make enduring, institutional change possible. It provides a goal and a core set of civic values—shared by both ordinary people and elites—which offer identity components (to become "European" while remaining, say, "French") and tangible material benefits; e.g., financial and political resources, freedom of movement, increased employment opportunities, and the security of being part of Europe. With such rewards clearly delineated, states can easily measure the worth of the sacrifices required to achieve them. Accession also offers a sense of future and provides a realistic time frame for meeting goals; furthermore, it uses an institutional architecture that presents clear sets of rules and practices that must be adopted, while still allowing for improvisation and adaptation to the national context. Finally, a series of nonnegotiable benchmarks, which must be met for accession to proceed, exposes entrenched elites (who quickly lose their power of illegitimate veto on change) and produces the simultaneous consent and alignment of both the elite and the common people to a goal, while generating new elites who must align themselves to this goal through democratic processes.

Weak and fragile states are the kind of challenge that requires solutions built on a fundamental agreement about a global approach informed by past successes and failures, our current context of globalization, and oriented toward adapting to our future. We have much to learn from those places that have transformed themselves in defiance of the pessimism of contemporary commentators—Singapore,

South Korea, Malaysia, Chile, and Dubai. And it is not only nations that can offer us lessons—the corporate world also provides many exemplary case studies in institutional transformation. Our own work in Afghanistan between 2001 and 2004 and subsequently in Sudan, Lebanon, Nepal, and Kosovo provides evidence that new approaches to state building, even in what appear to be the most hopeless cases, can be devised and implemented.

We argue that the elements for a new approach to state building are now available, if combined in the right way and tailored appropriately to context. During the last fifty years, OECD countries and global firms have created more wealth than in all of previous history, thereby demonstrating that the creation of wealth is limited only by human ingenuity and enterprise. From a global perspective, poverty and deprivation can no longer be viewed as an inescapable and inevitable condition. There was a time when people who were indifferent to or ignorant of the rise of fascism, the Holocaust, or the atrocities of Stalinism could perhaps have pleaded ignorance: How could they know what was going on half a world away? Such excuses have been erased by the globalization of the news media, which transmit video from the remotest corners of the world into the homes of those who live in OECD countries. Radios, television, and cell phones now convey the news of the action—and the inaction—of rich countries to the villages, hamlets, and shantytowns where the majority of the world's people live and work. People are increasingly able to watch each other and reflect upon the bonds that not only unite them in a common humanity but also divide them into various groupings of identity and interest. The language of human rights has become extremely widespread; the idea that all people are individuals is no longer a matter of serious debate in global civil society. Talk of "the empowerment of the poor" is now commonplace; the value of democracy a given. This presents an epochal shift from the nineteenth-century view that the poor will always be with us—to be led, of course, by those lucky enough to have been born among the world's small number of allegedly stable and virtuous elites.

Prosperity is thus within the reach of all of humanity, but to attain this goal we must first address its necessary precondition—effective states that perform the necessary functions for their citizens in our complex world, as well as an international community with the stamina to tackle the challenge of making the world a whole—a genuine international community that agrees to create a collective well-being. To develop a strategic framework for closing the sovereignty gap and to determine which states are (and are not) measuring up, we will need a consensus as to the precise definition of an "effective state" in the twenty-first century. However, instead of turning to existing theory or seeking answers from the stories of failure, we decided first to look instead at places where order—against all odds and expectations— emerged from chaos. Then, rather than despairing of ever finding solutions, we looked for patterns and distilled lessons from the approaches that have been proved in action. In some cases we were privileged to be able to put these techniques to work ourselves, and refine them on an ongoing basis. What we learned has prompted us to write this book.

TWO

Reversing History

CONVENTIONAL WISDOM HOLDS that the process of institution building will be lengthy and difficult (if not impossible) in those countries that have yet to consolidate rules and networks of trust, enable the performance of the private sector, and truly entrench the social contract. A frequent refrain in the news media and in our bookstores is, on the one hand, that state building is a new challenge that we know very little about and, on the other hand, that it takes hundreds of years for functioning institutions to emerge, as it were ex nihilo. (In 2006, a British Ambassador said we would need to stay in Afghanistan for "decades."[1]) It would be both irresponsible and wrong to believe that we cannot carry out—or do not know enough about—state building or that the necessary institutions cannot be created in a reasonable timeframe. In fact, the past fifty years show that there has been considerable innovation in the creation of institutional order in settings as varied as Europe, East Asia and the southern states of the United States. Since World War II, global history has provided a vast political and economic laboratory in which we can identify numerous examples of innovation in governance. Part of our myopia in this regard is a result of the fact that we look at the wrong places and at the wrong times to try to learn lessons. We should not look only at what has become a standard list of postconflict state-building experiments—from Kosovo and East Timor to Afghanistan and Iraq. In fact, numerous other countries have confronted devastation, chaos, and entrenched poverty but have transformed themselves into prosperous and stable members of the global community, and some of them are far closer to home than one might think. In each of these countries, a group of capable leaders emerged to forge order out of turmoil, reform the institutional architecture, and create the flexibility that permitted their countries to embrace the emerging opportunities of the outside world. Each country, in its own way, carved a new path toward modernity and prosperity, thereby overcoming the legacy of the past and reversing history.

In the spring of 1947 Will Clayton, the U.S. undersecretary for economic affairs, explained that "It is now obvious that we grossly underestimated the destruction to the European economy by the war. We understood the physical destruction, but we failed to take fully into account the effects of economic dislocation on production—nationalization of industries, drastic land reform, severance of long-standing commercial ties, disappearance of private commercial firms through death or loss of capital....Europe is steadily deteriorating. The political position reflects the economic. One political crisis after another merely denotes the existence of grave economic distress. Millions of people in the cities are slowly starving."[2]

In the mid-to-late 1940s officials in Europe and the United States demonstrated vision and leadership of the very highest quality when they created institutions and procedures that have shaped the international system ever since. As Keynes presciently pointed out in *The Economic Consequences of the Peace*, the Treaty of Versailles laid the groundwork for a new round of wars.[3] However, after World War II, once the immensity of destruction had been grasped, leaders in the West responded with one of the most imaginative acts of generosity and partnership ever witnessed. European policymakers, in close partnership with their American counterparts, put all their imagination and leadership to work in order to lay the foundations of a new European project, one as breathtaking in its scope as some of the greatest innovations of the Enlightenment.

As General Marshall himself pointed out, the Marshall Plan was "directed not against any country or doctrine but against hunger, poverty, desperation, and chaos." He explained that "Its purpose should be the revival of a working economy in the world so as to permit the emergence of political and social conditions in which free institutions can exist." In an early example of the idea of national ownership of development, he recognized that any plan must be led by the country concerned: "It would be neither fitting nor efficacious for this Government to undertake to draw up unilaterally a program designed to place Europe on its feet economically. This is the business of the Europeans. The initiative, I think, must come from Europe. The program should be a joint one, agreed to by a number of, if not all, European nations. The role of this country should consist of friendly aid in the drafting of a European program and of later support of such a program so far as it may be practical for us to do so."

Long before "strategic partnership" became commonplace in business literature, it was the political leaders of the mid-twentieth century who truly demonstrated the concept in their response to World War II. These men made use of an "open moment"—a rare period in which the status quo can be ruptured and possible futures imagined, based on constructive, citizen-centered politics—to adapt global governance arrangements through flexible, unceasing dialogue. Dean Acheson, secretary of state under President Truman, reflected twenty years later that "what remains interesting in those talks is not what we agreed upon but how, through all the complexity and confusion, we found a path to agreement. The task was to fix on the broad line along which we wanted to move, and then by increasingly specific development, find what was common ground and what was not.... We did not begin with papers, which so often divert readers to trivia, but with dialogue."[4]

Jean Monnet and Robert Schuman became the architects of what is now the European Union when they offered a plan for cooperation that centered around steel and coal (known as the European Steel and Coal Community) and became a pragmatic solution to the conflict between Germany and France. Step by step, the foundation they laid has led to pooled sovereignty and to the redefinition of Europe as a common market, a community, and a union. As a continually evolving political and economic organism, not only has Europe managed to deal with the unification of Germany, but European Union membership has also become the catalyst for the consolidation of democracy and the market economy in southern, central, and eastern Europe. In the process, a series of effective governance instruments has been developed and refined. The major colonial powers in Europe either learned the hard way that empires were unsustainable political arrangements or voluntarily divested themselves of empire to focus on Europe. The European Union, by providing for freedom of capital and labor, has allowed these commodities to flow across borders almost seamlessly. As a result, interstate conflict in Europe has become inconceivable. The relationship between European states and their citizens has changed drastically, and the current consensus on European values is a product of these decades of careful institution building.

In East Asia, while many leaders opted for national models for industrialization, Singapore emerged as the most successful development model in the region. The island state was widely considered an unviable project as a nation, as Denis Warner wrote in the *Sydney Morning Herald* on August 20, 1965: "An independent Singapore was not regarded as viable three years ago. Nothing in the current situation suggests that it is more viable today." An island without any natural resources, populated largely by indentured Chinese and Indian laborers and Malays, Singapore was accepted into the Federation of Malaysia in 1963 and asked to leave in 1965 with the expectation that it would accept much humbler terms of membership. The British navy, which provided 20 percent of GDP at the time and seventy thousand jobs, withdrew between 1968 and 1971. Singapore had long faced an active communist movement that controlled the trade unions. Throughout the 1950s and 1960s a sizeable minority of the electorate (20–30 percent) supported this movement, which developed into a full-blown insurgency by 1965. Corruption was endemic and economic development still minimal. As Lee Kwan Yew wrote in his autobiography, "We faced tremendous odds with an improbable chance of survival."[5]

The Singapore of today is an acknowledged global economic power. By 1995 Singapore's per capita GDP of US$26,000 had surpassed that of Britain (US$19,700). Under Lee Kuan Yew's leadership, a remarkable strategic vision took shape that provided the framework for the steady and systematic transformation of Singapore as a state, an economy, and a society. Having studied the experience of Malta's dependency syndrome, Lee Kuan Yew and his colleagues explicitly rejected this seductive model of sliding into addiction to foreign help. The goal from the beginning was the short-term use of aid, which moved toward an eventual break with the need for such assistance. While Singapore avidly pursued soft loans from the World Bank and other institutions and used them to great effect until it "graduated" from the bank in the 1990s, its core plan was development toward self-sufficiency. "Assistance should provide Singapore with jobs through industries and not make us dependent on perpetual injections of aid," Lee pointed out. "The world does not owe us a living. We cannot live by the begging bowl."[6]

This strategy had two basic principles. First, faced with hostile neighbors in the immediate region, Singapore opted to leapfrog the stages of development as prescribed by the national economic planning theories of the time and instead decided to connect to the international economy through investment from multinational corporations (MNCs) from farther afield. Recognizing that Singapore had "hardworking people, good basic infrastructure, and a government that was determined to be honest and competent," Lee set out to bring in the MNCs so as to "give our workers employment and teach them technical and engineering skills and management know-how."[7] This principle produced a necessary economic fillip and was supported by a second transformational policy. This was to avoid being a factory for Western goods and instead to provide a first-world oasis of service standards in a third-world context.

Lee Kuan Yew remarked that "All first-generation independence leaders were charismatic speakers, but their administrations seldom followed up with implementation."[8] By contrast, Singapore's procedure rested on the government as the key mechanism for the formation of development plans and policy implementation. This in turn required the creation of capability within government bodies and agencies. At the top, Singapore had a management team that combined the talents of a political visionary in Lee Kuan Yew, an economic architect in Goh Keng Swee, and a capacity builder in Hon Sui Sen. This team systematically invested in producing a cadre of managers and leaders to carry their vision forward through the creation of a merit-based system of recruitment and promotion.

The first plank of their implementation strategy was a series of efforts to create clean government and systematically curb corruption by focusing particularly on large-scale graft. By instigating integrity at the top of a very dishonest inherited machinery, Singapore started a process of expanding the new standards throughout the governmental system, a course of action that took decades to complete. In 2007 Singapore was ranked fourth out of 179 countries in Transparency International's Corruption Perception Index.[9]

With clean governance, Singapore became a credible partner for both labor and investors. This has led to a new type of economic and social partnership in which the government contracts and manages infrastructure projects that have laid the foundation for improved standards of living for the Singaporean population. Reliable airports, roads, telecommunications, and office complexes provide an efficient working environment for the business community. Through a national program, massive state investment in housing enables citizens to move from slums to newly constructed apartment buildings and also serves as a vehicle for a collaborative relationship between the public and private sectors. The provision of housing and jobs on a large scale in turn has produced a "fair state" rather than a welfare state.

Concerning infrastructure management, two features of the experience in Singapore are noteworthy. First, the government entered into supply chain management arrangements to ensure that contractors had reliable access to supplies at predictable prices. Second, it sought to develop engineering capability by investing in a housing corporation and then worked with contractors as partners throughout the year to coproduce the buildings promised to citizens and businesses on time. As a result, the government of Singapore acquired a reputation for delivering on promises and in the process created a superb private-sector-led construction industry. Today, PSA International (formerly the Port of Singapore Authority) is winning contracts for management of ports throughout the world—from Belgium to Panama to Vietnam. In 2006 the volume of containers handled in overseas terminals exceeded that in Singapore's own terminals, indicating the extent to which PSA International has grown and the manner in which it is managing to harness and capitalize upon world trade.[10] Singapore's institutional capacity has itself become a source of revenue.

Underpinning investment in infrastructure was a distinctive approach to the management of financial flows. The government created a set of corporations through which a mandatory proportion of a citizen's wages was directed into savings and pensions accounts in the Central Providence Fund, which in turn financed housing and other public investments. Thus the social contract in Singapore has been dynamic: The construction of new homes and other buildings provided jobs, and opportunities for the population were enhanced and supplemented by campaigns for wage increases and large-scale skills training, which were constantly upgraded to keep pace with changes in the economy.

For Singapore to realize its goal of becoming a first-world oasis, it needed to invest in the talent necessary to underpin economic growth. As Ngiam Tong Dow, a leading civil servant at the time, commented, "The economic imperative was the driving force of our education policies."[11] Investment in human capital has ranged from technical education in industrial training (particularly in higher-end precision engineering and process industries) to specialized financial services. High-achieving students were sent to Oxford, Cambridge, Stanford, and Harvard; top generals received business degrees and were circulated out of the army to run corporations; and investment in talent was in general widespread. After nine years as prime minister, Lee Kuan Yew himself went on sabbatical to the Kennedy School of Government at Harvard to reflect on the next phase of Singapore's development.

To position itself as a financial center, Singapore used its "location" in time—its time zone—as an asset. In 1968, noticing a quiet period in global financial markets in the hours between the San Francisco market closure and the Swiss market opening at 9 AM, Singapore realized it could manage this time period to create twenty-four-hour, around-the-world service in money and banking. To create trust in its ability to fulfill this role, Singapore "had to fight every inch of the way to establish confidence in our integrity, competence and judgment. The history of our financial center is the story of how we built up credibility as a place of integrity, and developed the officers with the knowledge and skills to regulate and supervise the banks, security houses, and other financial institutions."[12] One might call this a blueprint for the creation of the necessary institutions in a failed state, even where the materials for these seem nonexistent. "The foundations for our financial center were the rule of law, an independent judiciary, and a stable, competent, and honest government that pursued sound macroeconomic policies, with budget surpluses almost every year."[13] In the 1970s and 1980s the Monetary Authority of Singapore proved its reputation as a strict and credible financial center when it denied a license to the Bank of Credit and Commerce International (BCCI), an unproven and poorly capitalized financial house.

Although the broad directions of the strategy were clearly articulated early in Singapore's transformation, the exact details developed over time through a careful balance of both orchestration and improvisation. Singapore's leaders remained open to new ideas and were willing both to seize new opportunities and, given the changing global context, to leverage the assets that had been created. Singapore "embarked on a journey along an unmarked road to an unmarked destination" that would turn crisis into opportunity through pragmatism and imagination.[14] For Lee Kuan Yew and his colleagues, strategy was a constant process of adjustment to the outside world. Even though the outcome may now have an air of inevitability, at the time it required constant refinement of strategy, as Lee pointed out: "We cannot afford to forget that public order, personal security, economic and social progress, and prosperity are not the natural order of things; that they depend on ceaseless effort and attention from an honest and effective government that the people must elect."[15]

During the process of Singapore's transformation, state functions changed. In the 1970s, for example, the budget was used as a mechanism to control line ministries and ensure full accountability and transparency. The only exception was the Ministry of Defense, which was given block grants—nonearmarked finances—to be spent as necessary. This arrangement was based on trust, given that the first minister of defense had been a former minister of finance, and his colleagues had full confidence in his accountability. In the 1990s block grants to all of the various ministries became standard. The challenge that Singapore currently faces is that its ministries, while totally competent, still cannot deal with an aging population and with it a narrowing tax base. This requires coordination across many line ministries, and Singapore's Ministry of Finance is exploring new mechanisms to ensure that the challenges of coordination can be met more effectively. Because of its immense accomplishments in the past, Singapore's present leaders are relentlessly focused on the future and are highly aware that the conditions that made their strategy unique have changed. China and India are courting international investment, thereby forcing Singapore to adapt to new global dynamics to consolidate progress. Singaporean leaders are now engaged in intensive discussion on the set of strategic initiatives that could ensure continued prosperity for the island nation.

To take what might be a more surprising (yet no less impressive) example of state transformation, let us consider the southern states of the United States. These states are, of course, units of a federal system. However, as late as the 1960s, this region was far behind the rest of the nation in economic progress, development, and even the legitimacy of its institutions. A great deal of the problem lay in its history: slavery, defeat in the Civil War, and an often-misguided process of reconstruction.

The South of the 1960s conjures up images of poverty, segregation, and the violation of civil rights. In Mississippi, for example, the median family income for African Americans during this period was less than $3,000 a year.[16] A picture that defined the era was that of police dogs unleashed against an African American man during mass youth protests in Birmingham, Alabama, in 1963. George Wallace, a well-known segregationist, was elected governor of Alabama in 1962; in his inaugural speech he stated, "In the name of the greatest people that have ever trod this earth, I draw the line in the dust and toss the gauntlet before the feet of tyranny, and I say segregation now, segregation tomorrow, segregation forever."[17] In 1963 Wallace opposed a federal mandate to allow African Americans to attend schools with whites; that same year he literally stood in the doorway of the all-white University of Alabama to block the attempt of two black students to register.

Wallace is just one example of the deep-seated enmity and exclusionary practices that pervaded Southern life in the 1960s: His behavior and sentiments were not unusual. In 1963, even after the civil rights movement had brought attention to the injustice of segregation,

69 percent of Southern whites felt that blacks and whites should attend separate schools. The state was used as an instrument of exclusion and repression for a significant minority of the population. It was not utilized as a tool to create a sense of citizenship or to balance the tensions between inequality and solidarity. In many ways, the Southern states in the mid-twentieth century would have been considered highly fragile and potentially failed states in any other context except within the federal union of the United States.

The governors of the Southern states in the twenty-first century now proclaim a very different reality and a diverse set of priorities. Instead of a repressive politics and an economy based on cotton, tobacco, sugar, and slave labor, the South has become politically open and receptive of new ideas and has developed into a global hub of commercial life and scientific creativity. In 2006 twenty million tourists visited Alabama and spent more than $9 billion there. Georgia's economy has grown by 18 percent since 2002 to a GDP of $363 billion. As Governor Perdue has pointed out, "If Georgia were a stand-alone country, we would have the seventeenth largest economy in the world." In 1937 Southern incomes were only half the U.S. average; today they are 91 percent of it.

In addition, the South is home to eighteen of the top thirty "best-performing cities" in the United States, as judged by a 2006 index; Atlanta is home to more Fortune 500–company headquarters than any other U.S. city except New York and Houston; and today, three times more blacks move to the South each year than leave it.[18] Spurning Wallace's legacy and recognizing the centrality of investment in higher education to the economy, Alabama's governor Bob Riley said in 2007 that "By 2010, more than 80% of all jobs will require skill levels beyond those gained in high school. Almost every worker will need training and education at, at least, the postsecondary level. That is why we must provide more opportunities for Alabamians to get the technical training they need to be successful in today's global market."[19]

These impressive accomplishments constitute a significant departure but not yet a complete break from the Southern legacy. Race remains a significant issue, and, as the lack of preparedness for Hurricane Katrina and the problems in reconstructing New Orleans illustrate, both the state and the federal government face the challenge of forming effective mechanisms for dealing with the environmental and social consequences of natural disasters. To get an idea of the new politics emerging, we analyzed the speeches of the Southern governors. While their words may be aspirational and inspirational and may not always be followed up by implementation, they nevertheless reveal the preoccupations of the South's citizens as understood and interpreted by their elected leaders. These speeches are not only rhetoric, as they become part of an ongoing dialogue between governing elites, people, and the press. For citizens of the developed world, such leadership and public discussion are now assumed; a comparison of these speeches with those of the national and provincial leaders of the forty to sixty failed states that we have mentioned—in which citizens' genuine concerns are rarely addressed—demonstrates that they are truly remarkable.

Positioning Virginia as the "leader of change in a changing world...poised to seize the boundless opportunities of a dynamic new age," Governor Jim Gilmore stated that Virginia is now the "Internet capital of the world. Half of the world's Internet traffic travels through Virginia."[20] North Carolina ranks as the best place for doing business in the United States, and its governor, Mike Easley, in 2007 rejoiced that "It is great to have the best business climate in America. It is great to have the best credit rating in America. And it is great to have made the most education progress in the country."[21] Justifying increased investment in education, Governor Kathleen Blanco of Louisiana went as far as to reject the notion of poverty: "Poverty is just too expensive. Wouldn't it be nice to spend more money where we want to and less money where we have to?"[22]

The South now has low taxes, weak unions, business-friendly state governments, great weather, and a quality of life that is attracting a greater and greater share of the educated workforce from the United States and elsewhere.[23] In his state of the state address of 2001, Governor Roy Barnes tells in detail the story of Georgia's transformation: "Through hard work and good leadership, we have all created a place where people want to live and work, and where companies want to do business." He continues:

> None of this happened by accident. I'm old enough to remember when most of the roads in places like my home...weren't even paved. People who wanted to live in an area like that usually had no access to public water or sewers, much less public parks, ball fields, swimming pools and libraries. The schools throughout our state were among the worst in the nation, so our workforce was undereducated and underpaid. In short, we lacked the kind of infrastructure and amenities that businesses were looking for, and that are necessary if we are to enjoy a great quality of life.

But over the last four decades, something remarkable happened. Georgia was blessed with strong leaders who avoided the kind of divisive distractions that held back most other cities and states in the South. Our leaders understood the need for roads, and for other improvements like water and sewer systems. These investments opened up new areas for development where people could afford to realize the American Dream of owning their own home. We made a good start toward preserving recreational areas like the Chattahoochee River. And we began to pay attention to our schools.[24]

Broader examination of the story of the South shows how a generation of leaders managed to create a break with the underdeveloped, backward past and created a new, hopeful, and dynamic future through a combination of investment in military bases (Georgia's thirteen military installations now contribute more than $25 billion a year to Georgia's economy and provide hundreds of thousands of jobs), public infrastructure (through a federal-state partnership), and higher education. Law and order are still issues in the South, but they are now less central as citizen concerns.

Going forward, Southern governors are acutely aware that a prosperous future requires the adoption of innovation and active positioning if their states are to be able to take advantage of the forces of globalization. The innovation economy depends on highly skilled labor, and the South aspires to be on the frontier of this new system. Analysis of recent state of the state addresses bears out this idea. Mike Easley knows that his job is to "keep North Carolina competitive in the global marketplace."[25] Governor Sonny Perdue of Georgia understands that in order "to lead, we must innovate. That means we must become a State of Innovation. That means making innovation our competitive advantage in every area of our economy—in our existing industries, in our homegrown small businesses and in the growth industries of the future, such as life sciences and nano-manufacturing." Building an innovation economy, he says, requires "three main ingredients: people, capital and infrastructure."[26]

Investment in human capital tops the list of priorities in the South. Indeed, the report on Governors' speeches by the National Governors Association documented that, in 2007, 90 percent of all governors described in their speeches their efforts to improve education or provide incentives to businesses to promote knowledge-based industries. North Carolina's famous Research Triangle Park, known as the "Silicon Valley of the East," was founded in the 1950s as a research site to stimulate cooperation among research organizations and foster development of new industries to help stem the "brain drain" that was occurring as area graduates left North Carolina to secure well-paid jobs elsewhere. Today the park is home to more than 150 organizations that employ more than thirty-nine thousand full-time staff members, and capital investment exceeds $2 billion.[27]

Governors consider it part of their job actively to court businesses. Governor Blanco of Louisiana explained that her "economic development team is aggressively pursuing more than one hundred leads with a potential capital investment of $13 billion."[28] Governor Perdue of Georgia says, "We are working tirelessly to cultivate new relationships with businesses around the world. Last year alone, we made more than 31 trade missions to 23 countries. But we can do more."[29] Mississippi has also invested heavily in public-private partnerships to upgrade its infrastructure.

Policymakers in the South realize that their electorates expect leadership as well as service: Governor Perdue admits that "They expect us to work hard, to work smart and to find innovative solutions that work for them." North Carolina's Governor Easley claims that "state government must keep working to be more efficient. I am bringing together the best minds of the public and private sector."[30] At the same time, leaders must overcome a legacy of bad governance. Governor Blanco faces up to Louisiana's past with the frank recognition that "Our political past hurts us. One of the most discouraging things I hear from out-of-state CEOs is their negative perception of Louisiana. Many of these CEOs have avoided our state for years. They believe that to do business in Louisiana requires them to deal under the table."[31]

Not surprisingly, a new theme that emerged in speeches several years ago is that of stewardship of the environment and the environmental legacy for the next generation. Governor Perdue of Georgia comments: "There's a Native American saying that I think sums it up: We do not inherit the earth from our ancestors, we borrow it from our children."[32] Governor Blanco says, "Let us be the generation of leaders that had the courage to invest in the greatest environmental restoration effort in American History."[33]

Through these speeches, a picture of the state as coordinator, planner, and steward emerges. Governors are implicitly or explicitly examining their role and constantly reassessing their functions in order to serve their citizens. Governor Mark Warner of Virginia has outlined a "top-to-bottom review of state government. This review will consider the consolidation of state agencies. It will examine the very functions of state government—because there may be some things state government is doing that we can no longer afford. It will seek out new opportunities to integrate new management techniques into state government. Finally, it will identify ways that increased utilization of technology can allow us to serve our citizens more effectively."[34]

All of the governors recognize that the budget is an instrument of policy. Governor Perdue correctly points out that "at its heart there is no difference between balancing the state budget and balancing the family checkbook."[35] Governor Mike Easley goes further: "Our budget is not just a numbers game. It reflects our values. For we know, where a man's treasure is, there also is his heart. Budgets are about educating our children, training our workers and helping the least of our people."[36] Looking into the future, leaders in the "New South" realize that they cannot rest on their laurels for a moment. According to Governor Perdue, "To understand the State of the State, we must not simply look at Georgia as a snapshot. Georgia is a changing, dynamic action video that is moving at the speed of a NASCAR race."[37] Jim Gilmore beseeched his audience to "acknowledge we live in a time of change,"[38] and Mike Easley further emphasizes that "we must get off the old familiar road and be willing to embrace change."[39]

Ireland's recent transformation is as impressive as that of the American South. In the Great Famine (1845–1849), it is estimated that between 500,000 and 2 million Irish citizens died, and more than 1 million fled the country. Out-migration continued for another seventy years.[40] Ireland was looked upon with disdain by writers ranging from Jonathan Swift (an Irish patriot himself) to Friedrich Engels, who asked Karl Marx, "How often have the Irish set out to achieve something and each time been crushed, politically and industrially? Ireland has been stunted in her development by the English invasion and thrown centuries back."[41]

By the 1960s, Ireland was one of the poorest countries in Western Europe: Protectionist, self-sufficiency policies and nationalization under Eamon de Valera since the 1930s had led to economic stagnation, and the country relied heavily on agricultural exports to the United Kingdom. In 1960 Ireland's GDP per capita was just 60 percent of the EU average. In 2007 it was 140 percent of the EU average.[42] In contrast, Ireland today has one of the fastest-growing economies in Europe. The scale of the change can best be captured by the details of state expenditure in the National Development Plan (NDP). For the period from 2000 to 2005 the NDP entailed an expenditure of

€51.28 billion, while that for the period from 2007 to 2013 has a planned expenditure of €184 billion.[43]

This striking change in the budget is a reflection of the transformation of the Irish economy and polity from a closed national system, which was in place until the 1960s, to an open society eager to embrace opportunities afforded by the European Union and globalization. Ireland now has the second highest per capita income of any country in the EU (Luxembourg has the highest) and the fourth highest in the world based on measurements of GDP per capita. At $44,500, Ireland's GDP is 140 percent of the EU average.[44] It now ranks twenty-first in the Global Competitiveness Index, seventh in the Economic Freedom Index,[45] and first in the Economist Intelligence Unit's quality-of-life index.[46]

Actors and observers point to four factors in this story of transformation. First, just as Singapore used its time zone as its key asset, Ireland sensed an emerging opportunity in the field of technology and positioned itself to be the technology center of Europe. As early as 1992, even before the Internet became a widely used global platform, Ireland became the eHub for the region and thus was able to take advantage of the Internet revolution to develop a cluster of related industries such as call centers and financial services. Partnering with the Irish diaspora, which had become prominent within U.S. technology companies, Ireland worked relentlessly to attract these corporations to the country as a European hub. These businesspeople were attracted by the system of low corporation taxes, Ireland's location between the United States and mainland Europe, the attractive regulatory environment and access to the EU's single market. In the age of the agricultural and industrial economy, poor infrastructure and services had prevented Ireland from becoming a hub for trade and investment, but the Internet helped to overcome these constraints. In 1960 an estimated 65 percent of Irish exports were agriculturally based; in 2000 the figure had dropped to only 6 percent as a reflection of the hundreds of thousands of new jobs created in the technology industry. Employment in the service sector increased by 27.6 percent between 1999 and 2005.[47] Dell, Hewlett Packard, Equipment Manufacturing Corporation (EMC), and Apple Computer all have manufacturing facilities in Ireland, and software companies such as Oracle and Microsoft have their European headquarters in the country.

A second driving force was Ireland's accession to Europe in 1973 and its eligibility for Europe's structural and cohesion funds. With accession, Ireland was able to integrate with European markets and became eligible for massive financial transfers. Net receipts from the EU averaged 4 percent of GDP between 1973 and 1986 and 3 percent of GDP between 1995 and 2000.[48] During the implementation of the 2000–2006 national development plan, Ireland was eligible for €3.8 billion in grants from the EU. Rather than plan specific projects to absorb EU aid, Ireland used this assistance as part of a carefully wrought, integrated plan for economic and social development that has allowed it to far outperform other European countries that have received similar or even greater subsidies and grants. John Bruton, Ireland's prime minister from 1994 to 1997, stated in discussions that Ireland mapped its assets—an educated labor force and its inherited administrative structures—and put them to work in new combinations to spur productivity and growth.

In addition, Mary Robinson has pointed out in discussions that structural funds were used as catalysts to engineer partnerships between communities, local government, and businesses that unleashed a wave of dynamism and creativity. National policy and European funds were aligned to serve needs at the local level, thereby capitalizing on the energies of the Irish people and providing an overarching framework that combined flexibility and innovation at the local level to allow new policies to emerge over time.

The third driving force of change in Ireland was leadership. Bruton understood the importance of reconciliation in Ireland within the broader European project—the two could feed off each other: "The success of the European Movement provides an excellent example for Ireland as we work to build reconciliation on our own island. The achievement of Europe in overcoming the bitterness of two world wars, and several regional conflicts which had similar characteristics to the Northern Ireland problem, should be an inspiration."[49] Negative, backward-looking economics were transformed into positive momentum by development; the politics of division and revenge were molded into a constructive, peaceful consensus by the promise of progress.

In the process, Ireland has recast its politics in developmental terms. Seeing its fortune linked to Europe and a globalizing world, it wants to take maximum advantage of opportunities for expanding its national vision and imagination. Instead of viewing the institutions of Europe and globalization as a straitjacket, it understands the new rules of the game as a context in which it must play. Ireland is forging a new social contract that strikes a balance between investment in innovation and social inclusion. Its latest development plan includes a staggering €59 billion for human capital and social infrastructure, including

€21 billion for housing and €20 billion for investment in enterprise, science, and innovation.[50] Ireland is embarking on a new type of long-term planning that is treating spatial boundaries in imaginative ways. A twenty-year National Spatial Strategy, focused on "people, places and potential," aims to achieve a "better balance of social, economic and physical development between regions" by consciously focusing on quality of life. Each county is seen as a fixed administrative unit, but the plan promotes new mechanisms for collaboration among Ireland's cities and counties to maximize their respective opportunities and create a number of new "gateways" and hubs of sufficient scale to drive development across the country.[51] Ireland has explicitly framed an intergenerational approach to take care of elderly people and people with disabilities, while investing in the future for its youth.

These descriptions of state transformation are by no means exhaustive. We cite them only to indicate that state transformation can be achieved when the necessary relationships and planning are put in place. Nor are these examples exhaustive in terms of scope. Stories of remarkable transformation in recent times are not limited to the cases we cite here. We could have described many others. During the course of our developmental work, we have studied transformations in places as varied as India, China, accession countries from southern and central Europe, towns and cities in Latin America, the Gulf states of Dubai and Qatar, and many countries throughout Africa. Investigating these stories has yielded an immense repertoire of techniques and technologies that could guide those who are seeking to initiate state reform, create stocks of institutional capacity, and ensure that their countries become an integral part of a globalizing world.

It is not just the state that has been innovating collaborative partnerships across state, market and civil society boundaries. Another strand from which our work at the Institute for State Effectiveness has drawn many lessons is the story of corporate transformation. The practice of transforming failed companies into profitable enterprises has been subject to extensive codification and reflection. The failure of large-scale institutions in the private sector is a persistent trend that is marked by the fact that only a few of the companies considered as sector leaders in the last five decades are still in vanguard positions. In a significant number of cases, however, companies have been able to stage comebacks from the verge of destruction or bankruptcy. Critical factors in these recoveries include company leadership and strategies to align goals with capacity and resources, both human and material.

Company failure is an issue that has received much attention from practitioners and analysts in the business field. A large body of techniques derived from empirical analysis and formulated as accessible guidelines for formulation of strategy is available, and a sufficient number of failed companies have been transformed or nursed back to health. They provide evidence of a strategic path for moving from organizational failure to organizational success. Of course, techniques and theories cannot be uncritically shifted from one domain to another; structural differences exist between the public and private sectors. In the former, public value rather than financial profit must be created, and the public sector must often satisfy its political, as well as its "customer," base. Creative adaptation allows for framing the question of state failure and state building in the light of corporate experience. The adaptation of certain private-sector techniques (e.g., balanced scorecard, backward mapping from an objective to the situation at hand, catalytic mechanisms, and identification of critical tasks) could be instrumental in developing and implementing the strategies and collaboration arrangements needed to close the sovereignty gap in developing countries.

The civil society space is also spearheading new types of public-private-voluntary partnerships. The "social entrepreneurship" movement—which harnesses private-sector techniques to a social purpose—yields many examples of the creation of immense value from collaboration between state, market and civil society players from the international to the local levels. Rather than leaving societal needs for the government or business sectors to address, social entrepreneurs—according to Ashoka, the global association created to support such people—use the citizen sector to "create innovative solutions to society's most pressing social problems" to offer "new ideas for wide-scale change."

Efforts to encourage fair trade now support small producers in Africa, Asia, and Latin America; the Starbucks-Care alliance in Latin America and the Grameen-Telenor collaboration in Asia are fostering entrepreneurship and development. In Ireland in the 1990s, social partnership programs that were negotiated between the government, trade unions, and employer organizations were an important part of the country's economic regeneration. Former president Bill Clinton's Harlem Initiative brought together small businesses, volunteers from business school, lawyers, and financiers to craft a strategy to make small businesses more profitable.

Investment by the Aga Khan's development network—a business and philanthropic organization of one of the Muslim communities—in hotels and telecoms in Afghanistan has also yielded a business model that is being widely replicated. Putting investment funds up both to open a five-star hotel and establish a telecommunications business in Afghanistan after September 11, 2001, when most entrepreneurs were eyeing the country with caution, the Aga Khan Foundation has made impressive profits while investing in the social fabric of the country. The government required that 70 percent of staff members be Afghan, and locals were trained in carpentry and interior design before work could begin. In the contract for the telecommunications license, the foundation also stipulated that rural—and not just urban—areas must receive service.

These stories of transformation demonstrate the possibility of either creating or recombining existing assets to develop stocks of financial, human, and intellectual capital that will enable a country to connect with global economic, financial, and knowledge flows. Such processes create a smooth interface between the polity, the economy, and the citizenry—an arrangement that creates a dynamic compact for effective governance with reinforcing and self-perpetuating loops. States that turn their focus from a narrow-minded focus on security to a much broader social agenda create an environment in which the private sector can generate capital and jobs.

In some cases, this has created unimaginable wealth. In every instance, a potential opportunity—time in Singapore, commercial and intellectual change in the American South, technology in Ireland—has been imaginatively seized and relentlessly exploited. The entire architecture was not conceived at the point of initiation but rather nurtured through the development of management teams and implementation systems that were able to translate visions into reality, step by step. These processes continue as governance is perceived not as static but as a continuously evolving process. The optimal relationship between the state, the market, and citizens is forever changing, and policies to account for this must do the same.

Critical to success in all of these situations have been the state's willingness and ability to ensure a credible partnership with both established and emerging corporations and to redefine the social contract by investing in its citizens. Efforts by national leaders to map systematically and gradually build up stocks within their countries have also been crucial. These stocks are not just financial but also consist of infrastructure, human capital, and natural resources, all of which promote development. At the forefront has been the determination to build stocks of institutional capability and to rethink governance.

These players create the image and reality of integrity and competence within the public sector. While some countries were fortunate enough to have sound institutional structures in place to adapt to globalization, many others have had to confront their histories of systematic corruption and force a break with the past to ensure transparency and accountability.

These examples demonstrate that the development of human capital has been essential to successful transitions. Until 1945, university-level and technical education was confined to very limited groups. For instance, in 1949, when Indonesia obtained its independence, only about sixty Indonesian engineers resided and worked in that nation of eighty-two million people. All successful transformations have required investment in large numbers of technical skills, ranging from infrastructure and engineering to leadership and management. When a country positions itself to connect to the knowledge economy, investment in technology and innovation is essential. The United States predicts that it will need more than four hundred thousand new software engineers a year to stay competitive—showing how much the pace of change in our world requires constant investment in and upgrading of skills.

Wealth and opportunity lie in linking these financial, infrastructural, human, and institutional stocks to the web of flows in the world around them. Leaders of successful national transitions reinvented their countries as "nodes of value" by creating the necessary institutions; they built linkages not only by halting the diaspora—enticing the technology gurus to return home from Silicon Valley to Ireland and Bangalore—but also by building institutional capital. They understood that socially and culturally their countries could be national, but economically they had to be global. Whereas Singapore, Dubai, South Africa, and China have allowed for flows into and out of their countries, Sudan, Algeria and Afghanistan, before 9/11, did not. Rather than assuming the boundaries of the nation-state, leaders have realized that hierarchy alone does not work and that they must find different ways of connecting the community, local, national, regional, and international levels of interactions. These leaders have also realized that the state is not entirely autonomous in its rule making; rather, it must find ways to ensure that its rules and processes are aligned with the systems with which they wish to connect.

Embarking on these paths of transition has required efforts to overcome the perception that capitalism is necessarily exploitative and that the relationship between government and corporations is inherently confrontational. Successful governments have forged partnerships between the state and the market to create value for their citizens; these partnerships are both profitable financially and sustainable politically and socially. While retaining the formal power to promulgate and enforce laws, the state has entered into relationships with other players—corporations, universities, civil society movements—to determine the type of rules necessary and mechanisms of credible enforcement. In the process, states have become not just the site of rights but also bearers of obligations to their social and economic partners in a manner very different from that of earlier forms of autocratic central planning or even the modern social welfare state. In each case, success has been based on the formation of collaborative partnerships that turn what used to be opposition and contradiction into cooperation and collaboration.

In the end, the most significant asset in this process is trust. As reputations evolve to ensure adherence to agreements, they become a key factor in the decision-making process of other economic and social actors when considering whether to enter into and then expand a range of partnerships. An entire series of devices ranging from the formal instruments of credit rating to indices of competitiveness, quality of life, and friendliness to business have emerged to allow for comparison between countries, counties, and cities. In a context where decision makers have numerous options available to them in terms of resource flow management, it is critical to attract assets actively rather than expect them to gravitate toward any specific country. Leadership for success is not about dominance in a hierarchy but about managing complexity and interrelationships; it is about good governance and about building multistakeholder relations and processes.

There is now an unprecedented glut of global financial capital. Connecting to it and utilizing it, however, require an institutional architecture that can be created only through patience, integrity, and vision. This cannot happen without a state structure that provides the necessary support and performs the essential coordination functions. While theory has not yet caught up with it, a model for the development of this framework has been emerging.

THREE

Webs and Flows of Cooperation

IN THE DEVELOPED world today we can travel on airlines, purchase goods from supermarkets, and send instantaneous communications around the globe without thinking twice. Consider life about sixty years ago. In 1945 the world had just suffered the most devastating war in history, global political and economic systems lay in ruins, and political leaders in the United States were terrified by the prospect of mass starvation in Europe. Everyday activities were difficult. But for many people today, these types of problems are still daily realities. In half the countries of the world, citizens remain impoverished, starving, and excluded from any means whereby they can improve their situation. Traveling by plane, moving freely through public spaces to buy groceries and communicating with anyone other than close neighbors are simply not activities that factor into daily life.

Underlying what seem like mundane transactions in the West is a series of extraordinary institutional innovations that are now so entrenched as to be unnoticeable. At their core is a nexus that binds the state, the market and citizens into cooperative arrangements that have generated unprecedented wealth and an enhanced quality of life. Underlying the global flows is a relentless drive for investing in effective value chains, processes, and logistics. We are both participants and consumers in these value chains: That is to say, we both produce value in our everyday work and create demand for goods and services, thereby allowing others to produce even more value for themselves. It is our participation in and dependence upon these webs of value creation that legitimize the social order in our societies.

To illustrate this idea, let us analyze several everyday experiences. As air passengers in the West, we take for granted the experience of flying from one place to another and all of the processes it involves. But at each point—from check-in to takeoff to touchdown—the citizen's choices and experiences are determined by public policy. Regardless of whether the passenger travels to the airport by train or taxi, the location of the airport, the choice of airlines, and the range of services they are offered are the product of decisions agreed upon over long periods of time. Another layer of choices is entirely hidden from view: service access, security arrangements, air traffic control, and supply chain arrangements for delivery of food. There are no roads in the sky, yet every airplane moves along a route that is much more closely regulated than a highway. And since air travel frequently involves crossing national boundaries, the rules for international travel require the collaboration of both countries and companies. More than four billion passengers flew through the world's largest airports in 2007.[1] This enormous daily movement of people is now choreographed through connections between public regulation or provision, corporate activity, and citizen choice.

A large airport is a multibillion dollar enterprise that involves technological processes with a highly complex value chain; it is facilitated by hundreds of private-sector organizations that have broken down services into individual, manageable blocks. If we consider that these airports and the flights among them are linked within one huge network, we can begin to understand that our simple flight from one city to another (even on a regional carrier from one small town to another) is based upon a vast and profoundly complicated web of interrelations, procedures, rules, and systems that are all produced, mediated, and regulated by the public sector and refined at every level over years and years of operation and experience.

Air travel is a remarkable example of networked governance that allows for global private-sector expansion: The origins and operation of each airline might be entirely different, but a space regulated by common rules creates an interface that makes worldwide commercial aviation possible. This system of governance for air travel is based on networks of trust. Countries that act as nodes for globalization are all part of this, and they cooperate in a way that allows us to fly to our chosen destinations. One need only glance at the flight maps in the pocket of any airline seat to understand the pattern of network hubs and the density of interactions that have allowed for the expansion of airline flights during the last decade.

Each of the countries in which there is reliable air service understands and trusts that the systems and processes in another country will provide the safety and security needed to allow flights to operate without a glitch among them. The rules for air travel, which governments agree upon, provide the boundaries that mark the lanes in which aircraft can fly. Flight-pattern regulations provide virtual white lines to guide pilots from one destination to another. The remote choreography of not only the hundreds of different airplanes in the sky but also the interlinking processes that are necessary to support their operation is astounding in its complexity and ingenuity. The takeoff and landing of even a single plane is the product of endless work and intense scrutiny that make control of the airways appear seamless.

Just as we can see flight patterns on airline maps, we can imagine similar flows of any number of goods and ideas in the modern world; the contours might be different, but the concept is very much the same. What makes this experience possible is the delicate web of interconnections between the public sphere, corporations and citizens. While it is not always immediately obvious to us, especially to those who wish to minimize the degree of its intrusion, the state plays a vital role in everyday life. The fact is, rules are resources, just as finances are resources that the state can use to regulate key aspects of life for its citizenry. Without these rules the system would fall apart. Imagine boarding a plane in which the pilot had no idea what rules governed which runway or how to decide which aircraft should land first. The absence of these publicly provided regulations would result in standstill or disaster. As an air passenger, one often feels like the consumer of private services, but it is an entire set of public investments that makes airline travel possible.

In contrast, taking a flight between dysfunctional states is a highly disruptive and burdensome experience; processes and systems are manual, and reliability and safety questionable. Rather than feeling protected, the passenger often feels apprehensive when shaken down by customs and security officials and asked to bribe the police who are supposed to be upholding the rule of law. Countries that suffer from weak systems and processes and poor governance are therefore blocked from participation in the seamless network of air travel found in the developed world.

While creating and operating a functioning airline industry is hugely expensive, it is not finances that prevent countries from joining the system of networked governance. It is lack of trust. The functions that a state must perform in order to establish an enabling environment for air travel are well known and have become standardized across domains such as aircraft licensing, maintenance, and airport design. The issue is simply that countries that are part of the normalized network judge many fragile states not to be trustworthy members and therefore exclude them from full participation. In March 2006, for example, the European Union banned ninety-four airlines from fourteen countries from landing at European airports.[2] Dubai has its own solution since it serves as a hub for travel to and from many countries in the region: It maintains two separate terminals, one for flights to developed countries, and another for flights on irregular airlines to countries such as Iraq, Iran, and Afghanistan. Countries that are off the grid are in many cases rich in economic and natural resources but poor in terms of rules and regulations—the resource that is vital for the effective functioning of everyday services from air travel to health care.

Consider another example from daily experience: a trip to the supermarket to buy groceries. We buy bananas from Costa Rica or salmon from Scotland without a second thought, but bringing these products to the shelves requires an intricate chain of transactions and procedures—again an intricate choreography of space and time—from the moment they are plucked from a tree or fished from a river to the moment they arrive at the supermarket, often on the other side of the globe. Today $10.1 trillion worth of goods are transported by sea, land, and air every year by means of a set of interlinkages that create complex global value chains connected by economic hubs.[3]

The process that created this transactional system began centuries ago but accelerated in the nineteenth century with the direct transport of wheat to markets in Britain each month from colonies around the world. This demanded an integration of railways, shipping (with the innovation of containers), harbors, and highways to allow the transformation of goods into commodities. The synchronization of ships and railroads enabled the movement of hitherto unimaginable quantities of goods. A comparison between railroads and carts indicates the nature of the constraints that were overcome. In 1884 W. H. Hunter estimated that, in India, it would have taken 220,000 carts using 750,000 men and bullocks to carry the volume of grain transported by one loaded train in a single day.[4] Between 1840 and 1930 railway line mileage globally increased by a factor of two hundred.[5] This period also witnessed a significant increase in the volume of international ocean freight, with a simultaneous decrease in cost, as well as the transition from sailing ships to steamships.[6] Changes in the speed of circulation were even more impressive than the changes in volume, for distances previously measured in months could now be measured in weeks. The consolidation of time as a measure of motion was a signal of the oncoming subordination of geography to political economy. Spatial configuration could thus be deconstructed and restructured by capital.

Despite the immense pathbreaking of the knowledge economy, our current phase of globalization is still dependent on extractive industries. Flows of oil and gas still run the engine of global economic activity, which underlies the flow of information, commodities, and capital. These flows are made possible by a complicated network of pipelines, tankers, refineries, and distributors to gas pumps and homes, which links the Middle East and other oil-producing countries, such as Russia and Latin America, to the consuming nations of the United States, China, India, and Europe. Oil and gas exemplify natural capital. Institutional forms of use of this natural capital have varied, with the United States allowing the right of extraction to private players and the Middle East and Russia vesting the right exclusively in the state to either extract directly or award extraction concessions. Mass production of cars began in earnest in the 1920s; today more than 590 million cars are on the roads.

Yet the full implications of dependence on a carbon economy and our failure to account for the full costs of using up natural resources for our health and security are just now being appreciated. The profits—known as rent—from this economy constitute a major factor in relations between states and their citizens, where a significant share of the revenue comes from extractive industry, skewing the relationship between representation and taxation. Globally, it has meant an oil- and gas-driven foreign policy in which consumer nations have courted authoritarian regimes.

The supermarket checkout point—where today we swipe our debit or credit card to buy goods—is a result of centuries of innovation in financial instruments that have allowed for the transformation of cash from coin to paper to a plastic card. Money now travels in a virtual flow from your bank balance to a supermarket account in an instant. Understanding of the risks and the design of risk-management instruments, such as insurance, have been essential components of these developments. Simultaneously, personal identities have become embedded in instantaneously accessible histories of past transactions to establish the degree of trustworthiness for entry into (and continued participation in) this system. Both in turn are linked to the development of banking and other credit instruments, where assets that previously had only concrete forms (e.g., houses) are transformed into mortgageable instruments. The pace of abstraction of money and assets has been significantly accelerated by our enhanced capability to manage information and transactions on a vast scale by means of information technology. The number of financial transactions that take place on an annual basis is almost unimaginable. By International Monetary Fund (IMF) estimates, the value of global financial transactions is more than fifty times greater than the value of global trade in goods and services.[7] This would put it in the range of $625 trillion per annum.[8] By contrast, not so long ago, Russians had to exchange shoes for food, and Afghans a basket of currency notes for a loaf of bread. But in places that are off the financial grid, such as Zimbabwe and Somalia, people must barter goods for food even today.

The purchase of goods in supermarkets is also based on an implicit network of trust—consumers trust that the products they buy are of decent quality and are actually what they appear to be. This network of trust is taken for granted until it breaks down, for example, when contaminated imports of Chinese toothpaste or pet food are discovered. The global food supply chain depends on safety standards that have been created and standardized through cooperation among and within countries that have developed a network of trust in each others' systems and procedures. Generally the system works flawlessly, and fears over contamination are rare. This is why, on a day-to-day basis, we do not always appreciate its complexity. It just works.

Again we can see evidence of a contemporary slice of the world on the move, in contrast to those countries at the margins of development, where the obstacles to participation in this system are huge, the shelves are bare, and the people are hungry. While in the West we trust that the food we eat has been stored, prepared, and cooked in sanitary conditions, in the developing world, food is often the source of illness rather than nutrition. When one visits these countries, the difference between functionality and dysfunctionality soon becomes very clear. A zone in which various regulatory regimes have been coordinated and processes made routine in order to create trust is quite dissimilar to one in which regulations are haphazard, processes are dysfunctional, and trust among stakeholders is very low. These obstacles are all institutional rather than the product of culture, geography, or religion. Singapore and Dubai (discussed further in the next chapter) are examples of non-Western countries that have found a path to state functionality and modernity. Indeed, the success of these places was not predictable. Fifty years ago there was deep skepticism that these countries would be able to move so quickly toward prosperity.

Moving, interacting, and transacting freely and without fear in a public place is an everyday experience for men and women living in stable countries. Indeed, they consider it a fundamental right. There the military is conspicuous only by its absence. A sense of safety is made possible both by the lack of overt use of force and by the assumption that force, as defined by law, can be used only to protect people; one's body is therefore one's own. Others respect that autonomy as well. These daily events again have layers and layers of history that are deeply embedded in the changes in the relation between governments and the governed. In democratic societies, the state has by and large become an embodiment of the people's will. The contrast with unstable areas, where ordinary people are afraid to venture into public places, given the ever-present threat of violence, could not be more pronounced.

All of these examples indicate that our world today is one of literal and symbolic connections between the public, the private, and the citizen and that value is derived from chains of relationships among these stakeholders. The scale and scope of flows of information, goods, and ideas, as well as the value that increased interaction has generated, indicate that the limits to wealth creation may be far less circumscribed than we once thought. This shift has happened rapidly yet subtly, and this new architecture has outstripped our traditional theories of both economics and politics. That is what makes this period in history both so unique and so difficult to understand.

Five aspects of this new, networked world are of particular interest. First, in most OECD countries, a framework has been devised that balances the activities of the state, the market, and the citizen. This recognizes a public sphere of accountability and the rule of law; the market as a competitive space in which law allows freedom to contract, as well as the means of regulation; and a space for civil society where voluntary association is permissible. The citizen in this world is knowledgeable and may participate in all three spheres.

Second, while public policy provides the boundaries for action, law does not regulate the minutiae of daily transactions. In contrast to the miserable failures of the fascist and communist regimes of the twentieth century, the world created by the post–World War II visionaries provided a flexible architecture that allowed for sufficiently predictable order through law, as well as sufficient freedom of action through creation of a space for innovation and competition. Law brought regulation to the marketplace and allowed enough flexibility for the market to become global. A set of intricate relationships among multiple players, undergoing constant reform and calibration, has become a vehicle for the creation of immense wealth. This framework allows for gradual change, constant flux, and even massive disruptions without incurring the collapse or overthrow of the entire order or of the institution of law. A series of arrangements has created a web of laws, rules, information, and practices that enable public players, private entities, and citizens to come together. Currently, debate in much of the world is not about the legitimacy of the order itself but about the specific balance of the market, the network, and the hierarchy.

Third, this world has been made possible by a massive public investment in the well-being of the citizen, in the infrastructure of communication, knowledge, and law, and in market-enhancing mechanisms. Public policy determines the set of rules that establishes the actual and conceptual pathways that allow value to be created and interoperability across boundaries to be achieved. Public policy is all around us, defining our daily experiences and life chances even if we cannot see it. We can coordinate and produce certain interactions between the market, the hierarchy, and networks of citizens, and each offers different possibilities for action. Rules have brought about a private-public-citizen nexus that simply was not possible previously. This opens up a new range of choices and possibilities for state functionality. In the process, these rules have transformed reaction into proaction. The consumer is now a "prosumer," the subject is now a citizen, and the listener is now the opinion former.

Fourth, the world is now evolving according to open systems. The location and nature of hubs of power are rapidly changing, overthrowing previous assumptions about the fixed nature of processes, entities, economies, and polities. In many cases, what used to be the edge of global interaction is now a hub. In this new polycentric world are stocks of human, intellectual, and financial capital in Dubai, Shanghai, Mumbai, São Paulo, Durban, and Moscow. That said, as our everyday examples (to which we return in chapter 4) indicate, many countries still face significant obstacles to joining these systems, and vast numbers of people remain excluded.

Fifth, T. S. Eliot famously asked, "Where is the wisdom we have lost in knowledge?" Despite Eliot's loathing of the mechanical, this question today could easily be reversed. As the processing of information has become mechanical, the journey to knowledge and wisdom has begun in earnest. In a networked world it is not memory of particular pieces of information that makes a person valuable but the capacity to recognize emerging patterns. In knowledge-based economies, human capital is becoming crucial—even more so than financial capital in many respects. In the last three decades we have accumulated a vast repository of wisdom on how to organize flows of information, ideas, goods, and services and how to establish and maintain governance processes. Because of the pace of change, we might not have paused to reflect on this wisdom in a coherent fashion; nevertheless, this accumulated, implicit knowledge resides in the practices around us. We do not need to rehearse the origins of the system as we seek to expand it. We only need make the bases of the practices explicit so that we can utilize functioning frameworks.

John Maynard Keynes, often referred to as the most influential economist of the twentieth century, would recognize the general picture of our contemporary world but would be surprised by some of the specifics. In 1930, when the world was struggling with the Great Depression, he took time to focus on global economic possibilities in his article titled "Economic Possibilities for Our Grandchildren." In contrast to conventional thinking at the time, he argued that economic problems would not be permanent ones for the human race. Predicting that the standard of life in progressive countries some hundred years hence would be four to eight times better than at the time he wrote, he stated that "the course of affairs will simply be that there will be ever larger and larger classes of people from whom problems of economic necessity have been practically removed." His trust in the future, he explained, came from not giving in to two of the prevalent pessimisms of the time: that of the revolutionaries, who put their trust only in violent change, and that of the reactionaries, who believed that any experiment was too risky to undertake.

Keynes saw himself in opposition to Marx. Instead of viewing the end goal as the "withering away" of the state, Keynes set about rethinking the role of the state as an engine of economic change, through both regulation and expenditure. He not only imagined a different world but also joined forces with a group of visionary leaders in Europe and the United States to argue for public policies that would ensure democratic polities and market economies as organizing principles, putting the state at the service of its citizens. This group created the international institutions that would reconstruct a world devastated by the Great Depression and by World War II.

Keynes and his associates were progressive, but at the same time they believed that the architecture for world affairs should remain international, not global; nation-states were still the key constituent blocks. The new wave of globalization with its intricate web of ideas, goods, and services would probably surprise him. Keynes had grown distrustful of globalization and wished to ensure that currency was nationally regulated (restrictions on the transfer of currency between countries was one of his cardinal principles). He defined polities, economies, and societies in national terms and believed that international organizations should mediate between them. Global NGOs and multinational corporations were small in number at the time; they were neither trusted by nor as powerful as policymakers. Keynes's world was one in which political leaders trusted in the state as the key building block and power was vested in very few decision makers.

Today, however, decision rights have become diffuse across multiple organizations. Economic choices are not determined by businesses or states alone. Now, in addition to states and corporations, a constellation of major players—from the news media, financial markets, universities, international organizations, and foundations—drives global decision-making processes. Each has been the site of tremendous innovation.

The growth in these forms of organization and the scale of their financial assets give some indication of the changes that have taken place since 1945. In 1994 Lester Salamon argued that the growth of private associations as part of an "associational revolution" could be for us what the rise of nation-states was for the people of the late nineteenth century.[9] Empirical evidence certainly seems to be confirming his theory. The top five international NGOs now have a combined annual budget of nearly $5 billion. The largest—World Vision—alone has a yearly budget of $2.1 billion dollars.[10] This is larger than the GDP of many African countries and even European countries such as such as Andorra ($1.8 billion), Liechtenstein ($1.7 billion), and San Marino ($1 billion). In terms of resources, these NGOs can now compete with international institutions in many contexts. The United Nations, for example, spends around $15 billion per annum, but this amount is spread over a much wider range of countries and issues than for many NGOs.[11]

Today the resources at the disposal of foundations, universities, and corporations in the United States dwarf government spending in many developing and even developed countries: In 2005 the top fifty American philanthropic foundations had combined assets of around $151 billion, more than the entire budget of the European

Union.[12] University endowments are now reaching unprecedented levels. For instance, Harvard, the world's richest university, had $28 billion in endowment funds in 2006 (more than double the annual education budget for New York City);[13] additionally, global corporations are wealthier and more powerful than ever before. The top five U.S. companies made more than $90 billion in profits in 2006, and in 2005 bonuses paid out on Wall Street alone rose to an all-time high of $21.5 billion.[14]

State building in the twenty-first century will take place against a backdrop of globalization and the emergence of these new players on the global stage. The political leaders of 1945 would probably not have predicted, from the data available then, the variety and type of assets now on hand for this task. The wisdom of accumulated knowledge, the stock of organizations, and the vast amounts of financial and human capital must all be used to create institutions that can function cohesively in the contemporary age.

Based on the architecture created by the leaders of the post–World War II era, such as Keynes, Marshall, and Acheson, a system that embraces democratic polities and market economies has evolved. This system has succeeded in creating prosperity for its citizens and triumphing against its authoritarian alternatives, such as communism and other state-led models of development. Yet our current globalized world presents both challenges and opportunities that do not fit neatly into the architecture that these visionaries created. The intensity, nature, and scale of interactions and flows that we describe have outstripped our academic theories and the categories through which we interpret the world. Too often we see the present through an eighteenth-, nineteenth-, or even twentieth-century lens. Instead, to gain a sense of the history of the future, we need to understand the continual evolution of global rhythms and processes. The emerging trends in the present mark a very real departure from our past, even that of only a few decades ago.

A common refrain we hear is that experiments cannot be carried out in the social sciences because the theories are too nebulous and the data too intangible. The different paths embarked on by the myriad countries around the world during the second half of the twentieth century, however, provide a basis for understanding institutional design and patterns of transformation, both successful and unsuccessful ones. Examining these successes and failures will not only enrich our understanding of both the past and the future but also enable us to understand the importance of human imagination in open moments in history. Just as for Keynes and his colleagues sixty years ago, this activity will help us draw a map of the history of the future. In chapter 2 we examined the success of particular countries in generating a new, coordinating state; in the next chapter we turn to countries that are characterized by syndromes of dysfunctionality and conflict that prevent their citizens from accessing global flows.

FOUR

Failed Politics

MOUNT EVEREST FOR a long time was the symbol of the unreachable. Yet after Edmund Hillary and Tenzing Norgay's ascent, it became a symbol of the human capability to set and reach a goal. For the people living in Everest's shadow, another objective is still unmet, however: harnessing Nepal's flows of waters to generate prosperity for its people and energy for the region. Currently, the unharnessed flows result in floods that continue to devastate the lives of tens of millions of people in the plains of Bangladesh and India. The technical solutions are within reach, and, indeed, plans to implement them have been on the table for years; what has been missing are the necessary consensus and resolve among Nepal's leaders, neighbors, and supporters to translate the ideas into reality.

Similarly, millions of people depend on the flow of the Nile for their livelihoods, but the level of the water in the river has been dropping. South Sudan has the potential to change the flow of the Nile significantly if it finds a way to capture and channel rainfall. The untapped flows of water in Nepal and Sudan are both a literal expression and a metaphor of the failure of countries to translate their latent assets into active flows of resources and connections that could save the lives of tens of millions and transform those of hundreds of millions. Dysfunctional states are the key obstacle to the realization of aspirations of untold millions of people to be active participants in a world that is both prosperous and secure. Instead, they still live in dire poverty because they are unable to connect to this unprecedented stock of global wealth and knowledge. These people would consider themselves lucky if their earning power grew from one to two dollars a day. Four dollars a day—the cost of a cappuccino in the wealthy part of the world—would indeed be considered major progress. Yet these people are poor not because they lack capacity or capability or because the natural or cultural conditions of their countries are less conducive to economic growth. Most of these countries have astonishing amounts of actual or potential wealth, but it is blocked from being put to constructive use. In contrast to the parts of the world that operate by means of organized flows, many developing countries function within a space of disorganized blockages, where dysfunctional state, market, and civil society organizations and institutions combine in a way that excludes citizens from opportunities.

At the root of this poverty is a double failure: that of national public policy—or politics—and that of international aid policy. Country leaders time and again have rejected stewardship of the public good in favor of zero-sum political games and accumulation of personal and family wealth. States simply fail both to perform the basic functions that would allow their citizens a life of dignity and opportunity and to fulfill the obligations of statehood internationally. These failures increase intra-country tensions and risks to international peace and stability, which may result in the outbreak of and frequent reversion to conflict. While alleviating some of the symptoms of suffering, the international aid system has failed to address the root causes and unwittingly contributes to the perpetuation of the problem. Instead of becoming (except in rare cases) a catalyst for a country's journey to stability and prosperity, the aid system has variously assumed the position of bystander, colluder, fashion setter, provider of substitute services, or dictator of policies. In this chapter we focus on the first failure—of national politics—and in the next we discuss the failure of the aid system to respond to the fundamental causes of poverty.

The cost of this double failure in state functionality is the denial of legitimate opportunity to the poor and excluded people of the world. Every day is a missed chance to remove the gaps and marshal the assets that would address the basis of poverty, enable poor people to create stocks of capital and link to the flows of knowledge and wealth. In our discussions around the world we have been repeatedly struck by the desire and commitment of ordinary men and women from all walks of life for order and stability. These people clearly articulate the demand for rule of law and accountable institutions; it is the supply side that is letting them down. To understand this better, we need to look more closely at the symptoms of state failure.

In the previous chapters we described examples of countries and regions that managed to break with the past and create institutions through reorganization of their assets, thereby managing to connect to the ever-deepening flows of our current globalizing world. As these countries were creating new histories, others were failing to do so— places that were stalling, going backward, or witnessing the breakout of terrible conflicts. Some of these countries had embraced authoritarian models of governance and vested all hope and power in the state; some could not agree on the rules of the game for exercising public power and fell into conflict; some became pawns in the geopolitics of the Cold War; and others ceded effective control of their economy to extractive industries and essentially became company towns.

The dysfunctionality of many of these places has its roots in the Cold War. The educated people of many developing countries acquired a deep distrust of the market from their teachers in elite European universities and instead placed their trust in an all-powerful state as the sole agent of development. Meanwhile, policymakers in the West chose to focus their attention on political freedoms and market economics to counter the Soviet Union. As the two opposed ideological systems engaged in a prolonged cold war, their disagreement sparked hot conflicts around the globe, linking faraway places such as Cuba, Angola, Afghanistan, Nicaragua, Mozambique, and the Middle East. For individual power-holders, foreign policy became the most crucial foundation for a superpower's support, with the explicit acknowledgment that "our dictators are preferable to theirs." Widespread corruption was not only acceptable; indeed, until the 1990s it was also tax deductible in European states, which viewed it as an acceptable cost of doing business. The use of the word "corruption" was even forbidden in World Bank parlance until the mid-1990s, when James Wolfensohn broke the taboo in a courageous speech on the impact of the cancer of corruption. Nevertheless, repeated articulation of the negative impact of such dishonesty has not stemmed the tide of corruption and the abuse of office.

The fall of the Berlin Wall, the opening up of Eastern Europe, and the implosion of the Soviet Union in rapid succession created an enthusiasm for a new beginning in world history. The victors of the Cold War lacked the imagination and the capabilities to rise to the occasion and construct a global agenda for prosperity. Countries that had been the scenes of devastating ideological conflict during the Cold War were forgotten, as the prosperous half of the world embarked on an unprecedented period of wealth creation and technological ingenuity.

The blowback came on 9/11 from an unexpected quarter. Osama bin Laden had taken control of a country before hijacking planes to turn an instrument of mobility and communication into an agent of destruction. This devastation was unleashed upon the twin symbols of trade and military power. Now, whenever we use an airport and are forced to undergo a security check, we are reminded of our vulnerability and the fact that we are living in a world that offers no safety from global threats. This tragedy has put the issue of tackling dysfunctional states at the center of the global agenda.

When social divisions exist (whether based on gender, class, ethnicity, race, location, or other differences), disagreements on ends and means can be expected. The issue is not the existence of disagreements but finding mechanisms for resolving them through compromise. Accordingly, politics can be either constructive or destructive. In chapter 2 we saw how political conflicts over issues of redistribution were reframed for a politics of opportunity. The provision of jobs and housing in Singapore, economic opportunity in the American South, and the focus on future generations in Ireland reframed politics to create a technical space, a space where change can be realized. But political disagreements can just as easily lead to stalemate, outright conflict, or sustained resentment against the use of state institutions for the benefit of a minority. Civil wars are an extreme illustration of the failure of politics. Overt hostility takes an immense toll on daily life, destroys a country's accumulated stocks, and inflicts a terrible cost on economic opportunity.

In this chapter we look at those countries that are wholly or partially off the global grid, denying some or all of their citizens access to flows in the global system. These failed models for development have caused an immense fall-out, ranging from very low standards of living and poverty to mass genocide and suffering. Conflicts have led to death and destruction on an unimaginable scale in countries such as Rwanda, Cambodia, and the former Yugoslavia. Others have witnessed a reduction in life expectancies. In almost all of these countries, the plight of women has been particularly harsh: They have been subjected to systematic rape, human trafficking, and, in Afghanistan, the imposition of gender apartheid under the Taliban.

We have had the privilege to be engaged in the reimagining of Afghanistan and the constitution of a legitimate government there from 2001 to 2004. Subsequently, we have had an opportunity to interact directly on the ground with the citizens and leaders of Kosovo, Lebanon, Nepal, and South Sudan and to engage in dialogue with principals and ordinary people from dozens more countries. From these debates and discussions we have discerned a series of common threads. While each country has unique features, the syndromes of dysfunctionality fall into distinctive patterns. And each country has latent assets that, given today's global stock of knowledge and money, could provide a basis for the eradication of dire poverty and want, were a different path to be articulated and systematically pursued. First we describe the conditions on the ground in a series of countries and then identify a series of common threads.

Right after the conflict in Lebanon in August 2006, one image dominated the media: that of Hezbollah moving rapidly to distribute money to homeowners whose houses had been destroyed during the clash. While the Lebanese government was preparing a donor conference and asking for resources and diplomats and aid officials were assessing the extent of the damages, Hezbollah had scored highly on the domestic PR front. However, the story that did not reach the news media was revealed to us in a conversation with the bankers' associations of Lebanon: Lebanese banks had managed to attract $80 billion in deposits, thereby becoming a major player in regional and international flows of money. Yet as the representatives of the bankers' associations revealed, they had not created the financial instruments for investment to transform part or all of this money into solutions to the poverty and deprivation in Lebanon.

Against the prevalent trend in the Middle East, Lebanon opted for an open economy and a relatively democratic polity in the second half of the twentieth century. However, a devastating conflict combining civil war, invasion, and interference by neighboring and global powers imposed a huge toll on the country between 1975 and 1990. Peace came with a restoration of the old order without resolution to any of the fundamental causes of the conflict. The Lebanese have always demonstrated an entrepreneurial spirit and thrived within the world economy, and its diaspora has created vast fortunes. Their economic problem-solving abilities, however, have not translated into equally productive politics at home. Because the citizens are divided by religion and class, politics in the 1960s and 1970s became an instrument for protecting privileges rather than creating an inclusive society and polity. Distribution of offices according to a formula called the National Pact (an informal arrangement not formally part of the constitution) could neither keep up with the changing times nor accommodate the evolving demography of various constituencies in the country.[1]

Simultaneously, as the center of Arab intellectual thought in the 1960s and 1970s, Lebanon, thanks to its political freedom and printing presses, became the focal point of disagreements regarding Arab nationalism and for the agitation of armed Palestinian movements.

When tensions could not be contained, full-scale civil war, followed by Syrian intervention and Israeli invasion, broke out. The Israeli army occupied parts of the south for twelve years, and the Syrian army and intelligence forces dominated the country until 2005, when they were forced to withdraw. Some of the most significant battles were fought in the capital city of Beirut. Warfare in the city is just one of the ways in which the stocks that Lebanon had so meticulously built up over the years were quickly destroyed. A political compromise was struck in 1990 to bring an end to outright civil war, yet since the fundamental nature of political inclusion was not resolved, the politics of identity, which was organized around religion, still dominates.

This has effectively resulted in two Lebanons in bitter contention over the how state, society, and the marketplace should relate to one another. The political stasis has meant that development and economic growth issues have not yet been faced. There is now an upper-middle-income Lebanon. While the average income per capita of $4,800 places Lebanon in the upper-middle-income range of countries, more than seven hundred thousand people (nearly 20 percent of its population) live on less than $2 a day. For more than a century, education has been the ticket for upward social mobility for the Lebanese people, who have formed one of the most entrepreneurial diasporas in the world; they can now be found from the Amazon to East and West Africa to the major cities of Europe and the United States. At the time of writing, the richest man in the world is a Lebanese Mexican. Yet ten of the poorest districts in the country have illiteracy rates ranging from 18 to 32 percent. In large swathes of the south, two crops, tobacco and olives, provide only a minimum living standard. For more than sixty years there have been plans to harness the waters of the Litani River, the main source of water in the south, but no movement has taken place to implement the ideas.

Lack of financing is not Lebanon's problem. Indeed, as we had learned from the Lebanese bankers, there was $80 billion on deposit in Beirut's banks. Yet these sophisticated bankers had not leveraged any of this wealth to investment in either the south or the rest of the country. While foreigners interested in investing in Lebanon could obtain guarantees through a range of international instruments, the country's chamber of commerce stated that no risk guarantees were available for Lebanese investment there. Beset by external interference and occupation and gridlocked by the number of veto points, the state has failed both to assert its authority across its territory and to channel its wealth so as to bind the citizenry into a social compact.

Lebanon, once called the Paris of the East, was the entrepreneurial and cultural center of the Middle East in the 1970s. It was ideally positioned to generate clusters of growth and creativity to become, as it were, the Silicon Valley of the region. Instead, it has been divided into a country of haves and have-nots, is characterized by a politics of stalemate and veto, and is still struggling with basic issues of maintenance of order and security from foreign invasion.

Sudan, the largest country in Africa and about half the size of the United States, is a country that has followed an authoritarian path. Between 1956 and 1972 Sudan had a reputation for the best civil service in Africa, one of the finest universities in the region, and highly trained public servants and military officers. With these assets, Sudan could have tackled its centuries-old history of regional disparities and turned itself into an economic powerhouse for the area. Instead, Sudan suffered a twenty-four-year conflict in the south, where the rulers in Khartoum felt justified in brutally unleashing the army on the population to compel obedience.

A combination of military officers and political ideologues attempted to impose Islamism on the country by employing divide-and-conquer tactics. Claiming that the Muslim north was superior to the animist south, they plunged the country into a prolonged conflict. Culturally, the response in the south was a massive movement toward Christianity; politically, it was the launch of a series of militant movements.

The extent of alienation in southern Sudan can be judged by the credentials of its most significant leader, John Garang, who not only had a doctorate in agronomy from an American university but also was a professor in Sudan's major military academy. Until his tragic death in 2005, he stood for the notion of one Sudan. His vision, in contrast to his opponents in the north, was of an inclusive Sudan. The Comprehensive Peace Agreement (CPA) of 2005, which brought an end to the conflict between the north and the south on paper at least, proposed a radical transformation of Sudan's institutions of power. The ten states in the south became a federal state in their own right, with their own president, ministries, and the equivalent of a central bank. This new entity acquired the right to a referendum on independence through a plebiscite to be held in 2011. The implementation of this new institutional architecture could mark a significant reversal from the politics of inequality to the acceptance of equality between individuals and groups.

In 2005 and 2006 we visited Yei, Rumbek, and Juba and witnessed firsthand that the south had seen no investment in infrastructure "since the birth of Adam," as Garang had long claimed. However, we found both the natural and human capital impressive. Situated in an ideal riparian position, southern Sudan has the potential to harness floods and tributary rivers for energy and irrigation. The country's existing oil resources are also located mainly in the south, but the vast potential in oil, gas, timber, and minerals is yet to be fully documented. Both Khartoum, the capital of Sudan, and Juba, the capital of the south, demonstrate the impact of the CPA. Khartoum is enjoying an economic boom, with neighborhoods rapidly being added to the city and structures going up in every corner. Its newly found prosperity makes the war in Darfur a seemingly distant reality to the average citizen. Juba, formerly a garrison town that was the center of active fighting between the Southern Peoples' Liberation Army and the Sudanese Army, is experiencing its own boom. Businesses from neighboring countries in East Africa are lining up in government offices to offer their services. The traffic on the Nile is increasing by the week, and the number and quantity of goods in Juba's markets are quickly expanding.

As a result of the CPA, vast sums of money were to flow from the oil revenues to the newly created government of southern Sudan. John Garang had laid out a vision of the future to the south Sudanese in legendary speeches, but the capacity for effective expenditure was absent, and the underlying systems for financial transparency and accountability were not in place.

As a result, this picture of a "New Sudan" has remained a dream rather than a reality. Sudan's future was always going to be heavily dependent upon the way in which the country's natural capital was handled. Nearly $2 billion was available to the south from domestic resources. Sudan had immense human potential; many of its leaders were trained bureaucrats and civil servants who had received excellent higher education. The citizens were behind an agenda of transformation and held high expectations for change. However, the mechanisms to translate these assets into credible programs were missing. Instead of harnessing this natural capital, the wrong actors took control in southern Sudan. Disreputable firms that represented extractive industries lined up to acquire assets through opaque arrangements. Too often governments with only minimal legal and financial capability are targeted by extractive companies or other concessions such as telecoms for rent-seeking deals. In southern Sudan this was precisely the case. The aid complex descended upon Juba en masse, but rather than offering a clear and simple road map as to how to create the necessary institutions or control and channel the influx of oil money and private-sector interest, the government became confused and paralyzed. The image of John Garang on the walls of government offices was obscured from view behind piles of plans from donor agencies. The aid system failed to offer solutions to widespread corruption and abuse.

The comprehensive agreement between northern and southern Sudan offers the potential for a new beginning. At stake in Sudan is the country's unity on the basis of a new social contract or, if that fails, the splintering of the country into two on the basis of a referendum. If the latter occurs, a new round of violent conflict might erupt that could resemble either the creation of India and Pakistan or the dismemberment of former Yugoslavia. Of course, the north-south relationship will have immense implications for both Darfur and the simmering conflict in eastern Sudan.

As in Sudan, exclusionary practices form the backdrop to one of the most unexpected political rebellions in the late twentieth century: in Nepal, an armed Maoist movement not only succeeded in challenging the established order but also became a major instrument in bringing down an autocratic government. In 2006 the unlikely alliance of Maoists and established political parties was formed to oust the king.

The mass social mobilization that brought an end to the autocratic regime of the king created an open moment in Nepal. For Nepal to take advantage of this opportunity, it needed to confront a series of critical tasks that ranged from defining the political system to creating a functioning market. The greatest risks for the future stem from the established habits and mental models of the political elite. Consumed with their own positioning and interest, they may sacrifice the country's medium-to-long-term interest for their own short-term gain.

A small governing elite was incapable of agreeing on a common agenda to steward Nepal from shared poverty to communal prosperity and opportunities for all. This is nowhere better illustrated than in the governance of Nepal's formal banking sector. Large loans have been granted repeatedly to a small group of influential people who have made a habit of defaulting on repayments. Past governments have either shied away from confronting the defaulters or have actively colluded with them. The judiciary, lacking a detailed understanding of financial issues, has been outmaneuvered again and again by lawyers who represent these entrenched interests. Foreign management was brought in to restructure Nepal's two largest banks, but faced with a lack of clear decision making and enforcement by the courts, it has been unable to make a major difference. The cost of this elite capture is born by small and medium-sized firms that must pay high interest rates in order to secure capital for their investments.

The stalled development of the financial sector illustrates a pattern that recurs across many other areas of Nepal's economic, social, and political life. Despite heavy aid dependency and the population's loud demand for services, Nepal has been unable to spend more than $400 million a year in developmental projects. Fragmentation of the elite, its lack of consensus on a common vision, and its apathy in implementing technical programs all reveal the disjunction between the people's aspirations and the narrow concerns of the elite. About four hundred individuals hold key positions in the government, economy, news media, and civil society; they know each other, yet they occupy separate spheres that do not connect to produce the systemic coherence and resolve necessary to solve their country's urgent problems. Nepalese politics has long been about the capture of government resources for purposes of patronage. Nepalese people of various walks of life repeatedly point out that at each level of government a system exists for seizing and diverting the country's resources to narrow rather than broad interests. Political parties have been part and parcel of this institutional syndrome.

By contrast, our discussions with a wide variety of stakeholders in Nepal indicate that, at the village level, the Nepalese have unleashed immense institutional creativity. In one hamlet after another, evidence indicates that the so-called tragedy of the common people has been reversed. Thousands of village-level associations have been formed, providing an opportunity for exercise of leadership and imagination to solve joint problems. Forestry, once a prime example of the depletion of natural capital, is thriving under community management in Nepal. Microhydroelectric production, again under community management, is providing reliable electricity to nearly 35 percent of Nepal's villages. Parents are actively participating in the management of schools, contributing both in money and in kind to the construction of classrooms, and, more important, taking part in the supervision of children and teachers. In all of these arenas, women are coming to the fore to assume positions of responsibility and leadership.

The challenge of connecting Nepal to regional and global markets clearly stands out as a priority. Over a million Nepalis are working in countries from India to the Gulf, and the remittances they send home have been of critical importance to their families. Nepal has also produced remarkable entrepreneurs who have managed to open up a distinctive niche for themselves in the globalizing economy and

make significant amounts of money in legitimate ways. The challen‚
confronting Nepal's current leadership was best captured by Chairm‚
Prachanda, the Maoist leader. In 2007 Prachanda stressed to us the
country's need for agrarian reform on the one hand, but he also asked
these questions: "There is China rising; there is India rising; how
do we understand globalization? What do we do about it? Maybe
the market is a good thing." At the village level, farmers repeatedly
emphasized access to the marketplace rather than redistribution—
through welfare programs—as their key priority. They want to be able
to grow new types of agricultural products such as ginger, bananas, and
saffron rather than only wheat, enhance their value through processing, and find new outlets in which to sell them; they do not want mass
redistribution, which would disrupt production by its inefficiency.

In Afghanistan, of course, another crop, poppy, is a persistent challenge to stability. Afghanistan has witnessed the repeated failure of
politics. The first coup in 1973 resulted from rivalries within the royal
lineage when one cousin overthrew the other. When the Communist
Party carried out a violent takeover in 1978, it soon fell into interne-
cine conflict and failed to agree on a common strategy, thereby bringing
about a ten-year Soviet occupation of the country. When the communist-
backed government collapsed in 1991, the heavily armed but factional-
ized mujahadin again failed to resolve their differences and plunged the
country into civil war. The Taliban consolidated power at the expense
of these discredited factions but offered no meaningful vision to either
their opponents or the citizens of the country. Instead, they allowed
Osama bin Laden to hijack the country for his own purposes.

Between 1978, when the Communist coup took place, and November 2001, when the Taliban were overthrown, Afghanistan (according
to a World Bank estimate) lost $240 billion in ruined infrastructure
and vanished opportunities. While the rest of the world was shrinking
in terms of spatial and temporal coordination, the travel time between
the capital city of Kabul and every single province in the country significantly increased. Whereas it used to take a maximum of three hours
to reach the city of Jalalabad in eastern Afghanistan and six hours to get
to the city of Kandahar in the south, in 2002 the roads were so bad that
it took fourteen hours to reach Jalalabad and nearly twenty-four hours
to get to Kandahar. Millions of Afghan children grew up illiterate in
refugee camps, where they learned that the gun rather than the ballot
was the key instrument for the acquisition of power and influence.

But Afghanistan—contrary to popular perception in some parts of
the world—is not a naturally poor country. It has significant deposits

of marble, copper, iron, oil, gas and precious and semiprecious stones, including lapis and emeralds. In the 1970s it was one of the largest exporters of dried fruits and nuts on the planet. With the right policies, it has the potential to develop a thriving domestic market and be a significant exporter of minerals, polished stones, jewelry, textiles, and fruit products.

The political elite of Afghanistan had a rare opportunity to found a functioning state. Most of them, however, chose to put private before public interest and carried on with their factional agendas and seizure of private gain. Had there been a coherent and functioning aid system, the story could have been different. While we investigate the aid complex in more detail in the next chapter, the following two incidents illustrate how international failure compounded national failure.

Once the open moment of 2002 was created with the departure of the Taliban and the establishment of the Bonn Agreement, hundreds of thousands of young people rushed to spend their precious earnings on English, computer, and business classes. Working during the day as drivers for the hundreds of aid organizations that descended upon the country, young men would go to spontaneously organized classes in the evenings. Lacking access to electricity, they would wake up at the crack of dawn to study. An extensive consultation exercise at Kabul University revealed that, more than anything else, students wanted to be able to connect to globalization and take advantage of information and opportunity. The top priorities for students in the Islamic Law School were to learn English and to become technologically proficient. These young men and women were not interested in the clash of civilizations. Secure in their own culture and heritage, all they wanted was to overcome the digital gap and become connected to the network of opportunities that would allow them to change not just their own lives but also the lives of generations to come.

Connection to knowledge and opportunity, however, is not what the aid complex offered. The first thing that the UN system provided—through the $1.6 billion of donor money channeled to the UN agencies in 2002—was an airline devoted to serving UN and other international staff and occasionally (after much lobbying) some Afghan government officials. Six years later, the UN was still subsidizing its airline. As it has never disclosed the cost of its operations to Afghan citizens or to the world at large, the actual figure for this subsidy is unknown, but it may be between $180 million and $300 million. Meanwhile, the state-owned airline that could by now have been worth a billion dollars (through investment of $100 million to $200 million) is near bankruptcy and is considered unsafe to operate in many countries. There is a clear double standard between the UN staff who need to fly on a safe airline and the leaders and nationals of a country who are confined to flying with an unsafe airline. These examples are multiplied hundreds of times over, as becomes evident to anyone who investigates the operations of the aid complex in practice. It creates a cocoon for its own staff, without becoming a catalyst for institution building within the host country that it purports to help.

The presidential election of 2004 offered the Afghan population the first opportunity in their long history to elect their leader through a direct process. It also gave them a chance to leapfrog history and create a unified database of the country's citizens based on reliable biometrics that would have enabled the state to function and increase citizens' access to certification of their own identities. However, not only were the Afghan elections poorly organized by externally driven operations, but the UN system also blocked this innovation by instead insisting on an expensive manual method that allowed significant fraud to take place.

Millions of people came out and stood in orderly lines to cast their ballots on a cold October day. There were moving stories of old men and women who asked to be carried from their sick beds (or at times their death beds) to take part in this historic process. They understood the importance of affirming one's will for the future and one's right as a citizen in the political process. Yet within hours of the voting, the validity of the election was jeopardized. The indelible ink that the UN staff had insisted was foolproof as a means of identity quickly proved to be washable. Hundreds of people were voting repeatedly. Instead of celebratory headlines heralding the commitment of the Afghan population to a democratic process, the international media cited electoral fraud and mismanagement. Disputes over the outcome of the election were avoided, thanks to the maturity of the candidates and the significant margin between the number of votes for President Karzai and his closest opponent.

Afghan authorities had detailed discussions with UN staff prior to the election and had urged them to use modern iris-based technology to enable the creation of a biometric database that would serve as the foundation for the country's future planning and social policy. All of the Afghans we polled during this process viewed this identity device not as a threat to their civil liberties but as a vehicle through which to realize their identity as a citizen of the state, as well as a means to access a range of benefits and for taking part in an array of transactions. The UN High Commissioner for Refugees (UNHCR)—the agency in charge of the return of UN refugees—had already used the system. Millions of Afghan men and women had cooperated and did not consider the process invasive.

Theoretically, the system makes one mistake in ten million uses. Fingerprints in an agrarian society like Afghanistan have a margin of error of around 30 percent. In the technological age, where investment in information provides a basis of further savings, the UN system refused our request and insisted on a manual process that was based on giving out cardboard cards and identifying recipients through inked fingerprints. Thousands of people registered to vote multiple times and acknowledged to the press that they had voted more than once. The same process was repeated during the parliamentary elections in 2005 at a cost of approximately $400 million. Cardboard is perishable, and a master list of citizens was not created, so the whole process will have to be repeated for the election of 2009.

The alternative electronic system could have been put in place for $140 million and would have generated an estimated $80 million in its first year by issuing passports, drivers' licenses, and identity cards. Identification of civil servants on a reliable basis was likely to eliminate the problem of "ghost workers" and therefore to reduce the civil service burden by a quarter and provide a basis for human resource planning. The system would also have provided a basis for an e-governance system, whereby citizens could track their interactions with the state. Simultaneously, the government would have been able to carry out user surveys on a wide range of interactions with citizens.

The UN's excuse for not using the electronic system was that one of their donors had supplied $10 million worth of cardboard and would have been offended if it were not used. The rules of the aid complex are constructed in such a manner that decision-making authority is arbitrarily vested in the system's officials. Our ideas were considered too far fetched, as most of the UN officials we encountered lacked elementary schooling in the current trends in information technology. As the UN secretary general's report of April 2006 revealed, the UN management system was completely out of date and needed significant overhaul. Faced with the urgency of either proceeding with a tight deadline for elections or being blamed for causing the postponement of the political process, Afghanistan had to accept an inadequate solution with the promise that at least the manual system, although costly, would be failsafe. To our knowledge, neither a single official has been admonished nor a single lesson drawn from this experience, as the 2005 elections were again conducted by means of the manual method.

Pristina, the capital of Kosovo, is a short flight from Vienna. Arriving in Pristina, however, one is reminded of East Timor or Cambodia, not a territory at the heart of Europe with a clear path toward the European Union. Thanks to a UN Security Council resolution in 1999, the United Nations Mission in Kosovo (UNMIK) is the region's formal governing authority, and the special representative of the secretary general has the right to approve or change any laws or actions of the provisional institutions of self-government (PISG) in Kosovo.

Given the international community's emphasis on the centrality of the rule of law, one would expect that eight years of UNMIK operations would have resulted in creating an exemplary demonstration of the rule of law. Instead, discussion with a wide range of citizens and officials revealed utter confusion on the subject. For instance, they found it difficult to determine what was criminal, legal, or illegal, for four different legal systems were operating simultaneously, without any mechanism for resolving conflicts among them or creating coherence. As of September 2007 there was still no single database of the Kosovar laws that are in force. Given this legal vacuum, it is little wonder that criminal activity—from money laundering to trafficking in goods and people—is thriving. The officials of UNMIK had the right to promulgate administrative orders that acquired the legal status of laws without going through a due process of their preparation. All UNMIK officials are immune from prosecution, for the promulgation and interpretation of law resides in UNMIK. The mission's status therefore resembles much more the predemocratic notion of a sovereign who promulgates laws but is not subject to them.

State and socially owned enterprises had been placed under a Kosovo trust agency run by UNMIK that embarked on their privatization. Allegations of misjudgment, misconduct, and outright corruption abounded across Kosovo. Moreover, according to the citizens we interviewed, no mechanisms were available for challenging decisions on the valuation of the enterprises or the process of their sale. The most depressing aspect of the scene in Kosovo, however, is in the failure to invest in Kosovars themselves. Out of every dollar, eighty cents has gone to technical assistance. And while some accomplishments have been made in the area of public finance, the sustainability of these operations is at high risk. Most of the seventy-three thousand Kosovar civil servants are paid a salary of 180 euros per month, and the brain drain from the major departments of government to the aid system and the private sector was estimated at 20 percent per year. The budget department, for instance, had no English speakers who could be sent to an International Monetary Fund (IMF) training program. At the same time, there was no evidence of the creation of vocational training programs that might have laid a foundation for private sector investment, and the universities were languishing. While citizens generally gave high scores to NATO's Kosovo Force (KFOR) for the provision of security, they complained bitterly about the lack of investment in education, infrastructure, health care and job creation.

The symptoms of destructive politics are well known. Major newspapers around the world offer dozens of illustrations from Afghanistan to Zimbabwe. A disconnect between governments and their people is the central theme of these stories. Examples range from families of heads of state appropriating state funds for private gain to government ministers participating in outright criminal behavior. Government ministers consider it a right to staff their ministries with their relatives or party affiliates regardless of qualifications. Heads of state, when out begging for aid, travel with huge entourages and spend hundreds of thousands of dollars purchasing goods for their private use. Some of the brightest minds in these countries are forced to either work for aid agencies or find opportunities in exile. Contracts for the natural capital that could be used to create human resources are signed under the table and result in the diversion of huge sums of money to private offshore bank accounts. Large extractive companies that wield despotic powers over ordinary citizens are often the unhappy result.

These practices are neither isolated nor random but form a syndrome of dysfunctionality. Narrow interests become organized around privileges and rents that they derive from governmental positions. The international system provides them the authority literally to sign away the country's rights without any accountability. In addition, they often use formal governmental positions to promote criminal networks, as a result of which government offices degenerate into little more than a springboard for organized looting. Under such circumstances, a significant percentage of contracts that go to either a head of state and that person's relatives (or to officials and their relatives) is the norm rather than the exception. As nearly every transaction with state officials involves bribes, the citizens, instead of being served by public servants, are at the service of the officials. A small example from 1980s' Pakistan is both revealing and typical. A respected Pakistani international civil servant needed some documents. The head of the relevant office greeted him warmly (as his former employee) and said that he would be happy to get the documents, but he did not want to break his oath to his new employers that no transaction could take place without a bribe. He therefore asked the international civil servant for a pack of cigarettes to satisfy his code of personal enrichment. Tragically, where the international community is directly in charge, as we have seen in Kosovo, similar patterns of dysfunctionality can emerge.

Six themes in particular stand out from these examples. First, the prolonged conflict that often follows state dysfunctionality produces an institutional syndrome that in turn has significant implications for the economy and polity once a conflict ends. The key elements of this conflict syndrome are the emergence of armed groups, the spatial polarization of identities, the consolidation of private networks of support, ungovernable flows of aid and people across boundaries, and opaque decision making by a small elite. The combined effect of the elements of this syndrome is increased erosion of the people's trust in the state's formal institutions.

Second, peacemaking has generally been geared toward ending conflict by accommodating the opposing parties (with their existing personalities) rather than by creating clear road maps and mechanisms to bring about functioning states, as well as enfranchising citizens to make decisions and create pathways for new leaders to emerge. Far from being green fields for novel design and experimentation, post-conflict conditions require a firm understanding of entrenched interests and the conditions of state institutions.

As a result, third, state dysfunctionality often starts in the very wake of a peace agreement or transfer of power. Individuals who are used to opaque processes and often come with complicated histories and networks take formal positions of power and view them as licenses for private gain. This type of behavior creates a crisis of trust in the citizens who expected better; they then use it to justify reversion to conflict.

Fourth, even when civil war does not break out and a peace agreement is therefore not required, the cost of failed politics and poor public policy is immense. The most often-cited example of this is the difference in the trajectories of Burma (the Union of Myanmar) and the Philippines on the one hand and South Korea and Taiwan on the other. In the 1950s there was a consensus that Burma and the Philippines, endowed with both significant natural resources and a group of educated leaders, were likely to be the future economic leaders of the region. South Korea and Taiwan, by contrast, were considered basket cases, as most of Korea's natural wealth was in the north, and Chiang Kai-shek's failed policies had been critical to the Communists' victory in mainland China. The Philippines and Burma, however, embarked upon a series of policies that resulted in the loss of their initial positive momentum and exclusion from the world economy. South Korea and Taiwan, on the other hand, adopted a series of measures that transformed the former into one of the largest economies in the world and the latter, despite its political isolation, into an economic power.

Fifth, money is not the critical driver of sustained poverty reduction and wealth creation. In all of these countries money abounds, ranging from the tens of millions of dollars in cash that leave Afghanistan for Dubai banks every week to the investment of Kosovar citizens in their housing to the bank deposits we described in Lebanon. This is abundantly clear in countries that have derived huge rent payments from minerals in general and oil in particular. Sudan, Venezuela, Indonesia, Congo, and Chad are all examples of countries with extensive natural resources. In contrast, Norway, Dubai, and Botswana are examples of naturally wealthy countries, in which oil rent has been well managed. We can therefore posit a direct relationship between politics, policies, and poverty. Constructive politics can produce the type of political cohesion that in turn enables leaders and managers to implement policies. Step by step, the capabilities of the state then increase. Conversely, destructive policies lead to weaker institutions, to the point where governments themselves become the biggest obstacle to development. If wealth is the result of the right set of policies, then the corollary thesis is that the perpetuation of poverty also correlates with bad politics and policies.

Sixth, in contrast to the webs of value creation we saw in chapter 1, this syndrome of dysfunctionality provides a basis for the perverse side of globalization: the spread of dense criminal networks in weak states that operate with relative ease and trade in everything from body parts to guns, fake CDs, women, and drugs. No amount of heroin seems to be sufficient to feed the growing drug addiction of the poor and middle classes of the West, creating in the process one of the most efficient supply chains in contemporary history. Under such circumstances, the rule of law is not a benign slogan but instead a major threat to people who participate in these webs of value destruction. When neither the state nor the market is functioning, it is extremely difficult (if not impossible) for nongovernmental organizations to assume civil society functions. They are forced—not by choice but by circumstances—either to partner continuously with a corrupt state or to interact with a criminalized economy. It is little wonder that NGOs have lost their moral authority.

The syndrome illustrates the wisdom of Machiavelli's assertion that beneficiaries of reform remain disorganized while opponents are organized, entrenched, and resourceful. Under such conditions, stalling change is enormously beneficial to entrenched interests. In fact, it is so ubiquitous that it has spawned entire cultural subgenres. The Indian film industry has vividly captured the stories of this syndrome in the state of Bihar. Politicians hired thugs to intimidate their opponents in return for a free hand to kidnap wealthy citizens and plunder government resources. Within a decade, the ruffians realized that they did not need the politicians to front for them and that they could run their affairs directly. Every aspect of the rule of law was rigged, from entrance exams for the police and civil service to awards for contracts and court decisions. The Indian public came up with a name for the syndrome—Goondah Raj—the rule of the mob. These films may capture an extreme situation, but the works of novelists (e.g., Chinua Achebe, who wrote *Things Fall Apart*; John le Carre, author of *The Constant Gardner*) vividly illustrate the same state of affairs. Literature seems to be ahead of the social sciences in capturing the realities on the ground. The deep-seated nature of this syndrome is the reason we argue that an entirely new type of statecraft—one that recognizes state building as a central goal and accountability to citizens as the critical mechanism—is required in order to understand and break these patterns.

As we described in chapter 1, the contrast between functioning and dysfunctional states is best captured by the notion of the sovereignty gap. The legitimate state, as we show later in detail, performs a series of essential functions for its citizens, thereby becoming an instrument for collective mobilization, cooperation, and trust. It can then tackle both the immediate-term societal needs and the longer-term generational and environmental requirements. In dysfunctional states, office holders focus primarily on personal aggrandizement while the state fails to perform essential functions. This failure to perform state functions then takes a high toll on the citizens of the country concerned, as well as those of neighboring states (and even the globe), who are affected by its economic, political, and environmental pollution.

There has been an assumption in democratic theory that people are the principals and the government their agent. The dysfunctional syndrome turns this legal axiom on its head by making the people the agents of unaccountable rulers. The absence of an accountable government does not amount to the absence of public opinion. Indeed, it is in the cafés, classrooms, streets, farms, and even government offices that complaints circulate about the toll exacted by dysfunctional government. Collecting intelligence in these countries is a waste of time because all of the truly valuable information is in the public domain. Understanding the state in these countries is not difficult, as there is no "black box" of government that separates the governed from the governing. Every deed and misdeed can be read like an open book. One needs merely to follow the interaction between people and their government and observe the obstacles through which the former are made to jump to obtain their identity papers or benefit from any of the services that are supposedly available to them free of charge. An even more obvious path would be to follow the money within government—to trace its leakages and blockages. When government officials have to bribe each other to obtain their salaries or when as much as 90 percent of the money allocated for school supplies or medicine disappears between the capital and a village school or clinic, there is no mystery to dysfunctionality.

Our interactions with citizens reveal that the people's judgment is the best measure of the extent of effectiveness or dysfunctionality of a governing system. They both take pleasure in and are able to rank their government's performance against the framework of functions. But for people to have a measure of their government against which they can judge its performance, they first need a framework of what it should do. The problem is not their willingness to voice their concerns and hold their authorities accountable but the deafness of the national and international authorities.

FIVE

The Promises and Perils of Aid

T HE NEW MILLENNIUM brought with it a renewed concern about poverty and stability. Discussions on how to eradicate poverty moved out of academia and development agencies to become the cry of street movements, rock bands, and eventually the communiqués of G8 meetings. Recalling the generosity of the United States after World War II in the formulation of the Marshall Plan, participants in these discussions have called for the richest countries to give an increased amount of money to the poorest nations. This request, however, has not been greeted with unqualified enthusiasm. A number of skeptical voices have raised questions about both the utility and the efficacy of the aid system.

The debate between proponents of "more aid" (i.e., believers in aid as the means to end poverty in our time) and "less aid" or "no aid" (i.e., believers in luck, fortune, and accident as the source of prosperity) has diverted attention from a central conundrum: what tasks is the aid system currently performing, and what capabilities does it have for performing them? Examining the aid complex from a design perspective reveals the way its people, processes, resource flows, and mental models result in different types of outcomes and levels of waste. Such an analysis is a prerequisite for answering two questions: on the one hand, is the aid system itself in fundamental need of reform? On the other hand, to what extent is the aid system relevant to addressing the issues of poverty and stability? To answer the first question we need to unpack the "black box" of the aid complex and look at the tasks it performs—from handling money, preparing projects, engendering change, providing advice, and producing (as well as substituting for) state functions.

The "black box" is composed of a number of organizations. There are the multilateral groups, ranging from the Bretton Woods institutions such as the World Bank (which is itself a conglomeration of five organizations) and the International Monetary Fund, to the United Nations and its many independent agencies. There are then various "bilateral aid" agencies, usually independent government bureaus of wealthy countries, sometimes under the direct authority of a ministry of foreign affairs. As countries join the ranks of the wealthy—Ireland, Spain, India, China—they tend to set up their own development agencies. The NGOs—like the UN agencies—are often contracted by donors to implement projects, although they also raise their own money directly from the public. Military organizations, especially the Pentagon and other military groups, have recently become major players in reconstruction by handling large budgets. These agencies are interlinked by loops of information sharing, meetings, conferences, and contracting arrangements, which lead to tensions, as well as cooperation.

We argue that the aid system, which was designed for a different era, is now deeply out of synch with the challenges of the contemporary world. Built on the basis of membership by states, the international system assumed functioning states as its constituent units. The premise of the aid system is that states lack financial capital first of all and need to build infrastructure second. As states weakened, the aid system gradually yet imperceptibly and systematically assumed a variety of functions that under the system's rules are the states' responsibility. As a result they address the symptom but not the root cause of state dysfunctionality. The central task that the aid system should perform—namely, generating prosperity by bringing a global knowledge of stocks and flows to countries without it—is not being performed. In view of the fact that it comprises extractive industries and technical assistance brigades, the aid system—instead of opening countries up to legitimate entrepreneurial activity—epitomizes the side of capitalism that is fundamentally exploitative.

HOW WE GOT HERE: THE EVOLUTION OF THE AID COMPLEX

It is worth looking at how the aid complex developed if only to see that it was not deliberately designed in the form in which it exists today; rather, it evolved through a series of historical contingencies.

The story of how we got here—the design of the postwar system to address insecurity through aid, the effects of the alignment with dictatorships throughout the Cold War, and the rapid expansion of the aid system and the project as key aid instruments—is well documented. But the impact of these policies, institutions, and decisions in progressively weakening state capacities has not been systematically examined. A brief analysis of the evolution of the international aid system since 1945 reveals that its focus on the state has not been sustained and that this has had consequences for both security and development.

As we described in chapter 2, after World War II, political leaders applied their impressive imagination to the task of rebuilding the Western world. The international architecture of global relations that they conceived of and translated into institutions served well to build the dynamic economies and polities in what is now the wealthy half of the world. Through the Marshall Plan, the United States pledged nearly 1 percent of its GDP in 1948 for the reconstruction of Europe, and over the four years that the plan was underway, the United States provided $13 billion in economic and technical assistance. The plan fostered the fastest period of growth in European history by fuelling agricultural regeneration and providing huge support to industrial production in Western Europe, which increased by 35 percent between 1948 and 1952. Meanwhile, countries in Europe created and consolidated democratic institutions. On both sides of the Atlantic, resources were well used to usher in an era of prosperity and expand citizens' rights. While infrastructure absorbed the bulk of the costs, this physical rebuilding was rooted in a long-term strategic and institutional approach. The leadership of U.S. secretaries of state George Marshall and Dean Acheson and diplomat George Kennan on one side of the Atlantic was matched by that of British politician Aneurin Bevan, the "pragmatic internationalist" Jean Monnet, and French minister of foreign affairs Robert Schuman on the other. The Marshall Plan still stands as a unique act of visionary statesmanship and an illuminating example of a strategic instrument for state building.

Let us reexamine some of the principles of the Marshall Plan as summarized by Acheson: First, its purpose "should be the revival of a working economy in the world so as to permit the emergence of political and social conditions in which free institutions can exist." Second, "such assistance, I am convinced, must not be on a piecemeal basis as various crises develop. Any assistance that this Government may render in the future should provide a cure rather than a mere palliative." Third, the United States did not seek to impose any plan or project:

"It would be neither fitting nor efficacious for this government to draw up unilaterally a program designed to place Europe on its feet economically. This is the business of the Europeans. The initiative, I think, must come from Europe. The role of this country should consist of friendly aid in the drafting of a European program and of later support of such a program so far as it may be practical for us to do so."[1]

What is remarkable here is that the Marshall plan's institutional framework made the recipient country the driver of strategy and policy as well as project manager; the United States' role was to act as collaborator and provider of balance of trade support.[2] Herbert Simon, in his *Sciences of the Artificial*, describes how the European Cooperation Administration—the administration charged with Europe's rebuilding—considered (but rejected as unworkable) four other models, including bilateral agreements, commodity screening, the project approach, and the direct management of policy, which we have come to call "substitution." These four approaches became the dominant ones used for most other nations (i.e., the "developing world"). The consequences of those choices are now clear, and they again raise the question of institutional design and practice.

Despite the intention of Western political leaders to bring the Soviet Union, their wartime ally, into the multilateral economic and political system after the Second World War, the globe soon became polarized into pro-Soviet and pro-Western camps. In developing countries, the Soviet Union championed an agenda of decolonization to gain support. This resulted in the espousal of various forms of socialism and positioned the state as a substitute for the market. Meanwhile, in China and Vietnam, the embrace of Communism led to fears that other countries in Asia would follow suit. In this global context, aid quickly became a means of rewarding rulers on the basis of whether their foreign policies supported or opposed one of the superpowers— rather than whether they were pursuing any particular developmental agenda. For its first forty-five years (until the collapse of the Soviet Union), the global aid system did not even regard good governance as part of its agenda. Indeed, both the West and the Soviet bloc actually preferred to work with dictatorial regimes, and both engaged in covert action to overthrow democratic governments from Guatemala to Czechoslovakia to Iran. Countries used aid not only to further political objectives but also to advance the positions of their own firms and organizations.

The international financial institutions (IFIs) explicitly placed politics and security outside their purview. Initially designed to deal with the postwar reconstruction of Europe, the IFIs gradually evolved into the international system's central instrument for financing developing countries. Over the years, the World Bank and various regional banks (e.g., African Development Bank, Asian Development Bank, Inter-American Development Bank) shifted their emphasis from funding infrastructure—"bricks and mortar"—to good governance. In the 1940s the consensus was that infrastructure was the missing ingredient for development, and the World Bank's articles called for reconstruction projects that would produce acceptable rates of return. Thus the first developmental projects financed by the World Bank involved funding for dams, roads, railways, and the like. These initial projects dealt only with infrastructure: They paid for physical structures but largely ignored the institutional issues involved, such as how the projects would be managed, operated, and maintained.

Likewise, there was an initial reluctance to provide funding for health and education, as economists doubted the economic returns these domains could provide. This was the concept of "human capital," which Adam Smith defined as the "acquired and useful abilities of all the inhabitants or members of the society" and which Gary Becker promoted in his 1964 book, *Human Capital*, which supplied a rationale for funding them. The developmental project harnessed resources to this task by funding physical components such as schools and clinics. World Bank president Robert S. McNamara's later focus on eradicating poverty resulted in new attention to rural and urban development in the late 1960s and 1970s, as well as the incorporation of these areas as sectors within the aid community.

When the development community began investing in human capital, its emphasis was on primary education, for girls in particular. While this investment is necessary, it is by no means sufficient. The skills required for management and leadership do not come about in the absence of a first-rate system of higher education. College education provides the wherewithal for students to fulfill specific functions upon graduation; it also creates responsible and skilled citizens who support development of the economy and polity. Such an approach links investments in human capital to the goal of forming a large middle class, which has historically been the vehicle for consolidating democracy. Moreover, it generates a demand for the rule of law and provides a solvent for ethnic, gender, and class tensions.

Until recently, however, the development community has strongly advocated a reduction in funding for higher education in favor of an increase in assistance to primary education. This approach grew out of an analysis of some Latin American countries in which state-funded higher education has been the preserve of the elite. Yet if a country does not train its children beyond the age of eleven, where are its managers, doctors, engineers, and teachers going to come from? In country after country, we have seen funding for universities blocked, yet hundreds of millions have been spent on technical assistance, with the justification that the country is unable to fill the needed technical positions with its own citizens. Rather than abandoning higher education altogether, we need to focus on how to make it an instrument of social mobility. This requires the creation of contextualized transparency and accountability mechanisms that facilitate access for poor and underprivileged people.

The vehicle used by international development agencies for addressing infrastructure and human capital has been the project. Latin America's balance of payments crisis after the emergence of the Organization of Petroleum Exporting Countries (OPEC) in 1960, along with the rise of oil prices in the 1970s, led to the invention of the "structural adjustment loan." These loans transferred funds to a government's budget in return for the imposition of a series of limits on the type and volume of a country's expenditures, as well as on the country's macroeconomic and monetary policies.

The lessons that emerged from practice were codified in what has become known as the "Washington Consensus," which is a package of ten policy prescriptions that broadly support market-based reforms. The first generation of reforms under the Washington Consensus mainly involved taking the state out of the economy and acknowledging an expanded role for a competitive private sector. Although strong political will was required to counter resistance from groups who benefited from restricted licensing or import substitution policies, the first wave of reforms was institutionally quite simple. The second generation, however, focused to a larger degree on building effective markets. In order to deal with the key issues of creating both organizational capacity and the regulations necessary for a functioning market, it became clear that governments had to play a central role in market building.

To confront these problems, the development community began to focus on "governance." While Africa and Latin America plunged into a crisis centered on inflation and negative growth and the Middle East was stagnating, East Asia registered impressive gains in terms of economic development and poverty reduction. This generated a body of literature and subsequent discussion on the distinctiveness of the developmental state that culminated in the 1997 World Bank World Development Report titled "The State in a Changing World." With this, the Washington Consensus has begun to broaden its focus on macroeconomic policies to include the set of institutions, networks, and relationships that are essential for state building. James Wolfensohn launched his visionary Comprehensive Development Framework and established the Poverty Reduction Strategy Paper as an internally generated process that was intended to be the policy vehicle for both the recipient government and other stakeholders in developing countries. The success of this initiative required donor procedures to be harmonized and aligned with those of the recipient government. Unfortunately, the reality of the aid system is that it continues to produce fragmentation and disunity rather than prosperity and harmony.

FLOWS OF MONEY

In recent years a core activity of the aid system has been the stewardship of very large funds. A key to understanding any system—as any good businessperson will confirm—is to follow the money, and the amount of money running through the aid system is immense. Overseas development assistance (ODA) equals $50 billion a year. Most agencies have audit reports and internal evaluations that specify their successes and failures. As commissions have investigated each of these in detail, the two recent interventions in Iraq offer a litmus test as to whether the multilateral or the bilateral system has been a more capable steward of the global system.

After the first Gulf War, the UN Security Council imposed sanctions in Iraq. To ensure that these would not harm the ordinary Iraqis, the Security Council authorized a program of "oil for food" and entrusted its management to the United Nations, which oversaw the process of selling oil and using the profits to buy a range of items to alleviate humanitarian suffering brought on by the sanctions. When the press raised questions about the efficacy of the program, the UN security general appointed an independent commission headed by Paul Volcker, former chair of the Federal Reserve of the United States, to investigate the program. The Independent Inquiry Committee into the United Nations Oil-for-Food Program found that oil surcharges were paid in connection with the contracts of 139 companies and that humanitarian kickbacks were paid in connection with the contracts of 2,253 companies. The commission found that Iraq received

$1.8 billion in illicit income, which resulted from surcharges of $229 million, after-sales-service fees of $1.02 billion, and inland transportation fees of $530 million. The Volcker Committee documents in detail the ways in which companies and agencies around the world colluded in this process.[3]

The internal audit review carried out by the UN Office of Internal Oversight Services (OIOS) for the oil-for-food program found an "overcompensation" of $557 million. It also detected a high degree of risk inherent in the program, which "often had not been adequately prevented or mitigated," as well as "serious deficiencies in internal control arrangements for the procurement of construction contractors in northern Iraq." Prompted by the oil-for-food investigations, the U.S. Government Accountability Office (GAO) launched a broader investigation into the UN's internal oversight and procurement controls. The GAO determined that "The UN is vulnerable to fraud, waste, abuse and mismanagement" because of "weaknesses in existing management and oversight practices" and in the UN's "control environment for procurement, as well as in key procurement processes."[4]

These types of irregularities are part of a systemic problem. Kofi Annan, UN secretary general during this period, acknowledged the findings. His report titled "Investing in the United Nations for a Stronger Organization Worldwide" makes for sobering reading. Attempts to deal with mismanagement and corruption have not, in his view, "been accompanied by sufficient support and controls to prevent mismanagement and possible abuse"; thus, they fall "short of the high standards that the United Nations needs to set itself." He states that "A damaged culture, which is seen as limiting creativity, enterprise, innovation and indeed leadership itself, has meant that many managers have simply lost the capacity to manage."[5] Annan refers to an external report conducted in 2005, which found "major weaknesses in culture, management oversight and controls," as well as a recent audit by the OIOS into peace-keeping procurement, which "raised significant additional concerns with regard to both mismanagement and possible fraud." At the same time, however, UN agencies argue that donor funding should be routed through them rather than via the governments in question in view of their assertion of the latter's inability to manage funds.

The investigations carried out by the OIOS indeed found cases of "mismanagement, embezzlement, and sexual exploitation and abuse" in peace-keeping operations. With the rapid growth in the budget of peace-keeping operations (from $1.25 billion in 1996 to more than

$5 billion in 2006), the scale of the management task—and thus potential abuse—is considerable.[6] The OIOS determined that, in the UN Office for the Coordination of Humanitarian Affairs (OCHA), the financing of tsunami-related operations provided "no effective monitoring of the expenditures" and that the "proposed oversight and reporting arrangements for the enlarged Fund did not ensure adequate transparency and accountability in the use of its resources." The OIOS repeatedly claims that it has insufficient staff to investigate properly the abuses and that it can carry out only one in-depth evaluation a year; with twenty-seven secretariat programs, each program would thus get evaluated only once every twenty-seven years.[7]

During the decade that the oil-for-food program was in operation, the UN assumed responsibility for a number of other programs around the world. The recent growth in UN agency expenditure is significant. The UN budget is now $20 billion a year, of which half goes to UN agencies for these types of programs. Programs have included the management of the transition in Cambodia (where most of the country's sovereign rights were vested in the United Nations), Bosnia, East Timor, and Kosovo. Each of these operations has involved billions of dollars in resources. To our knowledge, none has been subjected to a full system audit, similar to that carried out by Volcker's commission. Given the acknowledgment of the significant weaknesses in the control system, it would be surprising if these programs did not suffer from some or all of the problems in the oil-for-food program.

Nevertheless, every year UN agencies launch either individual or consolidated appeals by sector or country, ranging from the post-Taliban Afghanistan appeal to that for tsunami-affected countries. Contained in each one are hundreds of projects that have usually been hastily prepared without internal review processes or meaningful consultation with the government authorities in the countries concerned. In Afghanistan we reviewed more than four hundred projects—costing $1.8 billion—that the UN had handed to the donors for funding in the spring of 2002 and found most of them ill organized. Between 2002 and 2004 the Afghan government and citizens continuously and publicly requested disclosure of the management of funds provided to UN agencies and the outcomes they had achieved. The UN agencies refused to comply with the request. Estimates were that up to 70 percent of this fund had been spent on the internal costs—for international salaries, white Land Cruisers, satellite communications, and specially chartered airlines—to set up a UN agency presence. The *London Sunday Times* of September 16, 2007, reported a Serious Fraud

Office investigation into alleged corruption involving programs run by the Global Fund to Fight AIDS, TB, and Malaria regarding contracts given by the United Nations Development Program (UNDP) to a firm in Denmark; the office, which is part of the UK government, suspected that "large sums of money may have been laundered through British Bank accounts."

Viewed from headquarters, these numbers are overwhelming, but they are essentially abstractions. What do the figures look like to the people of a developing country, the majority of whom are living on less than a dollar a day? Villagers in a remote district of Bamiyan province (the central valley in Afghanistan), into whose red rock the fifth-century statues of Buddha were carved but tragically destroyed in April 2001, described their understanding of how the materials provided by a multimillion-dollar UN agency housing program literally went up in smoke. Hearing a radio announcement that a new program was going to restore shelter to their area, the villagers had been very excited. But what arrived was not what they had anticipated. Disappointed at the apparent waste of public funds, they set out to find out what had happened.

The money, they discovered, had been given to one agency, which had taken 20 percent for head office costs in Geneva. The project was then subcontracted to an NGO, which had also appropriated 20 percent for head office costs in Brussels. All in all there were five contractual layers, and at each one, 20 percent of the financing was lost to overheads. The villagers said that only a small proportion of the original donation remained with which to buy wood, which came from western Iran. Trucked in by Ismael Khan's trucking cartel at a premium to their villages, a few wooden beams were eventually delivered, but they were too big for the mud walls of the houses, so the villagers chopped them up for firewood.

Demand for UN reform is neither a right-wing nor a left-wing issue. The most significant stakeholders in any reform are the poor. From the people in refugee camps in Darfur to those in hamlets in Rwanda and Cambodia, every cent that is wasted affects their lives. Now the burden of proof is on the UN and the nations that contribute to it to demonstrate its fitness for the purposes those nations ascribe to it. The future of the United Nations is too important to be left to its own bureaucrats without a global public discussion. The United States has been leading demands for improvement in the accountability of the UN for years. The GAO's investigations into the operations of the United States Agency for International Development (USAID) in Iraq, however, make it clear that accountability in management of resources has also been a major challenge for the United States. The same patterns were evident in Afghanistan. In November 2005 both the *Washington Post* and the *New York Times* documented USAID's school-building program across the country. Having promised the government of Afghanistan that it would build several hundred schools (and in one meeting USAID said that it would build eleven hundred schools within two years), it asked other actors to discontinue their programs. However, the agency ended up building only eight school buildings within this time frame—of which six have already collapsed. The costs are not just financial but can also be measured in terms of loss of trust and hope, which are far more significant. Afghan citizens interviewed in the spring of 2007 expressed their sense of betrayal by the international community because of the waste, inefficiency, and corruption.

MANAGING PROJECTS

The developmental "project" has become an established practice; the World Bank, regional banks such as those mentioned earlier in this chapter, UN agencies, NGOs, and bilateral agencies alike have all now adopted the project as the critical instrument of development. Efforts to determine the total number of projects are fruitless, as many of these agencies have hundreds (if not thousands) in progress. At its best and when aligned to a national vision, leadership, and management capability, the project can be an effective instrument. But when they are externally driven, poorly designed and managed, and have little connection to the national system, they are not only a source of waste, corruption, and indebtedness but can also directly undermine state institutions.

At the World Bank, the "project" was originally based on a model of coproduction between technical experts and government managers. Robert McNamara—president of the World Bank from 1968 to 1981, after having been president of Ford Motors and U.S. secretary of defense—then applied Fordist models of production to the project, turning it into a standard vehicle for World Bank work throughout the world. This has brought scale to the enterprise, but it has not necessarily also brought the high standards that result when the market is the test of effectiveness.

The preparation of the project is often funded through a technical assistance grant and farmed out either to a consulting firm, a UN agency, or an NGO. Meanwhile, the rules for purchasing goods and services have evolved into a distinctive practice: procurement. Since developmental agencies and bilateral donors have adopted different procurement rules, recipient governments are required to master an often arcane series of regulations to disburse money, which uses up officials' precious management time and fragments national rules and practices. If the European Union, USAID, the World Bank, and the Asian Development Bank are to finance a road, they will have to break it up into segments and then contract, design, and supervise each segment separately.

Project implementation often takes place through specially created units that appear to be more efficient in the short term. Their staffs are not subject to the regular government rules regarding salaries and benefits, and they are often international consultants. Occasionally donors agree to direct implementation by government agencies, but the accepted approach to project implementation for infrastructure is generally to contract it to a domestic or foreign contractor. All projects that cost more than a certain amount in each country have had to go through international procurement. Although sometimes bid documents can express a preference for a firm from the local private sector, international firms tend to have an advantage in these bidding contests as they have large departments devoted to winning contracts.

Unless donors maintain large staffs in a particular country, supervision tends to take place sporadically since development agency teams visit the project between two and four times a year during oversight missions. Meanwhile, a government submits regular reports to the donor on each phase of the project. Since projects often utilize a combination of domestic and international funding, one recurrent problem has involved obtaining domestic resources. Not surprisingly, this often results in further implementation delays.

Since the World Bank needs to lend a certain amount of money every year, bank staff and outside commentators have often pointed out that the ability to disburse large sums is a critical driver for the behavior of bank staff, whose rise up through the ranks is implicitly linked to their ability to lend. Until the early 1990s, concern over the quality of projects took a distinct second place to the volume of lending. The bank then created a quality assurance group that reviews the value of the projects either just after their approval by the board or in the early phases of implementation, thus enabling management to take quick remedial action. Each country's effectiveness can be judged by its ability to utilize the money it has borrowed—on time and in full. But given the presence of the sovereign guarantee (through which the state guarantees that it will repay its debts), the ability to spend money is not linked in any way to the quality of the lending instrument.

Originally intended to provide infrastructure, the project approach retains its engineering blueprint in being standardized and driven by the construction schedule. Developmental agencies were slow to recognize adverse social and environmental impacts. It took massive social protests by both the environmental movement and displaced people to incorporate attention to social and environmental issues into project design. Even today, most engineering plans use the same blueprints for infrastructure from the 1950s, without considering the phenomenal advances in strategy and technology that use alternative energies, better materials, and more efficient transportation methods. Instead, it is all too common to see the name of one country on a project document intended for another because of the fact that the requests for proposal (RFPs) are copied from one report to another without even changing the place names.

Often the project is a legal agreement between the donor and the recipient government. In the case of the World Bank, its own rules take an acknowledged precedence over national law. This allows the bank to cancel the project if the country does not meet established conditions. Yet funding for project operation and maintenance has been a recurrent problem in weak states. Frequently budgets are not the central instruments for managing policy and ensuring that projects are operated and maintained as well as built, and so millions of dollars can often be lost where all that was needed was thousands allocated in a timely way. Despite their shortcomings, completed projects by the World Bank are rated 72 percent satisfactory, but fewer than half of them are sustainable.

As a result, the aid system has created a web of relationships between multilateral and bilateral donors, UN agencies, private contractors, and NGOs. Funds go directly from the donors to NGOs and private contractors, sometimes channeled through UN agencies that then subcontract NGOs and private contractors. Usually a chain of intermediation develops (as the villagers in Bamiyan discovered), where each organization in the group charges a fee for its contract management services but then turns around and subcontracts the same function to another level. In the case of USAID in Afghanistan, the chain had as many as five links for the construction of a school. When one of the bilateral donors decides to engage in a particular sector, its entire process of firm selection bypasses the government counterpart. In Washington,

D.C., the phenomenon has been given a name—"beltway banditry"—referring to the organizations that inhabit Route 495 outside the capital, whose specialty is writing contracts and obtaining resources from USAID and other government agencies. Large "body shop" companies have grown up to absorb these contracts and subcontract others. Earmarking large sums (sometimes of hundreds of millions of dollars) by European donors for disbursement to and through the NGOs has created similar incentives in Europe.

Nongovernmental organizations can be active partners in this process, as they are often asked to implement the projects for which UN agencies and private contractors win large bids, or they can make their own appeals. Like UN agencies, they have grown rapidly over the last ten years to take on roles that substitute for state functions, often building and managing schools, clinics, and food distribution directly. These NGOs range from the good to the bad to the ugly, and their employees include both the dedicated and the narrowly opportunistic. For example, the Swedish Committee in Afghanistan kept schooling alive under the Taliban by mobilizing resources and a network of dedicated staff to maintain education, including to girls. As a whole, the behavior of the NGOs in responding to the tsunami, by contrast, has brought harsh criticism. Failure to agree on basic coordination, refusal to account for large expenditures, and poor-quality construction plagued the rebuilding effort. Consequently, three years after the tsunami, residents of islands such as Banda Aceh still live in dire conditions. Like UN agencies, very few NGOs issue transparent accounts to the public in the countries of either their headquarters or their beneficiaries.

The aid system as currently configured tends to undermine rather than support state institutions. The thousands of small projects designed to aid a particular school, village, or district end up recruiting the very teachers, administrators, and doctors they are designed to support to work instead as secretaries and drivers for international staff. The world spends billions of dollars on contracts with international firms for projects in developing countries, but since the emerging local private sector cannot understand the complicated contracting rules to put a bid together or fulfill the bid criteria, they cannot compete.

In many developed countries, state expenditure is used to invest in domestic capabilities and spur private initiative. The clusters of people and organizations that underpin a country's growth, as we saw in chapter 2, resulted from a combination of imagination, research capabilities, and public and private money from governments, firms, and universities. The donor-driven project approach, by contrast, has been an exercise in the perpetuation of dependence. After sixty years of aid, local contractors in some countries are still serving as subcontractors to foreign firms for small works. We have reviewed hundreds of donor strategies but have not seen one that has focused on sustained development or utilized a cluster approach to developing domestic contracting capability or financial services. Neither have we seen one that fosters the development of design, research, or coherent project preparation capabilities.

A review of transitional countries (e.g., China, Singapore, Malaysia, Dubai), shows that they built up their capabilities systematically and can now undertake both the design and implementation of large-scale projects through either a domestic organization or an international partnership. In countries that have transformed themselves, groups of citizens have become stakeholders in the process, thereby reinforcing their interest in orderly change and system stability. These stakeholders see increasing state functionality as crucial to their interests. And as the trust between citizens and state and the prosperity of the country grows, so the state's revenue-raising capacity increases.

Quite the opposite is the case in aid-dependent countries, where interests are not channeled in a coherent way toward stability. The presence of donors is an inescapable part of the landscape. Hundreds or even thousands of signs feature the logos of donor countries and organizations, forever reminding the inhabitants of their perpetual dependence. This underlines the fragmentation of authority, accountability, and rule of law. Each donor has different procurement procedures and contracting arrangements; each is organized along functional lines that push for certain types of projects regardless of whether they are national priorities; each organization asks for exemptions from prevailing law; and each drains the talent of the government and the private sector while lamenting the government's lack of capability. Donors prepare their own (often conflicting) priorities for investment and, after years of OECD declarations, have never been able to agree on coordination arrangements. Because donors differ in their degree of emphasis on gender, human rights, or social protection, the reality becomes a quilt of confusing practices and strategies.

The predominance of the project as the key aid instrument has created a series of structures that run parallel to the government. Hundreds and occasionally thousands of these projects may coexist in a recipient country, each structured according to different rules and procedures. The existence of these project organizations has resulted in the creation of dual bureaucracies: the government bureaucracy (often overstaffed, underpaid, and feeling deeply threatened by the layoffs or reorganizations entailed in structural and sectoral adjustments) and local staff working for donor-funded projects, international organizations, UN agencies and NGOs. The latter are paid many times the wages and benefits of government civil servants and make a career out of moving from one donor-funded project to another. Tension between these two bureaucracies is therefore not surprising and has become a constant of developmental practice on the ground.

In Afghanistan, for instance, approximately 280,000 civil servants work in the government bureaucracy and receive an average salary of $50 per month. Meanwhile, approximately 50,000 work for NGOs, the United Nations, and bilateral and multilateral agencies, where support staff can earn up to $1,000 per month. Unsurprisingly, there has been a brain drain from the government's managerial tier to menial positions in the aid system. If the disparity in wages resulted from a competitive market, then people might consider it fair. The problem is that the finances of the aid complex generally fund both bureaucracies, and the rules for remuneration are set by bureaucratic fiat rather than by open processes of competition.

The thousands of projects, each with their own rules, procedures, and requirements, fragment the rule of law. To prevent corruption, projects and sectoral adjustment operations involve agreements on specific rules for procurement, accounting, and auditing. While these issues are highly technical, they have major institutional consequences. Procurement determines the purchase of goods and services and is potentially a key instrument for nurturing the private sector. It should ensure the most economical service provision and build rule of law by making transactions more transparent. Such objectives cannot, however, be achieved when country officials must deal with myriad rules and regulations set by a donor. Often the rules are designed to protect or promote particular industries within the donor's country, and procurement takes place for each project under the donor's legal system; as a result, the officials are required to understand and juggle dozens of different legal systems. Experience shows that transparency and accountability can best be achieved when local processes become the main focus of attention and when all efforts center on adhering to a harmonized set of rules and regulations.

The largest adverse impact of the aid system has been the undermining of a country's budget as the central instrument of policy. When hundreds or thousands of projects are funded through parallel systems, implemented by the private sector, NGOs, and UN agencies, and supervised by donors, the budget of the recipient country tends to become undermined. The projects' separate decision making, contracting, management, maintenance accounting, and auditing rules fundamentally circumscribe the budget's role in deciding a country's priorities and allocating resources to implement them in a disciplined way. Donors still have little understanding of the budget's significance in unifying a state's laws and policies and in establishing accountability between a state and its citizens. Without being embedded in a budget, the project finds little synergy and is rarely scrutinized for its cost-effectiveness. Without incentive to raise revenue to sustain the costs of society, attention is focused on attracting more money from the aid system; in Kenya in 2005, the first draft of the government's aid policy opened with the statement that Kenya's goal was to attract the maximum possible amount of aid from donors rather than develop a healthy economy.

TECHNICAL ASSISTANCE

The aid complex establishes not only a dual bureaucracy but also another distinctive layer of "officialdom," which comprises international consultants whose stay in developing countries ranges from several days to years. The technical assistance model was developed in 1945, when many colonial governments had left their colonies with meager technical capability. The initial objective was to help recipient countries prepare, implement, and supervise projects according to internationally accepted standards. Lee Kuan Yew states that most of their key advice came from a Dutch economist, Albert Winsemius, who returned to Singapore every few months for intense discussions with the leadership, unpaid except for his travel expenses. He advised the Singaporean leaders that the country needed "large-scale technical, managerial, entrepreneurial and marketing know-how from America and Europe."[8]

Technical assistance has now become a multibillion-dollar global industry that employs thousands of people and has spawned businesses and corporations that specialize in and derive their profits from these activities. The Commission for Africa reports that Africa spends an estimated $4 billion every year on one hundred thousand expatriates.[9] Moreover, USAID has given hundreds of millions of dollars for technical assistance to a handful of firms. Chemonics (one of USAID's subcontractors), for example, handles contracts worth $185 million, 90 percent of which comes from USAID.[10] The firms are selected by USAID with no (or only minimal) consultation with the government or ministries of the countries in which they are going to be placed; consultants often arrive without the knowledge of who their ministry counterparts are or what they are going to be doing. Regardless of their record in one country, the same firms are given contracts (which often run into hundreds of millions of dollars) in other countries on a sole-source basis despite well-known problems and inefficiencies. Indeed, the *New York Times* reports that "members of Congress say understaffed (US)AID is far too reliant on large construction companies and Washington-based consulting firms."[11]

Since international consultants are not usually found in formal positions of authority, they are not accountable for the organizational transformations needed to overcome the capacity constraints. Moreover, there are no established processes for vetting and evaluation, which thus raises a question about the quality and salience of the advice they provide. The time horizon of short-term consultants usually results in generalized advice derived from rules of thumb and so-called best practices. Tailoring their guidance to context and the patient process of nurturing the growth of local institutions through firsthand familiarity are not usually part of the culture of technical assistance.

It is not clear that economists have the best skills for advising on institutional transformations. In his 1930 essay titled "Economic Possibilities for Our Grandchildren," Keynes said, "Do not let us overestimate the importance of the economic problem, or sacrifice to its supposed necessities other matters of greater and more permanent significance. It should be a matter for specialists—like dentistry. If economists could manage to get themselves thought of as humble, competent people, on a level with dentists, that would be splendid." Nor is it clear that diplomats, who have little familiarity with budgeting and the details of policy implementation, are in a better position. A gaping lacuna exists in the curricula and skills training of those who are sent to advise on matters of immense import: the creation and nurturing of institutions in countries that face severe challenges.

As with NGOs, the best suffer from the record of the worst. Certain individual experts can be extremely good in specialized technical domains, but the critical challenge they face is institutional transformation, and they are not trained for that. The World Bank's own findings indicated that, until 2001, technical assistance was the least satisfactory part of its project portfolio.

MANAGING ADJUSTMENT

In shifting from the project to structural adjustment as a vehicle for intervention, the aid system discovered the state without realizing it. Funds in a structural adjustment or program loan (now called "development policy loan" by the World Bank) are directly allocated to the country's budget in return for adoption of a reform package usually designed by World Bank or IMF staff. The disbursement of both sectoral and structural adjustment loans is linked to the fulfillment of certain benchmarks. Program loans are usually divided into tranches. A country must meet a set of conditions before the loan is submitted to the board of the bank, which results in the disbursement of the first tranche of the loan. Each subsequent disbursement is also subject to the country's fulfillment of certain conditions. If a country is unable to do so, the bank staff must determine whether disbursement still needs to take place. Compared to project lending, financing through such operations proceeds relatively rapidly. These loans are considered essential to providing liquidity to a country in crisis; thus the bank board has typically approved them. While the majority of bank lending is still absorbed by projects, adjustment lending came close to matching it at the height of the East Asian crisis in the late 1990s, when the World Bank lent $2.4 billion to Indonesia.

To tackle the specific issue of governance, donors also set up a series of complementary projects that ranged from judicial reform (linked to the rule of law) to civil service reform; the focus of these plans evolved from firing civil servants to promoting measures for enhancing their capacity and accountability. All of these undertakings emphasized the importance of ownership—the extent to which those holding power in a country are committed to an agenda of change, along with the culture and process of governance.

In the wake of the 1970s' oil shocks, the World Bank and the IMF determined that many states were overly involved in their economies, which in turn were in crisis because of balance of payments problems and inflation. To resolve this issue, they devised the idea of structural adjustment. Subsequently, the structural adjustment loan became a vehicle for promoting the Washington Consensus, the first generation of which, as mentioned earlier, aimed to take the state out of the economy. Though politically difficult, these reforms were largely stroke-of-the-pen events that created the conditions of entry for new players. Nevertheless, this model did not work well in Africa, Latin America, and Central and Eastern Europe.

The World Bank slowly came to realize that a working economy requires a functioning state. Taking the state out of the economy is easy; finding ways to regulate the economy without the state is impossible. The second generation of these reforms, which created new institutions, proved considerably more difficult: their success depended on the cooperation or consensus of various stakeholders within and outside the government. The changes envisaged in these reforms created potential winners and losers, and the organized resistance of the losers was intense. As a result, the country would pretend to reform, with the bank pretending to believe that conditions were met. While the bank used fast-disbursing mechanisms and cookie-cutter approaches derived from a fixed menu, success would have required learning about specific contexts and tailoring programs in light of them, as well as partnering with domestic groups. For reform to take root, the politics of governance has to be generated domestically rather than imposed externally.

We reviewed fifty-four World Bank adjustment (conditionality) operations in forty-two countries between 1997 and 2001. All of these selected from a menu of six core issues: privatization, market regulation, enabling laws, reduction of the fiscal gap, administrative reform, and decentralization of governance. The operations in Africa focused on the fiscal gap; those in Latin America on decentralization; those in East Asia on market regulation (because of the financial crisis); and those in Central Europe on privatization and administrative reform. The task managers identified social and institutional risks rather than economic ones as the main threat to the successful outcomes of the adjustment process by a factor of four to one. Perhaps it is no coincidence that only one in five World Bank borrowers recorded continuous per capita income growth from 1995 to 2005.

Unlike many other development agencies, the World Bank has now grown quite comfortable operating at a macropolicy level. The challenge is how to translate the objectives of reform into outcomes, as this requires mediation through state institutions. Neither by constitution, skills, or practices is the bank currently suited to this challenge, as it does not understand the state's essential functions, how they interrelate, and how they come to be performed. According to its own annual review of development effectiveness (ARDE), the bank's business models are under pressure from dysfunctional states where the bank's advice is rarely practicable, as well as from middle-income countries, which often find its advice irrelevant. In China, for example, officials and researchers indicate that the bank did not take advantage of the growing sophistication and knowledge of its Chinese counterparts and instead provided generic, textbook advice rather than discussing policy options relevant to China's actual needs.

UN PEACEKEEPING, MILITARY RECONSTRUCTION, AND HUMANITARIAN INTERVENTIONS

Three other components of global institutions currently impact the process of governance. The political-security nexus is the core mandate of the United Nations. In the last sixteen years, the United Nations has been the catalyst for a large number of peace agreements, which manifest its role in the security arena. A reading of peace agreements shows that the functions that states must perform lie at the core of both the problem of and the solution to conflict; many participants in peace agreements cite bad governance as the root cause of conflict and state that functioning institutions are the key to stability. Recent peace agreements demonstrate not only this awareness of good governance but also aspirations for democratic governance. Nevertheless, implementation has nearly always fallen short of these lofty ambitions because the skills, resources, time horizons, and staying power necessary for their realization have by and large not been mastered.

Since the United Nations does not command permanent forces, decisions on deployment require both consensus within the Security Council and a coalition of countries willing to contribute troops. The result is the very infrequent use of preventive deployment. The failure to deploy in Burundi, Rwanda, and the Balkans caused enormous loss of life that could perhaps have been mitigated. The imposition of peace in the Balkans has been accomplished only through massive deployment of troops throughout the relatively small territories of Bosnia and Kosovo, with clearly defined rules for the use of force. With no clear exit in sight, these operations are financially costly. Even when the numbers have been smaller, as in the case of coalition and NATO deployment in Afghanistan, the annual costs are now exceeding $15 billion a year.

The fundamental point is that international military forces are going to be a significant player in the projection of security in some of the world's most volatile regions and the chief instrument for training of the local security forces. Given the military's capability for systematic and long-term thinking, these forces bring a much-needed alternative perspective to development and easily grasp the need for a state-building doctrine. Our interactions with several leaders of NATO/ISAF (International Security Assistance Force) in Kabul led to increasing international alignment on strategy. General Rick Hillier, Canadian commander of the international forces in Afghanistan in 2004, ordered his strategic planning team to determine the drivers of stability in Afghanistan. On finding that credible institutions and a public finance system topped the list and that they were far more important than planning the itinerary of his tank patrols, he assigned his core team directly to support the Ministry of Finance. Problems of continuity, however, are introduced by the frequent change of command and turnover of personnel.

A new phenomenon that can have disturbing consequences for long-term stability is the emergence of security firms that provide protection for various developmental projects but recruit and train young men who have been reared in a culture of violence to work on short-term contracts. As with development projects, this situation fragments an essential function. Costs for these mercenary armies can be very high. And without their adherence to the culture of loyalty to orders and propriety in the use of force, these fighters can, on the one hand, escalate the use of force too quickly and, on the other, desert on short notice when the going gets tough. In addition, mechanisms for demobilization are not in place when a particular job is done.

Organizations that specialize in humanitarian assistance have emerged as a distinctive third component. Persistent conflicts and natural disasters have produced waves of refugees who are often forced to live in camps, and organizations have emerged to manage the situation and supply food aid to them. The cost of transportation and distribution of food accounts for as much as 40–60 percent of the total cost, whereas food could be purchased for much less within the region. As we discuss later, a strong nexus of farmers (who benefit from subsidies in the United States and Europe), shipping interests, UN agencies, and NGOs ensures the continuation of this system. Young men, given no other economic options, often become recruits for gangs and armed militias within the camps, thereby putting the women and children living among them at high risk.

The division of conflict resolution into three phases—humanitarian, reconstruction, and developmental—offered the humanitarian community an opportunity to expand its assistance beyond food aid and camp management to a wide range of activities and long-term engagement with vulnerable populations. But humanitarian organizations too often develop and raise money for "quick-impact projects" that neither meet the criteria of economic feasibility and financial viability nor address the fundamental issue of sustainable paths out of poverty. Rather than looking for ways to reintegrate citizens into regular lives, they often perpetuate the symptoms of conflict, and camps sometimes remain in place for decades. Given the lack of accountability and management in UN operations as we pointed out earlier, the humanitarian field—where the emphasis is on quick action—is particularly prone to abuse.

THE AID COMPLEX

Good intentions are wasted without positive effects. Even though the development system sometimes acknowledges that weak states are a central issue, it continues to fall short in efforts to strengthen fragile institutions. Without an approach based on a clear analysis of the state's core functions, it continues to deal with the symptoms rather than the cause of the problem.

Today the aid system is facing a crisis. While vast public relations teams produce glossy reports that describe the success of development projects, the reality on the ground is clearly different. While the state's current organizational capacity is low in many cases—leading to the aid industry's further justification of mechanisms to bypass government systems—it is not clear that the aid system has a better track record than the state when it comes to cost-effectiveness, corruption, efficiency, and competent service delivery. Further, it is clear that aid has in many places undermined the state. The aid system's mode of operation has effected a series of institutional consequences, and it has never had the explicit goal of state building.

The ineptitude of the donor complex in advising a country to use its assets to escape poverty is illustrated by the case of Nepal, where for quite some time the aid system has experienced a crisis of confidence (the first critiques in Kathmandu date to the early 1960s). Donors have either colluded with the existing patronage networks or created institutions that operate parallel to the government, thereby giving rise to another series of entrenched interests and reinforcing a cycle of dependence. Four decades later, the aid complex still remains substantially unchanged. A civil society leader in Nepal recounted how the aid system reinvents itself with new methods and languages, and the Nepali leaders spend their time learning those languages to meet the criteria of the moment. But as soon as they have mastered them and rewritten their documents, the approach changes, and the cycle begins all over again: poverty reduction, sustainable development, millennium development goals, capacity building. A Ministry of Finance official was amazed that visitors from the outside questioned how the aid system operated and shared stories of its immense wastage. For example, a Japanese aid project bought bricks on the market at 150 rupees per unit through its particular procurement system, whereas the Nepali government could have obtained the same bricks for 6 rupees per unit if allowed to use its own procurement system. Under the project rules, however the Japanese procurement system had to be used.

Institutions are best characterized by both formal and informal rules of the game. When the informal rules dominate the formal rules, they distort or subvert them and give rise to an institutional syndrome through which substantive actions are in constant conflict with the stated rules. Aid mechanisms have now assumed the character of a syndrome, the unintended but very real result of which is to undermine state effectiveness and the relationship of rights and obligations between citizens and the state. Instead of a level playing field, it creates a crooked one, and instead of promoting partnership, it pits people against each other in unequal positions.

Despite having operated for sixty years in some countries, the aid system still retains a short-time operational horizon. The key driver tends to be the annual budget cycle in a particular donor country or organization, through which donors decide on the amount of money to be divided among different countries and determine the allocation through the aid system's various instruments. The longest time horizon is three years, which is the framework for the World Bank's country assistance strategy and the lending program of regional banks or bilateral aid organizations. Since there is a variation in each country's ability to absorb and allocate money according to the established rules, the system is highly unpredictable. Moreover, the rhythms of the aid system vary considerably. The last month of a particular donor year can provide a bonanza to some countries, as the aid system has a strong incentive to report that it has been able to spend the allocated funds. This is one reason that donors contract UN agencies, as funds transferred to them can be categorized as expenditures.

In recent years the aid system has begun to realize the need for a medium-term expenditure framework and alignment of donor procedures with country timetables and systems. Such a framework requires that the state budget become the central policy instrument. Internal procedures must also be strong enough to allow for predictability, transparency, and accountability. Nonetheless, despite hopeful signs and the donors' verbal consensus on the urgency of harmonizing their procedures, the reality is still one of fragmentation: in 2007 in Nepal, Kosovo, and Afghanistan, donors' talk of coordination and harmonization glossed over a reality of thousands of projects still operating to the donors' tunes (e.g., budget years, procurement, and reporting rules) rather than the host country's laws, systems, and procedures. Those preparing the budget had little understanding of the country's laws and procedures; those preparing the laws had little understanding of the budgets and flows of money. In some countries, donors exhibited synthetic understanding of neither the budgets nor the laws that would be required to create systems out of dysfunctional elements.

From the user's perspective, the fragmented system is costly. Ministers who are responsible for coordinating policy must create consensus not only with other cabinet members but also with dozens of donors and agencies and hundreds of NGOs, each with their own budgets, priorities, rules, and preferences. In Afghanistan, the minister of finance in the post-Taliban period spent more than 60 percent of his time on coordination. Had the aid system united around a single flow of financing and rules, the number of reforms carried out within the government's core systems would have risen exponentially. Moreover, each donor agency tends to build alliances with different ministries, further fragmenting cabinet unity. Instead of becoming catalysts for orderly policy management, donors become instruments of division and chaos.

In Haiti, the aid system has been forced to acknowledge its adverse impact on the state and argue for an explicit agenda of state-building. In a framework for interim cooperation jointly prepared between bilateral actors and the government in 2004, donors stated that over the past decade they have provided more than $2.5 billion but that "it must be noted that the results fall short of the expectations and the needs of communities. . . . The donors recognize a lack of coordination, of consistency and of strategic vision in their interventions. The donors have often set up parallel project implementation structures that weakened the State, without, however, giving it the means to coordinate this external aid to improve national absorptive and execution capacities."

A paper by the U.S. National Academy of Public Administration aptly named "Why Foreign Aid to Haiti Failed" seeks to explain "why, after consuming billions in foreign aid over three decades, and hundreds of millions specifically for governance and democratization programs, not to mention billions for other programs, Haiti remains politically dysfunctional and impoverished." While laying the blame squarely at the door of poor governance in the country, it describes how aid has made either little impact or has had adverse impact on governance. It cites the Director of the World Bank's Operations Evaluation Department as describing the outcome of World Bank programs between 1986 and 2002 as "rated unsatisfactory (if not highly so), the institutional development impact, negligible, and the sustainability of the few benefits that have accrued, unlikely." It describes a Canadian aid agency as admitting "Considering the resources invested, scattered Canadian projects do not seem to provide a critical mass of results, do not foster efficiency and effectiveness of the action taken, and make it difficult to achieve sustainable results." It describes how *USAID's Strategic Plan for Haiti—1999–2004* was merely a listing of projects underway with the annotation that they were 'accomplishments.' Yet the policy areas—environment, privatization, justice, security, fiscal and monetary management, elections—were disasters with billions spent and adverse results produced." The report concludes that "Aid...continued to be ineffective as a result of aid suspensions and cutbacks; inappropriate conditionality, unclear policy focus and program design; poor alignment, accountability and harmonization; ineffective capacity building; faulty implementation; lack of coordination; and delusions about what constituted program success. No donor stepped forward to lead. These issues, perpetually in play, may have caused donor fatigue, wherein aid organizations tired of Haiti."

Arguing the need for state-building as the critical task in Haiti, authors of the 2006 World Bank Economic Memorandum state that the generalization that we make in this book regarding the onset of a vicious circle of state failure seems tailor-made for Haiti. We had argued that states that do not perform their functions in an integrated manner fall into a vicious circle of "the creation of contending centres of power, the multiplication of increasingly contradictory and ineffective decision-making processes, the loss of trust between citizens and state, the delegitimization of institutions, the disenfranchisement of the citizenry and ultimately the resort to violence."

Donors, however, have had difficulty in breaking away from their acknowledged failures. The Inter-American Development Bank's Office of Evaluation and Oversight, for instance, documents that despite the donor cry of "mea culpa" the donors continued to work through project executing units in 2007. It argues that the "Bank's strategies failed to present a proper diagnosis of the situation beyond description of some of the many problems. The failure resulted in the inability to effectively prioritize among the different pressing needs that the country faces. The analytical background for the strategy, if it exists, is not reflected in the document." Not surprisingly, it concludes that "the current portfolio lacks a strategic perspective."

Only in the wake of 9/11 has it become clear how much the current functioning of the international system acts as a constraint rather than an asset in the fight against terrorism and other global threats. The aid system has had the perverse effect of fragmenting states' ability to perform key functions. Further, the aid system itself is organized into a series of "stovepipes" that keep economic, political, and security issues separate from one another. The international system devised in 1945 is structurally and practically outdated. This is not to argue that international institutions are not an indispensable part of any practical and sustained attempt to combat the most serious challenges in the contemporary world, but in their current shape and form they are contributing to problems rather than resolving them.

The aid complex—the series of ways in which the international aid architecture works—undermines states' capacity to perform essential functions. To address the most serious of the world's problems (among them poverty and global terrorism), the aid system must orient itself around the task of building effective, functioning states. This means that organizations with different cultures, objectives, time horizons, and staff incentives must all be coordinated. Reforming the governance of the aid system is just as significant a part of the global governance agenda as improving the systems, institutions, and procedures within developing countries themselves.

We must remind ourselves that the goal of the aid system was to promote productive investments. Both postwar Europe and Japan had an abundance of human capital and the institutional capacity to put it to the task of reconstruction. It is therefore not surprising that an understanding of the political economy of aid effectiveness was slow in developing. The aid system's adverse impact on the state has not been intentional. Without the polarizing alliances of the Cold War, the aid system might have come to focus on state building much earlier and might also have had the freedom to define its goals and instruments for promoting good governance years ago.

At the level of individual projects or sectoral and structural adjustment, the aid system has met with much success—for instance, in Japan, Korea, and Indonesia. Many dedicated professionals have devoted their lives to making a difference and helping poor people. We can and must learn from these successes. In more recent years, as we saw in chapter 2, it is those countries who followed an unconventional path driven by leadership, management, and untried and imaginative thinking that have broken out of the poverty trap. There is a great deal of tacit knowledge in the aid system that must be turned into active knowledge to provide the basis for state-building strategies. The developmental project retains its relevance. The challenge is to bring innovation to its design and embed it institutionally in a larger strategy geared toward generating trust between citizens and states. In the last part of the book we will return to how the aid project can play a constructive role in development.

PART TWO

DEFINING THE STATE FOR THE TWENTY-FIRST CENTURY

SIX

Toward a Multifunctional View of the State

D URING THE SUMMER of 2007, important but seemingly disparate headlines filled our daily newspapers, radio shows, and television programs. Global financial market volatility, as a result of subprime mortgage lending in the United States, was a topic of much concern; the war in Iraq was, as always, a topic of impassioned debate; and the collapse of a large bridge in Minnesota and the second anniversary of Hurricane Katrina led to deep reflection in the United States. If we think about these and many other newsworthy events in a slightly different way and not as a series of unrelated occurrences, it becomes clear that they all have something in common—the idea that the state has a certain set of responsibilities to its people and an array of mechanisms it can use to fulfill these responsibilities. From the intervention of the central bank to monitor money supply, to the ability of the government to wage war, to the role of federal agencies in the provision of infrastructure and reconstruction after natural disasters, it is now accepted that the state has a central role in society. This idea has become so entrenched within our Western psyches that it is not state intervention itself that we question but its efficiency or inefficiency and the form it should take. It is now well understood that citizens have certain rights and the state has certain obligations.

This was of course not always the case, and it is instructive for us to think briefly about exactly how we now have such a broad conception of state activity and responsibility. The word "state" was first used in its contemporary sense to convey a delicate balance between might, power, and authority in sixteenth-century Italy: "Might in order to be able to be able to defend itself from outside dangers and to impose upon its members, if necessary, conformity by force; power, insofar as that force is exercised in the name of and in accordance with certain rules; authority, inasmuch as that power should be considered legitimate and entail an obligation on those who are called to obey its commands."[1]

Throughout the intellectual history of the state as an idea, two concepts of power have coexisted: power as a zero-sum game that entails the imposition of one actor's will upon another (commonly associated with Max Weber[2]) and power that arises when a group comes together and cooperates in attaining a collective goal (this concept has evolved from Hobbes's view of the state as an independent, omnipotent, indeed God-like entity empowered by a "social contract" from the people[3]).

In violent times, the central problem for the state was consolidating force. The birth of modern political theory in the sixteenth and seventeenth centuries, the time of Machiavelli and Hobbes, coincided with an era of pervasive violence in Europe that accompanied the birth of the absolutist state. Machiavelli, arguably the first modern political thinker, separated the practical and self-interested political goals of a "prince" from the church's moral commands. He was writing at a time when the rich principalities of Italy were falling to France, Spain, and the Holy Roman Empire, whose armies sacked Rome in 1527. Hobbes, surrounded by the upheaval of the English Civil War, had good reason to imagine the state as a Leviathan, a political entity that stood above the law and could keep the peace, albeit with the contractual consent of the governed. In 1918, during the Bavarian revolution, Max Weber articulated his celebrated definition of the state as a human community that "successfully claims a monopoly of the legitimate use of force within a given territory." He noted that "today, the relation between the state and violence is an especially intimate one." In those very violent times, it is not surprising that the idea of the state was conceived of in relation to the use of force.

Although Weber's remark is often cited in the literature on political thought, the state's violent role does not, in fact, represent the full expanse of Weber's thinking. A closer reading of his work reveals that the emphasis on the use of force is on its *legitimate* use. Weber anchors legitimacy in traditional authority, charisma, or legality "by virtue of the belief in the validity of legal statute" and "functional competence based on rationally created rules." He also articulates a clear functional view of the state, describing its "basic functions" as the legislature, the police, the judiciary, and the various branches of civil and military administration.[4] Weber's words reflect three centuries of thinking about the issue: the state was independent and the sole form of constitutional power in Europe. Initial conceptions of the state were thus relatively circumscribed: the state was the mechanism through which to consolidate, organize, administer, and maintain the use of violence.

Writing in 1848, British thinker John Stuart Mill offered a more flexible view of state functionality.[5] Mill differentiated between the necessary and optional functions of government—"those that are exercised habitually and without objection by all governments"—and those "which have been considered questionable as to whether governments should exercise them or not." Mill also asked: "Is there not the earth itself, its forests and waters, and all other natural riches above and below the surface? These are the inheritance of the human race, and there must be regulations for the common enjoyment of it. No function of government is less optional than the regulation of these things or more completely involved in the idea of civilized society." He added that society must consider the following: "First, the means adopted by governments to raise the revenue which is the condition of their existence. Secondly, the nature of the laws which they prescribe on the two great subjects of Property and Contracts. Thirdly, the excellences or defects of the system of means by which they enforce generally the execution of their laws, namely, their judicature and police."[6]

Mill argued that expediency alone determines which functions the state should perform. In the 1930s American philosopher John Dewey identified the public as the mechanism for determining government functions. The crisis that Dewey faced was reorganizing collective power to solve one of the market's greatest failures: the Great Depression. He argued that there had to be common agreement on precisely what the government's functions are and how the government should perform them; furthermore, he contended, such a consensus could come only through public debate. According to Dewey, the very definition of "the public" resulted from an open discussion of the means and ends of government. The state was not about a small group of leaders dictating to a passive citizenry what had to be done. On the contrary, the state receives its mandate—its very legitimacy—through its accountability to the people, the constant and rightful monitors of the state. Legitimacy, however, is not static, based on voting leaders into office. Rather, it is an ongoing process of public discussion and the formulation of alternative policies and actions. This is a dynamic, self-reinforcing relationship: without vesting authority in the state, collective power cannot be mobilized, and without elections that determine the rulers and their policies, there can be no new alternatives. Therefore, Dewey argued, the state's functions can never be frozen but must be dynamic enough to change with the times.

A more recent illustration of the kind of state dynamism Dewey had in mind is Britain in the last fifty years, where the dominant social welfare model of the state was first changed by Thatcher and then reconfigured by Tony Blair's Labor Party. It is a fascinating exercise to think back even further to the budget speeches of British chancellors of the exchequer, or finance ministers, over the past two hundred years. In doing so, we can identify how the nature and scope of state functionality have changed and the way in which the rights and obligations of citizenship have become progressively entrenched within British society. For example, during the presentation of his budget in April 1853, William Gladstone argued that the key areas of expenditure for the state, which he estimated at approximately £52 million, were payment of the army, payment of the navy, and payment of public debt. Like Disraeli, whom he had succeeded to the post, he considered public taxation to be a temporary expedience to finance occasional war rather than a vehicle for the state's assumption of an increasing series of functions.[7] In the 1853 budget Gladstone did not justify taxation by suggesting that the function of government is to provide an extensive range of services but instead argued that the burden of foreign war is better covered by levying an income tax than by incurring further debt under unfavorable terms. He advocated a steady decline in the rate of income tax and its cessation in 1860 but wanted this tax to be held in reserve in case the country should need to depend upon it in the future as it had in the past. His attitude, therefore, was not that taxation should be used for redistributive purposes or for investments in infrastructure and public services; taxes, for the most part, remained indirect.[8] Income tax became institutionalized in the United Kingdom only after the 1841 election, when Sir Robert Peel reinstated it in the 1842 budget in response to the growing deficit and dwindling funds. An income tax was then imposed for three years, with the possibility of a two-year extension, but a railway funding crisis and increasing national expenditure ensured that it has been maintained ever since.[9]

Gordon Brown's 1998 budget speech indicates how radically the role of the state can change. Taxation has expanded in order to support a wide array of functions that are now accepted as the state's responsibility. Instead of seeing taxation as a burden upon the population that can be justified only by its power to finance civil government, foreign war, and onerous debts, Brown views public spending as crucial to meeting the British population's demands at the end of the twentieth century. He argues that the state must "encourage enterprise; reward work; support families; advance the ambitions not just of the few but of the many."

Clearly the role of the state had expanded exponentially by this time and become responsible for numerous functions from the population's economic well-being to social welfare to the provision of individual opportunity. Brown's way of talking about the budget is entirely different from Gladstone's. He refers to "ambition" and "opportunity" rather than "ordinance" and "shipping," concepts which would have been simply unfathomable in Gladstone's time. Brown acknowledges that the state's role in setting the parameters for economic activity has not always been positive: "The great economic strengths of our country have been undermined by deep-seated structural weaknesses—instability, under-investment and unemployment. So behind the detailed measures of this budget is the conviction that we must break for good from the conflicts and dogmas that have held us back and have for too long failed our country."[10] But there is no question (as there may have been a century earlier) that the state must play an expansive role in regulating the economy and providing citizenship rights. Moreover, by 1998 there was absolutely no argument over the direct or indirect nature of taxation as Gladstone recounted in 1853—the relationship between the population and taxation was very much a direct one in the form of personal and corporate taxes.[11]

If we fast-forward to Gordon Brown's 2007 budget speech, we can identify even further the expansive role of the state in British life. Brown explained that "in 1997 capital investment in schools, hospitals, security and defense and infrastructure, stood at just £18 billion. I can announce that investment will rise from £43 billion this year to £48 billion next year and then in successive years to 52, 55, 57, and then 60 billions, more than three times what it was in 1997 as we invest in our future."[12] He outlined investments in education and skills (in part to boost global competitiveness), reform of the National Health Service and the welfare system, maintenance of economic stability by controlling inflation, taxation reform to promote international competitiveness, and promotion of full employment. Social justice was a key element of the 2007 budget, which encouraged single parents to go back to work, supported those who had lost their pensions when their companies became insolvent, helped first-time home buyers, and supported families and children—particularly the poorest and most vulnerable. While his budget aimed to promote growth by fostering a business-friendly environment, it also reflected a desire to balance this priority against an agenda of fairness and opportunity for citizens.

The chancellor went on to describe four instruments of change—better use of assets; reduction of administrative costs; efficiency savings; and decreased debt and unemployment—thereby truly indicating a new positioning of the state vis-à-vis the economy in the United Kingdom. Brown understands the role of the state in the twenty-first century in the context of globalization. His primary aim is for Britain to lead global economic competition "and particularly to secure our place in the high value-added, investment-driven growth sectors of the future from modern manufacturing and the creative industries to business and financial services and the city—Britain must champion open markets, flexibility, and free trade—an open and inclusive globalization, not protectionism." Brown's view is that investment in "the great new drivers of growth, innovation, and education will need to rise towards 10 per cent of national income." Competition in the global marketplace requires taxation to enable investment in a range of public services.[13]

Brown also referred to the state in relation to a range of global challenges that simply did not factor into thinking on state functionality in Gladstone's day. Efforts to tackle adverse climate changes are situated squarely within the state's responsibilities. Additionally, the threat of terrorism, coupled with the technologies and networks made possible by globalization, demand expenditure on security and intelligence services so that the state can maintain its control over the means of violence and reaffirm its legitimacy. Given the expanded role of the British state and the standards to which it is held accountable, the total expenditure in 2007 was a massive £552 billion. Even accounting for inflation, proportionally this dwarfs the £52 million in expenditures described by Gladstone in 1853.

Dewey was correct: the functions of the state evolve over time in response to the public consensus on the scale and parameters of the state's activities. While Dewey's ideas are important to bear in mind, examination of state practice is clearly richer than analysis of state theory. And state practice is best revealed through a dissection of public finances since these indicate most clearly the state's rights and obligations to its citizens, as well as those of the citizens to the state. We chose here to examine the evolution of the British budget, but the same exercise could be carried out for any number of Western countries—from Scandinavia to the United States—and in each case it would show an expansion in citizenship rights and the obligations of the state. Indeed, as Franklin D. Roosevelt made clear in his "four freedoms" speech of 1941:

> The basic things expected by our people of their political and economic systems are simple. They are: equality of opportunity for youth and for others. Jobs for those who can work. Security for those who need it. The ending of special privilege for the few. The preservation of civil liberties for all. The enjoyment of the fruits of scientific progress in a wider and constantly rising standard of living. These are the simple, the basic things that must never be lost sight of in the turmoil and unbelievable complexity of our modern world. The inner and abiding straight of our economic and political systems is dependent upon the degree to which they fulfill these expectations.[14]

The public cannot be mobilized in the way that Dewey envisaged unless it has a clear moral purpose. Historically, morality has been expressed through an agreement about either a common goal or a binding legal contract. The first great political thinkers of the Western tradition, Plato and his student Aristotle, argued that the Greek "polis," or city-state, was a moral entity created around a shared purpose; the Romans institutionalized the state as a universal contract, thus giving birth to the notion of public law.[15] The nation-state was an attempt to combine the two—common purpose and public law. According to one dominant interpretation, the modern state—at least prior to the rise of the totalitarian phenomenon—was inherently about emancipation. The rise of the absolutist state had as its counterpoint the rights of individuals. Today's consensus on an effective state as a necessary precondition for the eradication of poverty echoes this origin.

Rather than cohering around the idea of the use of force, the state today coalesces around the rule of law. The common thread running through the history of political thought is that a distinctive form of collective power resides in the rules. Rules are resources that can be used to generate collective power; without active citizens, however, who reflect on and consent to these rules, there can be no legitimacy. The people judge the state's effectiveness not in the abstract but on the basis of how well it performs its legal functions, however broad or narrow their scope may be. The governed and the government are bound together by a common view of public value and interest, embodied in a compact—whether explicit or implicit—of rights and obligations. Both the challenge and the opportunity today are to see the foundation of the state not as situated in violence but as in agreement on a set of rules that allow for an orderly process of change that makes violence unnecessary. We can refer once again to Franklin D. Roosevelt, who guided the United States through the Great Depression, a period in U.S. history that could quite easily have resulted in violent, not orderly, change: "Since the beginning of our American history we have been engaged in change, in a perpetual, peaceful revolution, a revolution which goes on steadily, quietly, adjusting itself to changing conditions without the concentration camp or the quicklime in the ditch."[16]

Therefore, the role of the state is multifunctional and dynamic rather than singular and static. This may seem obvious to us now, but that is precisely because the network of rights and obligations that binds us, as citizens, to our government is defined by the rule of law and has become entrenched in modern Western societies. This has not always been the case but instead, as we have seen, is the result of a gradual process of evolution. In an era in which citizenship rights around the world have been consolidated and globalization has fundamentally altered our relationship to the marketplace, many states have adapted, thereby bringing the balance among state, market, and civil society into a new equilibrium. Citizens have deep expectations of fair play and now daily judge their governments through a proliferation of polls, indices, and business surveys that examine its Moody's credit ratings, political approval ratings, the livability of cities, and the extent of transparency, red tape, and the government's proclivity for peacefulness.

In developing countries, the state has often failed to acquire the flexible architectures needed to enter into a dynamic and collaborative partnership with the citizenry and the market. Instead, many suffer from rules that do not prescribe orderly processes for change; as a result, violence becomes the means through which that change occurs. The state then erodes from within and ultimately provides very few functions for its citizens. Hence we propose state-building strategies that support an inclusive political, social, and economic order embodied in the rule of law in these countries. These strategies cannot come about, of course, without a very clear delineation of state functions. We have examined the expansion of the state in the United Kingdom and the United States, but what precisely are the functions that a modern state should perform in an optimal scenario?

Only when we can reach agreement on this can we move toward developing a strategy to build those functions. Concord on the key functions that a state should aim to perform would both create a mechanism for measuring the sovereignty gap in a tractable fashion and allow us to generate strategies that would work back from the desired outcome to the specific situation in a given context.

SEVEN

The Framework

The Ten Functions of the State

TODAY STATES MUST fulfill their citizens' aspirations for inclusion and development and also carry out a constellation of interrelated functions. Given the historical and geographical variability of state functions, it might seem bold to declare that there are ten of them (why not nine or eleven?). Nevertheless, based on our reading of history, our engagement with international development, and our firsthand experience with the challenge of state building in one of its most difficult contexts, we have concluded that states in the world today should perform ten key functions.

Our overriding objective is not a platonic search for the essence of the state but a quest for realistic mechanisms for the realization of collective ideals. For while there can be legitimate debate as to the characterization of these functions, we maintain that consensus on a specific set of functions provides the vital ingredient for international agreement on the best way to design creative responses to the challenge of state building, in partnership with national and local players. State functions change over time, and the range of those considered necessary at a particular point is subject to the consensus at a specific moment. Our proposed list is designed to generate the kind of discussion that will build such a consensus. Therefore, these suggestions are not written in stone, but we hope they will provide a basis for a common understanding of state functionality, one that also allows for improvisation.

RULE OF LAW

Perhaps the most crucial function performed by the state is law making (i.e., establishing the rules by which society operates). Laws define both the powers and the limits of the state and the people within that state. In any particular territory, one can judge the degree of the rule of law by the extent to which the state is constituted by formal rules to which people actually adhere.

The rule of law is a "glue" that binds all aspects of the state, the economy, and society. Each of the state's functions is defined by a specific set of rules that creates the governance arrangements—decision rights, processes, accountabilities, freedoms, and duties—for that function. Rules provide both resources that enable innovation to occur and constraints that limit behavior. In some societies, the state has the right to take away life and property if doing so is determined to be in the public interest. As a result of the rule of law, citizens understand a distinct set of rights and duties that guides their behavior toward other citizens, as well as toward the larger community of citizens represented by the state.

The complexity of tasks a state must perform requires internal mechanisms to monitor each branch of the government. It also necessitates systematic checks and balances between the executive branch, the legislature, and the judiciary, which encourage—and sustain—trust in the system of governance. The resulting discovery of potential and actual abuses allows reform to take place in an organized way within the existing rules of the game rather than prompting calls for the wholesale rewriting of those rules.

All societies have tensions; the key is whether these disputes are resolved through the process of law or are dealt with outside it. Finding existing rules exclusionary, both Mahatma Gandhi and Martin Luther King Jr. led calls for fundamental change in those rules through civil disobedience, which took place within the framework of the rule of law. An entire social movement arose in the United States when Rosa Parks refused to adhere to an unjust law. Revolutionary movements, by contrast, call for the overthrow of an entire order. But these movements, as the Russian and Cuban examples show, often fail to constitute systems based on the rule of law. When policy change occurs within accepted rules, stakeholders find it easier to realize their agendas through the formal system and are thus less likely to subvert or overthrow the government. Although the policies of a particular government may favor one coalition of stakeholders over others at any particular moment in time, the fundamentals of a democratic polity and market economy remain unquestioned. These permit the state to perform its functions in the public interest over the long term. The challenge for a legal system is to provide certainty through an orderly and binding interpretation of existing laws, while at the same time providing flexibility through mechanisms for peaceful change and adaptation of rules to new circumstances. The process for promulgating and changing rules is critical in its own right. A high degree of openness and flexibility in this process is essential to maintenance of the rule of law and lasting rule changes.

Citizens provide the ultimate source of legitimacy for a social order. Laws are promulgated by the government through a hierarchical process, but it is the citizens' adherence to those laws that changes legal prescription into legal practice. History is replete with examples of laws and court decisions that exist only on paper—from bans of music file sharing online to animal poaching laws. Informal systems arise precisely when a segment of the population does not consider the formal rules acceptable. In the case of property, the Peruvian economist Hernando de Soto has demonstrated that the problem of urban slums did not originate with migrants to the cities but with the nature of the laws that required these migrants to wait years before obtaining land or building permits through the formal system.[1]

Considered in isolation, each law may seem to specify clearly rights and obligations. The test of coherence, however, is at the systems level—namely, how laws relate to one another as a body of rules and the extent to which alignment of the system is achieved. When new laws are promulgated, they must clearly state which laws are repealed, where contradictions exist, which laws have precedence, and how conflicts can be resolved. In many countries where technical assistance imports off-the-shelf laws from all parts of the world, the legal system can very quickly become a quagmire of contradictory rules and processes.

When rule of law takes hold, it creates a reinforcing loop of stability, predictability, trust, and empowerment. First, rule of law stabilizes government and holds it accountable. Second, it sets a predictable environment in which other players can make plans over the long term. Third, it creates confidence in the public, which trusts that, when change is necessary, it will take place within a framework of continuity. Finally, it empowers those in civil society and the economy to take initiatives, form associations, create companies, and work within the confines of the state more broadly. It changes the nature of politics from a divisive to a collective endeavor; people can disagree, but their disagreements are resolved through a peaceful process.

Singapore has consistently ranked in the top cluster of Transparency International's Corruption Perceptions Index (CPI). As we saw in chapter 2, Singapore of the 1950s was afflicted by corruption and extremely poor governance; the story of that nation's transformation "from third world to first," as the political patriarch of Singapore, Lee Kuan Yew, aptly called it, is about using the formulation of rules as a source of good governance to create both wealth and social benefits.[2] The result has been that citizens of Singapore identify with their legal system, which has transformed a small island without any natural resources into a global economic powerhouse.

In contrast, distrust in the enforcement of formal rules increasingly leads to a universe of parallel rules that constitute the actual norms of society. Criminalization of the economy, informal judicial processes for property and other disputes, patron-client relationships as vehicles of entry to government service, and illegal natural resource concessions and licenses for imports or exports are all symptomatic of this dynamic. Tax avoidance becomes the norm, public land and property are expropriated by officials, the state becomes predatory, rulers perceive themselves to be above the law, and violence becomes the key mechanism for change. The poor lose hope and trust in the system, and their time horizons become very short as they focus on survival. Talent is diverted from the acquisition of skills and capabilities that would normally be the source of collective prosperity.

When political leaders claim and cede power through orderly processes, seeking mandates from citizens at regular intervals, they build trust in the legitimacy of the state's power. But throughout history, succession to high office has been a source of conflict. In the United States, George Washington's wise decision to refuse the offer of the presidency for life after two terms set this bar high. He was followed by a series of equally eminent statesmen, well educated in the history of violent succession from ancient times, who all ensured that power was handed peacefully to their successors. By the time Franklin Delano Roosevelt led the United States through the Depression and World War II and was rewarded with an unprecedented third term at the ballot box, Congress turned the nation's discomfort with government by one person into a constitutional amendment that limited the presidency to two consecutive terms. This law has helped to guarantee the legitimacy of the U.S. political system. The circulation of the political elite strengthens loyalty to the system rather than to one person. The right to vote for their leaders puts citizens in a position to transform their personal judgments into collective decisions on the direction of the country, which also allows them to identify with the political system and hold it accountable. The toll taken by dictatorial regimes, where the dominant occupation of officials is to perpetuate their own positions of power, has been a significant factor in the decline of promising countries—the Democratic Republic of the Congo under Mobutu; Indonesia under Suharto; the Philippines under Marcos; Zimbabwe under Mugabe; and Yugoslavia under Tito. The recent trend of heads of state agreeing to transfer power according to the rules first in Latin America and now Africa is encouraging.

Globalization of the economy requires a process of co-production of rules involving the state, firms, and citizens to produce rules that are compatible across boundaries. When the life chances of individuals depend on their place within global corporate chains, the practices of these corporations, ranging from wages to environmental issues, become global, not national, concerns. As we argued in chapter 1, global flows require rules that different stakeholders can agree on, understand, and adhere to. Any violation of such rules can result in huge costs for the credibility of partnerships. Countries and companies that do not invest in understanding the rules that make global flows possible pay an enormous price—even to the point of exclusion from the global circuits of prosperity.

A MONOPOLY ON THE LEGITIMATE MEANS OF VIOLENCE

As mentioned in the previous chapter, Max Weber singled out a monopoly on the legitimate means of violence as the very definition of the state. Control over the use of violence brings three distinctive processes together. The first is the establishment of a monopoly over the means of destruction and the use of force. The second is the establishment of the legitimacy needed to subordinate violence to decision making. The third is the use of force, according to certain rules, against those citizens of the state who challenge its legitimacy.

The absolutist state in Europe provided the historical background for Weber's definition. Aiming to destroy feudalism, the state monopolized violence by creating standing armies that took orders from their rulers. The major innovation in this regard was Napoleon's creation of a merit-based, conscripted citizens' army where the citizenry, rather than mercenaries or the aristocratic classes, provided the manpower for a nation-state's battles. The military gained legal status, and the use of force became defined by rules and regulations. Once the state exercised the legitimate use of force, violence became unacceptable as a means through which to challenge policies. Dissidents who resorted to hostilities placed themselves outside the pale of legitimacy—thereby permitting rulers to use force against them.

Consolidation of the rule of law as the vehicle for solving disputes impartially and predictably and for expanding citizenship rights means that the need to resort to force domestically has decreased substantially. Societies that have created large middle classes seem to have reached a consensus that use of the army against citizens is unacceptable. Instead, the definition of security in these societies has been broadened to encompass both human security and social security. There policing has become the face of order. A striking example of the routinization of authority and the state's impartiality is the unarmed police force in England. English bobbies embody moral power precisely because they are unarmed. Even after the London bombings of July 2005, no shift in the social consensus occurred on the use of arms by the police. Costa Rica has gone even further and resisted the pressure to create an army. Like Switzerland, this Central American country derives its national security from the very absence of a defense force. The strict adherence of the Indian army to its constitutional role is another remarkable example of the subordination of power to law. Senior officers of the Indian military abide by their limited terms of office, particularly that of the chief of staff, and no former Indian general has ever sought elected political office.

A related trend is the development of security institutions into managerial systems. New York City is perhaps the archetypal example of this shift. Infested with crime and violence until the early 1990s and even on the verge of bankruptcy in the mid-1970s, the city rallied remarkably. At the core of the recapture of its security was a zero-tolerance regime, a strategy of cleaning up the city and making improvements block by block, and a management system that changed measures of police accountability to preemption and prevention rather than response. Once the value of this system was demonstrated in New York City, it was widely copied in other parts of the United States.

A monopoly on the use of force has several important effects for a state. First, it allows freedom of movement for ordinary citizens in general and the merchant community in particular. Before the establishment of the absolutist state, movement always carried a cost, as various power holders around the country routinely demanded payment for protection, whether on roads, rivers, or the sea. The cost of such protection fell to the state, thereby establishing public safety and the role of the night watchman as one of the enduring state functions. This centralization of power also made property secure and ensured that transactions became governed by rules rather than by arms. Feudal lords maintained power by keeping retainers to pillage for goods, which were then used to maintain these self-same retainers. Absolutist states put an end to this practice by establishing the military as a specialized hierarchical organization that requires a standardized system of taxation and expenditure.

Over the last three decades the negative consequences that arise from the loss of this monopoly over legitimate force have also become clear in many parts of the world. Organizations ranging from militias to mercenaries and mafias have emerged to challenge the state, aided by the global trade in small arms. Some companies have even acquired their own forces to ensure their control over mines and other extractive industries. In other cases, the military has emerged as a center of unaccountable power, subverting the rules of the game and preventing the formation of civil and political movements. The high cost of protection has reemerged as a significant factor in economic activity by imposing severe constraints on freedom of movement for people and goods. When the state fails to establish its monopoly over the means of force, parallel organizations have also stepped in to collect the revenue legally due to the state.

Extreme centralization of power—as exemplified by Stalinist Russia and Hitler's Germany—and attempts in recent years at restoring central authority in Rwanda, Cambodia, the Balkans, and Taliban Afghanistan—have frequently led to periods of equally extreme violence against the people. Genocide, ethnocide, ethnic cleansing, and the subjugation of groups considered undesirable (e.g., gypsies, the Chinese in Indonesia) are all too common in recent history. Xenophobia has been harnessed to justify hatred and to dehumanize entire categories of the population. Where the military has not been subordinated to the rule of law, the result has been the militarization of political, economic, and social life. Latin and Central American armies have also dominated many aspects of the economy through specially created military corporations that often control public land.

The historical experience of totalitarian and authoritarian regimes makes it clear that checks and balances on the use of force are critical to guarantee essential freedoms and the rule of law for the citizenry.

The market and civil society both play a critical function in the exercise of such checks and balances. In some countries in which the military dominates the polity, military expenditure actually surpasses social spending.

It is not only the illegitimate use of force that presents a danger but also the size and sophistication of the world's most powerful military machines. During the Cold War, technology and science became inherent components of military strategy and doctrine in both the United States and the USSR, thereby leading to the emergence of the military-industrial complex, which in certain key areas operated without effective public oversight. Today global military funding dwarfs any other category of state expenditure: In 2006 governments spent $1.16 trillion. United States defense expenditure accounts for 46 percent of these costs ($528.7 billion). The NATO expenditure on personnel and equipment alone—combining eighteen countries' contributions—was $300 billion in 2006.[3] By doctrine and training, the U.S. army and European forces were designed to fight industrial wars. Today's insecurity emanates from networks of people rather than from organized, hierarchical states and their armies. It remains to be seen whether these conventional forces will have the flexibility to win these wars and how well they can adapt to the new security context.

ADMINISTRATIVE CONTROL

Administrative control should be managed by government professionals who are accountable to the citizenry and recruited through an open process. They achieve control by organizing a state's territory, functionally and spatially, via a unified body of rules and practices. Several processes are central to this dimension of sovereignty. First, a hierarchy of divisions marks the state's territory into administrative units. Each of these divisions performs specialized functions, has continuity over time, and is overseen at a higher level. The range of functions performed by each level changes over time as the state assumes new roles and sheds old ones.

The bureaucracy initially drew its inspiration as a hierarchical and specialized organization from the model of the standing army. The original impetus for the bureaucracy was control, and the system focused narrowly on the job to be done rather than delivering value to the public. The administration was established through a professional staff that specialized in the various functional areas. States vary as to how they manage the rules and processes for recruitment, including the degree of centralization, but among developed countries, a common denominator is transparent, meritocratic recruitment processes. Rules often specify how professional staff should be protected from undue influence and divide the bureaucracy into various working areas, ranging from the foreign office to tax collection. Each of these domains has different regulations and processes, as well as a distinctive culture. In the late nineteenth and early twentieth centuries the state in many parts of the world assumed direct responsibility for delivering an expanding range of functions, which required increasing specialization on the part of its bureaucrats, while state budgets rose exponentially to pay for these services.

Individual states differ significantly in their administrative practices. What is common within successful systems, however, is the uniformity of a particular set of rules within an individual state—and tight adherence to them over time. Frontiers and border points are strong testing grounds of this uniformity across a state's territory. The greater the degree to which a frontier location conforms more broadly to a country's administrative practices, the higher the nation's degree of uniformity. Before the revolution, France was a divided country, which made internal commerce very difficult; travelers had to pay tolls merely to move between different parts of the country. The revolution, however, created a uniformity of rules and practices as systems were integrated across the territory. Before the railway arrived, England had multiple time zones; it was the new train schedules that ensured that time would be standardized. Equally, the Rio Grande is a small river that divides Mexico and the United States into very different sets of rules. In their book, *The Hidden Frontier*, Eric Wolf and John Cole document the manner in which two neighboring mountain villages only one mile apart operate according to completely different rhythms of life because one falls within Austria's borders, the other within Italy's.[4]

In developed countries, this standardization of practice has led to predictability, which generates trust in the impartial administration of the rules. Change takes place through routine, continuity, and well-known practices. This uniformity of rules and regulations throughout a country is vital to the formation of a distinctive identity for its citizens. Meanwhile, the emergence of honest, effective, impartial bureaucracies has helped to establish an environment for growth. In some countries, the bureaucracy has become quite adept at assuming new tasks and generating the specialized knowledge and routines necessary for performing them.

Overall, citizens can judge the effectiveness of administration by the extent to which it creates public value. An important attribute of an administration is the degree of its accountability to the people and more specifically to their elected representatives. Over the last century, the bureaucracy has clearly emerged as a technical sphere of governance. A standard set of auditing, accounting, and procurement procedures that allow for internal and external oversight routinizes accountability. As states increasingly subcontract with private firms to provide services, procurement and contract management have taken center stage, and a movement toward transparency in this process is under way in many countries.

The effects of a dysfunctional administration have also become clear. Unpredictable rules—often either idiosyncratically interpreted or corruptly applied—can generate a climate of distrust and contribute to a crisis in state legitimacy. Pervasive corruption not only undermines confidence but also deters investment. Government failure to establish uniform and trusted practices across state territory allows large swathes of the country to fall into the hands of local militias and warlords or global commercial interests that function with impunity. The politics of identity is affected by the degree to which administrative practices are seen as fair or unfair. Lack of inclusion because of unjust administrative practices—evident in Guatemala, Mexico, the Philippines, southern Sudan, and the Terai region in Nepal—can become grounds for violent attacks on the system. Finally, failure to adopt modern governance technologies and accountability practices creates a corresponding failure to adapt to the globalized economy and therefore become a beneficiary of expanding opportunities. Today, the bulk of direct foreign investment goes to only ten countries in the developing world—those that the market believes can provide a predictable and well-managed environment, leaving the bulk of other countries outside the flows of the system.

Corrupt practices such as the sale of offices, patronage, and tax farming were severe problems in England throughout the nineteenth century. A fundamental shift toward the meritocratic recruitment of bureaucrats, however, had the effect of endowing the highest echelons of the bureaucracy with moral prestige. In the Prussian bureaucracy and the colonial Indian civil service, reforms in the last quarter of the nineteenth century and the first half of the twentieth helped to reduce corruption and establish accountabilities—with the press playing a major role in upholding this accountability. Whereas early bureaucracies focused first on control and then on efficiency in the delivery of services, now the administrative challenge in many countries is coordination across boundaries. The objective of a discernable new trend in administrative practices is to synergize and coordinate different administrative units, civil society, and the private sector. The new issues facing us today, such as population ageing, global warming, and health pandemics, do not fit neatly into functional areas. Accordingly, they require us to think and act outside old boundaries and across geographic lines and organizational boxes.

A number of administrative breakthroughs occurred during the last half-century that have dramatically improved the quality of life and enhanced governmental accountability in developed countries. In Japan, for example, prefectures and municipalities have acquired significant autonomy in administration, budgetary matters, and local legislation. Local governments there have assumed responsibility for social insurance and health care, and they work in tandem with the central government to provide Japan's welfare state.[5] Collaborative governance requires very different skills from previous types of administration, and a fundamental shift by the bureaucracy from managing microrules to directing complex networks of knowledge, people, and resources. In turn, accountabilities must be configured differently—overseeing networks is quite unlike administering rules.

The revolution in information technology and the centrality of human capital have far-reaching implications for organizing administration in terms of efficiency, transparency, and accountability. The flow of information among complex hierarchies has always posed a particular problem for administrative control. Gathering and assessing information on millions of daily transactions using a manual system is expensive, and the very nature of hierarchy constrains upward and downward flows of knowledge, as each level guards information in order to exercise power or influence. E-governance has deeply democratic implications: suddenly information becomes a domain through which we can engender equality; no longer can the bureaucracies of hierarchical organizations refuse to divulge information. The Indian states of Karnataka and Andhra Pradesh illustrate the potential of e-governance: individual citizens are able to follow their legal cases through the administrative or judicial process online, thereby undermining the bureaucracy's tendency to withhold information. More recently, the government of Karnataka has moved e-governance to education, property records, tax returns, vehicle registration, and policing. It is now possible for concerned citizens to monitor government action through collaborative auditing.

The new potential for direct citizen interaction means that old assumptions about administrative division—both into levels and functions—can be revisited. Representation of each ministry at central, regional, provincial, and district levels is not necessarily required now that information can travel to and from citizens directly. Many countries are now redesigning their representational architecture. In Finland it will soon be unnecessary to file paper income tax returns. Pensioners who do not have new investments are exempt from taxation paperwork. Both state and private pensions are recorded in a database, as are home and automobile ownership and other assets. Employers in Finland digitally transmit the personal ID codes of all of their workers to the internal revenue service and attach the details of their salary information. Databases show demographic details, pension income, student grants, payouts from insurance companies, and assets. Computers then calculate the appropriate taxes based on this information, and a large proportion of the workforce then receives an annual tax proposal that outlines the total tax owed.[6]

The community is reemerging as a significant focus for prioritization and the source of initiative and decision making. Just as consumers have become "prosumers" in the digital age, instead of passive recipients of state redistribution schemes, citizens can become active collaborators in the production of public value. In our new era of "convergence culture," the legacy of the tightly hierarchical model of governance is no longer binding. A model of citizen-centered governance, in which public servants are truly held accountable for the well-being of citizens and communities, is now feasible. It may be a cliché, but it is important to remember that the future is not just the continuation of the past. Within our globalizing world, change is neither episodic nor cyclical but continuous, pervasive, and fast paced. Leadership and management in such a context are going to require balancing the needs of the present and the future. The capability to discern and respond to emerging patterns will mark the difference between either continuous prosperity or sustained failure.

SOUND MANAGEMENT OF PUBLIC FINANCES

Sound management of public finances is the vehicle through which states can realize public goals. Efficient collection and allocation of resources among contending priorities turn ideas and aspirations into concrete outcomes. The record of state activities lies most clearly in its budget, which is both the medium and the message. The budget brings the rights and duties of citizenship into balance. Each entitlement must have a line of expenditure, and each expenditure must be matched by a source of revenue. Thus, the discipline of preparation, implementation, and alteration of budgets allows the translation of public goals into measurable programs and projects. Public expenditure takes place through rules for the procurement of goods and services, accounting, and auditing. Adherence to these rules is a critical indicator of the state's effectiveness and accountability.

The scale of both revenue and expenditure in OECD countries reveals a sea change in societal consensus on the state's role and functions. The willingness of citizens and corporations to assume the obligation of paying taxes is an especially impressive outcome given that, for a majority of global history, tax paying was not an obligation for most citizens.

In 2005 Sweden collected 50.6 percent of its GDP in taxes. The EU average was 40.5 percent, while the U.S. proportion collected was 25.6 percent ($2.4 trillion in 2006).[7] Income tax collected from individuals in the United States alone has increased from $45.6 billion in 1962 to $1 trillion in 2006. This increase in revenue underpins a concomitant rise in expenditures, with the state emerging as the primary employer. For example, as a proportion of total employment, public sector employment in the United Kingdom was 20.4 percent in June 2005.

In many countries, the expenditure aspects of public finance have now evolved into a highly specialized arena in which each subfunction—budgeting, treasury, accounting, procurement, and auditing—has become specialized in its own right. Given the complexity and scale of public expenditure, the key lies in the coherence of the checks and balances to constitute what we call a "national accountability system." That system sets out the specialized subfunctions and processes that must be performed to ensure accountability and transparency. Our analysis shows three phases in such systems: first, control, in which the goal is a minimum degree of accountability and fewer major leakages in the collection of funds; second, efficiency, whose main goal is an improvement in outcomes; and third—after internal trust in the civil service has been established—a relax on controls to allow far greater imagination in the use of public resources (i.e., a shift from process to results).

David Osborne and Ted Gaebler's *Reinventing Government* reports that 25–50 percent of federal employees are "useless personnel"; in the late 1980s the federal payroll, including benefits, totaled $600 billion per year, which implies that $150 billion to $300 billion of payroll funds were spent on the salaries of "useless personnel."[8] The term "public value" was invented by Harvard professor Mark Moore.[9] Since then, concern about realizing public value and attempts to limit the tax burden have spurred efforts to do more with less, ranging from Al Gore's Reinventing Government program to the activities of parliamentary oversight bodies around the world. Australia has a "Charter of Budget Honesty" that allows its treasury to estimate the cost of major parties' election commitments. The U.S. Government Accountability Office scrutinizes the government's use of public funds and evaluates government programs. In the United Kingdom, the House of Commons and the House of Lords select committees provide nonpartisan analysis of government policy and executive decisions. Indeed, the United Kingdom recently published an analytical framework for public service reform that focused on improving public value.[10] Private-sector organizations such as Accenture have even been exploring the way in which value is created in public-sector bodies.

Commitment to make every cent work for the public interest has been characteristic of those public servants who have transformed their countries. For example, during a visit to the World Bank meetings in 1968, Goh Keng Swee, Singapore's minister of finance and defense and the architect of its economic system, asked a staff member to give him a memorandum on the creation of a bird park when they returned to Singapore. When the staffer asked why not a zoo, the minister responded that "bird seed costs less than meat."[11]

One of the main characteristics of public finance as a specialized branch of administration is its temporal rhythm. The annual budget, which is the most distinctive symbol of this process, creates a routine by utilizing specific cycles—hourly, daily, weekly, or monthly. As taxpayers and recipients of public benefits, citizens follow these temporal routines on an ongoing basis. The regular rhythms of public finance have their origins in ensuring prompt and consistent payment to standing armies. Since ancient Roman times, the state's failure to pay armies regularly has often resulted in armed men turning into sources of disorder rather than guarantors of order. That danger alone made it necessary for states to collect revenue in a timely, systematized, and thus predictable fashion and to focus on those revenue sources that would be the most dependable.

The social conflicts of the nineteenth century, however, pitted labor against capital and threatened to disrupt emerging capitalist economies. Social policy, ranging from regulation of working hours to benefits for unemployed and vulnerable workers, emerged as a vehicle for social harmony. This eventually spawned doctrines of citizenship rights. When different categories of the population began to consider these rights as distinctive entitlements, there arose a concomitant obligation to pay for those rights. Both individuals and corporations assumed the duties of citizenship and therefore parted with significant portions of their earned income to underwrite their rights in the form of taxes.

The effects of sound public expenditure programs have led to the acceptance of the social, economic, and political order in the developed world. Despite periodic concerns about government waste (military procurement in the United States during the ongoing Iraq war is one pertinent example) or abuses of public power for personal gain, the degree of trust in public servants as guardians of the public purse has remained relatively high in the wealthy half of the world. Trust in government accountability has allowed the government to perform new functions and take exceptional measures that are considered necessary for the public interest. When Fernando Henrique Cardoso became finance minister of Brazil in 1993, for example, inflation—then at 2,500 percent—was his most serious challenge. High inflation produced a culture in which corruption went unnoticed or unpunished since the value of the currency was continually eroding. To combat this problem, Cardoso produced a new currency, the real, which the central bank attempted to maintain within a broad range of value against the dollar. To cut public spending, he and his advisors then managed to create political support for a special fund that took control of some $30 billion of earmarked government spending. Cardoso opted for a six-month period in which businesses would list the price of goods and services in both old and new currency in order to curb inflation, build a stable currency, and allow the government to address the structural issues behind inflation more comprehensively. In his memoir, Cardoso emphasizes the incompatibility between capitalism and corruption.[12] The real issue was therefore not only about combating the immediate problem of inflation but also about changing mindsets by demonstrating the government's ability to manage monetary policy and more fundamentally to establish and then enforce rules.

In Afghanistan after September 11, our relentless focus on managing public finances was the key to establishing order and gaining the trust of citizens and the international community. A reform program tackled treasury, budget, currency, and revenue in a carefully crafted sequence. It established systems that allowed for rule-directed disbursements, increased revenue collection, and a focus on the budget as the central instrument of policy. As a result, information could be collected on a weekly basis, and reports to the cabinet were disclosed to the press and shared with other stakeholders. As we explain in more detail later, the distribution of direct block grants to villages across the country allowed the communities themselves to budget, manage, and account for the money, thereby giving them firsthand experience in public finance and heightening their awareness of the challenges involved in effective public expenditure.

Failure to manage public finances in an effective and transparent manner undermines the state because it weakens bonds of citizenship and trust. This sets in motion a vicious circle as public assets are diverted to private ends and powerful interests refuse to pay taxes. Reliance on indirect taxes and widespread tax evasion and corruption thus increase. Royalties from extractive industries vanish into the personal accounts of rulers and public officials. Public debt and external aid underwrite the routine functions of the state and thereby signify an increased dependence on external actors. The net effect of all this is loss of trust in the state as an institution. As multiple revenue collection centers emerge, sovereignty is soon parceled out and fragmented. During the transitional government in Liberia, between 2003–2006, the accountability systems were in such disarray that both government and donors had to resort to weekly budgeting in order to maintain the most basic controls on costs. Travel budgets for ministries and senior officials constituted one of the country's greatest expenses. In Sudan, failure to agree on the identity of the military and civil service meant that, more than two years after the peace agreement, few civil servants were receiving regular pay despite the availability of $2 billion a year in oil rents. In Iraq, failure to put in place checks and balances on oil revenue collection has led to the loss of billions of dollars.[13]

The yearly budget cycle, derived from the period when government functions were limited to the maintenance of law and order, is increasingly becoming a constraint. In fulfilling the functions of government that require medium-to-long-term policy and planning horizons, some of the most imaginative governments around the world are, at the local and national levels, expanding their time horizons for planning and expanding budget periods as necessary. But a significant problem remains: the tension between the short-term electoral cycles and the medium-to-long-term planning periods that are now necessary for public stewardship.

INVESTMENTS IN HUMAN CAPITAL

Investment in human capital has been the key to the formation of a middle class in the developed world. It was the mechanism used to overcome the conflicts of the nineteenth century and provide a ground for stable democratic politics. As professions emerged, spurred on in part by the expansion of universities, they became critical to social mobility. Economic productivity and growth now depend on an educated and healthy population. As human capital becomes more critical to wealth creation than other forms of capital, public investment in universities also becomes more important.

Conflict and antagonism marked the relations between labor and capital during the nineteenth century; the phrase "satanic mill" aptly captures the human cost of the emerging industrial order. As opportunities for education widened, however, they changed the definition of social problems. Over the course of the nineteenth century, education in Europe underwent a revolutionary transformation as compulsory universal schooling by the state either replaced or incorporated the private and religious institutions that had previously fulfilled this function. In 1763 Prussia became the first region to enact legislation that enforced primary education. University attendance in Prussia expanded during the early 1800s and continued to rise—with some periods of stagnations—until the outbreak of the First World War, growing from roughly 13,000 students in 1860 to 63,000 by 1914.[14] Many scholars have argued that the British imperial decline, which began around 1870, stemmed at least in part from the failure to systematize university and vocational education in the same way as the Prussian Empire.

During the last few decades, the proportion of adults in higher education in the wealthy world has increased dramatically. University enrollment rates hovered at 2–3 percent for the first half of the twentieth century in the United Kingdom and the United States. In the United Kingdom today 50 percent of the citizens have some form of higher education, and in the United States there is now remarkable consensus on the centrality of educational opportunities as the vehicle of social mobility and affluence. By the middle of the twentieth century, labor was valued as the most important ingredient in the creation of wealth. Today, changes in information technology—and the general recognition of the importance of human capital—have brought about a radical reorganization of management forms in the private sector that tend to emphasize autonomy and creativity of human input rather than the rigid discipline of times past. Intellectual property has become the key driver of prosperity, and the value of human capital has risen commensurately in a world in which software designers are among the wealthiest individuals in the world.

The benefits of investing in human capital are virtually instantaneous. In the United States after World War II, the GI Bill of Rights disbursed university tuition fees and low-interest mortgages to veterans, thereby creating a new meritocracy and massive housing developments around the country. By the mid-1950s most American workers considered themselves middle class and had the house, well-paying job, and car to prove it. Within a decade, the "baby-boom" children of even the least educated World War II veterans were winning scholarships to the nation's elite universities, which soon launched them into the professional classes and the kind of wealth that their poor immigrant grandparents had never even dreamed of. One generous and far-sighted government program had seeded the longest wave of prosperity in history—and almost single-handedly legitimated capitalism in the United States. Spending on education today is unprecedented. From the 1929–1930 school year to the 1986–1987 school year, total real expenditures per pupil in U.S. public schools rose by 500 percent.[15] The United States now spends 2.6 percent of its GDP on education. Australia has recently spent as much as 6 percent of its GDP on education.[16] While spending in Europe is less significant as a share of GDP, it is still sizeable: It was estimated that in 2007 Britain would spend £60 billion on education.[17] Annual worldwide spending on education is assessed today at $1 trillion, with a "market" of some one billion students worldwide.[18]

Unsurprisingly, the definition of education has also changed since the industrial age, when the repetition of a function over a course of years and even decades was the norm for most employees. In the globalized economy of today—where the obsolescence of a particular body of knowledge within months or years is common—ways of learning and problem solving are emphasized over command of a specific body of knowledge. Education in the developed world is becoming a field for continuous learning and the lifelong updating of skills.

Investment in public health has been equally critical. Throughout history, medicine has been mainly curative. Preventative health emerged as a distinctive field only in the twentieth century. The research in public health that has spurred this advance has been significantly funded through the public coffers. For example, since the late 1990s, health care spending in the United States has outpaced growth in the GDP, inflation, and population. Total national spending on health care has risen to $1.67 trillion, or $5,670 per person.[19] This public spending has also been bolstered by private investments in public health. The University of North Carolina, for example, manages a public-private genome sciences initiative of more than $245 million.[20]

Because of these investments in human capital, networks of voluntary associations and organizations that hold both the state and the market accountable have emerged and become consolidated within developed societies. A large middle class of professionals has been pivotal in the growth of this intermediate space between the state and the market. In the process, these voluntary groups have been critical in articulating and peacefully resolving social issues through the political process.

The consequences of failing to invest in human capital are equally clear: an excessive degree of inequality, social immobility, and thus persistent poverty. Without access to health care and education, there can be no middle class. Growth becomes negative, stagnant, or slow and thus has no impact on development. Several of the poorest societies have had some of the highest rates of brain drain. Also, with the outbreak of the AIDS epidemic and failure to invest adequately in its mitigation, life expectancy in Africa has fallen to 1960s' levels and threatens to wipe out the gains of the last five decades.[21] Child mortality and childbirth death levels are still extremely high, populations continue to grow, and life expectancy in the poorest countries remains very low.

In Afghanistan in 2002, World Bank and UN officials insisted that the government should not invest in higher education and moreover should invest very little in secondary and vocational education despite the fact that Afghanistan had seen its professional class decimated by war, disease, and flight. Citing the focus of the millennium development goals (MDGs) on primary education, they considered higher education and vocational training a luxury that Afghanistan could ill afford. But without training doctors, teachers, engineers, and managers, it was not clear at the time whether Afghanistan could get back on its feet. Five years later, the fact that the country's operational budget is overshadowed by the cost for technical assistance (TA) to make up for the "poor capacity" of the government testifies to the debilitating expense of failure to invest in the training of professional staff, future leaders, and administrators.

In many parts of the world, the neglect of higher education has led to poor-quality administration and spiraling TA bills. The price for TA amounts to roughly $20 billion per annum, with consultants often paid around $200,000 a year.[22] Nor is this technical assistance provided by Western donors of high quality in many cases. The U.S. Government Accountability Office reported in January 2007 that "the United States has provided the Iraqis with a variety of training and technical assistance to improve their capacity to govern. As of December 2006, we identified more than 50 capacity development efforts led by at least six US agencies. However, it is unclear how these efforts are addressing core needs and Iraqi priorities in the absence of an integrated US plan."[23]

It is now an inescapable fact that since innovation drives competitive economies, the cultivation of flexible mental models, collective problem solving, and pattern recognition are vital skills. Emphasis has shifted from natural advantage to competitive advantage. Since human capital is key to wealth creation, the private sector has found it necessary to reorganize and to provide staff members who are the most skilled and entrepreneurial individuals possible. With the failure of public institutions to keep up with industry's demand for skilled technology workers, businesses are stepping back in to help with the learning process. In Africa recently, companies have joined forces with other stakeholders in initiatives such as "Brain Gain" and "Engineering Africa" to overcome the shortage of skilled people by developing specialized training programs.

The key to competitiveness is not necessarily a particular firm or industry itself but the cluster of institutional relations within which a specific industry is spatially located. Industry and centers of research and knowledge were once seen as apples and oranges; today both knowledge and creativity are recognized as the engine of competitiveness. Prime examples are the group of richly endowed educational institutions in the Boston area that includes Harvard, MIT, Tufts, and Boston College; the M4 research corridor in England; the Paris-Sud concentration of high-technology firms in France; and Tokyo-Yokohama in Japan. As Manuel Castells has noted in *The Rise of the Network Society*,[24] centers of technological innovation in the United States are located in "greenfield" sites (undeveloped land); in the rest of the world, old and established cities are the setting for such developments. Now that the centrality of these clusters is recognized, policymakers in many countries are actively attempting to create their own clusters of growth. The Research Triangle in North Carolina, described earlier, is just one example. Jawaharlal Nehru, India's first prime minister, was often criticized for investing heavily in the Indian technological institutes. Advocates of primary education argued that this was a waste of precious resources on an already privileged elite. Today it is widely acknowledged that an entire set of industries, now driving India's growing economy—from information technology to call centers and financial services—are the by-products of Nehru's investment.

The information revolution is calling into question our centuries-old assumptions about the relationship between information, knowledge, and wisdom. Gathering information in order to identify patterns was until recently one of the most time-consuming and expensive acts imaginable. Information that a search engine can instantly make available today would have taken years of work based on a robust infrastructure of universities and libraries just a few years ago. Historically, a significant part of education was directed toward the processing of information, and people were prized for their capability to reproduce information when it was required. This task has now become digitized, and machines are freeing us from the need to memorize.

Now that huge quantities of data can be processed at very little cost, the key challenge becomes the cultivation of knowledge to categorize information and to discern patterns in it, particularly regarding new and emerging phenomena. The difficult task for policy in the spheres of public, private, and civil society is to acquire the collective wisdom to respond to existing challenges such as global poverty and inequality and to emerging challenges such as global warming with wisdom and foresight. The emergence of online communities as a vehicle for problem solving indicates that collaboration and cooperation can yield results that are far beyond the reach of individualized approaches.

CREATION OF CITIZENSHIP RIGHTS THROUGH SOCIAL POLICY

Experience has shown that the creation of citizenship rights—through social policies that cut across gender, ethnicity, race, class, spatial location, and religion—is critical to stability and prosperity. When the state uses social policy as an instrument for the establishment of equal opportunities, the social fabric created can lead to a sense of national unity and a shared belief in common destiny. This belief overcomes fragmented identities that oppose the status quo. Social policy turns the state from an organization into a community of common sentiment and practice: a nation-state. Subjects thereby become "citizens."

At the core of this crucial transformation has been the right to vote. In the United States of the early twentieth century, only landowners were allowed to vote, but by the end of the 1900s everyone over the age of eighteen could cast a ballot. By regulating the working day and establishing minimum wages, the state intervened in the struggle between labor and capital. Welfare mechanisms such as social security, pensions, disability, and child support provided safety nets to recognize especially vulnerable categories of citizens. The twentieth century witnessed a fundamental change in attitudes toward poverty. In England, the shift in mental models from the nineteenth to the twentieth century is remarkable. In the nineteenth century, poor people were not only held morally responsible for their own poverty but also considered deserving of severe discipline in poorhouses. Anyone found idle could be imprisoned. George Orwell, in *Down and out in Paris and London*, vividly describes how, as a poor person, he could not sit in the streets in London without being taken to the poorhouse. All the more astonishing, therefore, was William Beveridge's call for a welfare state to establish a minimum standard of living "below which no one should be allowed to fall."[25]

The repositioning of the state vis-à-vis the market economy that took place in the wake of the Great Depression on both sides of the Atlantic made the state a central player in the well-being of the citizen. In OECD countries, direct and indirect expenditures on social issues are defined as "the provision by public and private institutions of benefits to, and financial contributions targeted at, households and individuals in order to provide support during circumstances which adversely affect their welfare."[26] In 2001 public social spending averaged 21 percent of the GDP for all OECD countries. Belgium, Germany, France, Austria, and Italy, which typically spend more than 11 percent of their GDP on old-age benefits, have been termed "pensioner states."

Social policy transforms the nation-state into a community of mutual rights and obligations, where each citizen has certain responsibilities vis-à-vis other citizens. In contrast to "atomized" industrial society, some developed countries have become embodiments of stakeholder societies. Instead of class, race, or religious issues, attention has turned to ensuring fair treatment across generations and throughout the territory. For example, Canada is diverse in both its geography and its people. The tie that binds Canadians is a social policy that has created a set of citizenship rights and obligations across the country's vast territory and social diversity, which have overcome the territorial and linguistic obstacles to unity. Structural funds in Europe have also focused on removing spatial barriers to opportunity. The EU cohesion policy, put in place to support poorer regions of the union, will invest $480 billion in poorer regions over the next seven years. This investment will create new consumers and new markets, stabilize fragile democracies, and reduce migration.[27]

The negative effects that result from the absence of inclusive social policies are quite clear. In weak states, tensions and cleavages along ethnic, religious, race, and class lines are exacerbated. At times the consequences can be tragic, leading in the most extreme cases to ethnic cleansing and genocide. Relations between rulers and ruled are tense, poverty becomes entrenched, and a distinctive category of ultrapoor people emerges. This ignites a widespread desire for migration, against which industrial countries are continuously erecting barriers. As social cleavages continue to deepen, conflict erupts. Militarization all too frequently concludes the vicious cycle by disrupting the state's ability to administer effective social policies.

Europe has now achieved a remarkable consensus on citizenship rights, and the United States has done the same—evidenced by the fact that both an African American and a woman are serious contenders for the 2008 presidential election. In developing countries, too, much progress has been made. The South African state has been transformed from an agent of exclusion based on race to the arbiter of a "rainbow" nation. However, gender remains the oldest and most stubborn category of social inequality. Recent analysis from the European Union indicates that mainstreaming of gender in social policy is still a major challenge. Race is equally problematic. Even in the wealthiest nations, including Canada, the United States, Norway, and New Zealand, indigenous and other racial groups continue to face major barriers to inclusion. Despite significant changes in the United States, the legacy of racism is far from resolved. Today in the United States, 25 percent more black men are found in prisons than in universities. As events in Rwanda and the former Yugoslavia show, the specter of ethnocide and genocide still haunt us.

While one set of social questions is being dealt with, the very dynamism of the global economy is creating new social tensions between permanence and change, young and old. Assumptions about stable jobs and families are obsolete in OECD countries. With 47 million Americans without health insurance, the continuing significance of social issues cannot be ignored. The unprecedented rise of India and China has focused attention on the need for a credible social contract between the haves and have-nots and the role of the state in fostering this growth. Tension also exists between our world of flows, where capital and commodities are on the move, and the restriction in movement of labor. When previously homogeneous societies absorb large numbers of immigrants from former colonies, the question of cultural identity vis-à-vis dominant cultural models arises. In countries such as Britain and France, the uneasiness in dealing with the small number of young Muslim women wearing veils is just one illustration of the nature of challenges to established cultural paradigms.

PROVISION OF INFRASTRUCTURE SERVICES

Adequate transportation, power, water, communications, and pipelines all underlie the state's ability to provide security, administration, investment in human capital, and the necessary conditions for a strong market economy. Since the last quarter of the nineteenth century, the state has been a significant player in the provision of infrastructure. First Germany and then other European states realized their backwardness in relation to Britain, and with large populations concentrated in relatively small areas, imaginatively developed infrastructure for transportation, services, and food delivery. Since World War II, federal, state, and local authorities in the United States have been major players in the funding of infrastructure from federal highways and mass transit systems to canals, dams and harbors. Between 1956 and 2004 annual public spending on infrastructure grew an average of 2.3 percent per annum, adjusted for inflation. In 2006 U.S. infrastructure spending totaled $76.3 billion.[28]

Water management for irrigation and power has long been a function of the state. The harnessing of the Mississippi and Colorado rivers (and the building of the Hoover Dam on the latter) provides inspiring stories of how states can manage infrastructure for the common good. The seventeen turbine generators at the Hoover Dam produce a massive 2,074 megawatts of power for Southern California, Nevada, and Arizona. The U.S. Army Corp of Engineers played a significant role in these projects by planning, designing, building, and operating these water resources. The Mississippi River Commission (MRC) implemented the Mississippi River and Tributaries (MR&T) project under the supervision of the chief engineer, who commands the U.S. Army Corps of Engineers. The MR&T project is "arguably the most successful civil works project ever initiated by Congress. Since 1928, the nation has contributed nearly $12 billion towards the MR&T project and has received an estimated $425.5 billion return on that investment, including savings on transportation costs and flood damages."[29]

The state has also played a critical role in the funding of technological research that has changed the nature of planning and development. The role of the Defense Advanced Research Projects Agency (DARPA; initially ARPA) in the development of the Internet is a striking example of the facilitation of global flows and commitment to open societies. First DARPA funded and managed the development of the Internet and then shared it with civil society, which has enabled it to become our common global information platform.

The developmental states of east Asia saw infrastructure as a central component of economic development. Japan paved the way in this regard and was followed by Singapore, South Korea, Taiwan, Malaysia, and Hong Kong. The recent rise of China is underpinned by massive investments in infrastructure, with the Chinese government spending $150 billion in 2003 on electricity, roads, airports, seaports, and telecom. As at 2007, it spends 10.6 percent of its GDP on infrastructure, seven times as much as India.[30]

The development of seaports is also critical. To build the port of Dubai, for example, the ruling family mortgaged the sheikhdom's future revenues to Kuwait. Their gamble paid off handsomely as the demand for the port far exceeded their original estimates. Not only is the Dubai port first-rate, but it has also acquired the management capability to emerge as a major global player in port management. Similarly, Dubai's air traffic quickly exceeded the anticipated demand, leading the sheikdom to explore opportunities in uncharted markets. Emirates began with a $10 million investment and is now one of the world's major airlines. The creation of the port of Gwadar in Pakistan, leased under a long-term management contract to Singapore Ports, is another bold venture to create infrastructure as a source of wealth generation.

During the last century, direct state production of infrastructure was carried out in conjunction with contracts with the private sector to build, operate and maintain services. Public funding for infrastructure has remained a central feature of advanced industrial countries, the first effect of which was the conquest of space by time. Because of the development of roads, railroads, canals, air travel, and now communications highways, the wide spaces where people and their products had once been isolated from potential markets are now integrated. The flow of goods and services has become more predictable, and time schedules for travel and planning are far more sophisticated and efficient than in the past. The reach of the market and administration has expanded, as people, goods, and ideas all move more rapidly. Providing infrastructure also helps to underwrite a state's legitimacy by overcoming spatial inequalities and allowing for the accumulation of engineering and technological knowledge.

When infrastructure services are lacking, spatial inequalities and areas of exclusion persist. This has a particularly marked effect on health: a lack of sewage systems, clean water, and other health services such as clinics and pharmacies takes a heavy toll. Without infrastructure, integration into the market is difficult, particularly within the agricultural sector, which is critical for eradicating poverty. Depending upon the international community to provide infrastructure does little to resolve this issue. International donors pay relatively little attention to operation and maintenance, which are crucial factors in connecting to a domestic infrastructure that provides access to a larger market.

A substantial number of countries lack adequate infrastructure services. In 2001 the World Travel and Tourism Council constructed a global infrastructure index that focused on access to roads, sanitation, and drinking water. Of the 117 countries it measured, only Australia scored 100; only the United States, Sweden, Canada, and Austria also scored higher than 80; 51 countries (44 percent of the total) scored less than 50; and 4 countries scored less than 20 (Afghanistan scored 0.00).[31] As long as those countries toward the bottom of this scale remain dysfunctional and fail to plan and implement new infrastructure projects, they will fall farther and farther behind and will be unable to link up to the global grid of flows.

Infrastructure is going to remain a major focus of global attention in the coming decades. The management consulting company Booz Allen Hamilton estimates that modernizing and expanding water, electricity, and transportation systems in the world's cities over the next twenty-five years will require $40 trillion, a figure roughly equivalent to the 2006 market capitalization of every share held in all of the stock markets in the world.[32] Given our increasing understanding of environmental and social issues, the very framework that underpins the value of different capitals—particularly natural and social capital—is changing. As Amory Lovins, Hunter Lovins and Paul Hawken presciently argued, the market and public policy can make natural capitalism work to their mutual advantage to reduce carbon emissions and increase energy efficiency while increasing the profitability of enterprise, particularly through the elimination of waste in the current use of energy.[33] Provision for and upgrading of infrastructure on a global scale is going to require fundamental changes to our design, prioritization, and implementation. Management of such a critical challenge must be based on new governance techniques, all of which must involve the state, the private sector, local communities, and civil society groups.

FORMATION OF A MARKET

The state supports the creation and expansion of the market through three major measures: setting and enforcing rules for commercial activity, supporting the operation and continued development of private enterprise, and intervening at times of market failure. The market is often considered an institution of human making but not one of design, an example of how individual greed can yield public good seemingly spontaneously. Yet an examination of the market, as Alfred Chandler Jr. demonstrates in his book *The Visible Hand*, shows that the market has often generated demands for greater control by the government both to create the enabling laws through which wealth can be created, leveraged, and preserved and to deal with market failures through public policy and action.[34] The Great Depression is the most vivid example of a time when an unchecked market brought about a worldwide crash, throwing tens of millions of people into poverty in the process. More recently, the crisis of the banking sector—from the savings and loans scandal in the United States to the calamities in Mexico, Brazil, Russia, Indonesia, Korea, and Thailand—vividly illustrates that the market requires regulation and strong rule of law for its functioning and continued expansion.

The state has often set barriers against the market, the most extreme example of which is the Soviet Union, where the market was outlawed. The marketplace has been restricted by other mechanisms such as guilds or the licensing and granting of monopolies such as to certain Indian companies by the government of India and to telephone companies in the United States. In some countries at particular times, certain services (e.g., railways, airports, airlines) are reserved for the state, and the market is not allowed to function. The state can impose huge costs on the market through corruption and inefficiency, but the market cannot function without certain services (e.g., security of people and property, rule of law, education). If the state does not perform these functions, the market is forced to assume them; if it cannot, the market functioning itself is constrained. The balance between state and market has evolved over time, and the market now takes for granted that the state will perform a range of functions.

Setting market rules involves multiple activities ranging from the establishment of standards for property rights (including intellectual property), banking, and insurance to the defining of the relationship between labor and capital. The state also sets standards for quality, enforces contracts, and puts into place credible dispute resolution and arbitration mechanisms. To ensure competition in the market, the state actively intervenes, thereby preventing monopolies from forming and large corporations from colluding to fix prices. After World War II, the emergence of the state as a purchaser of goods and services and a provider of subsidies to industry became central to the relationship between the state and the marketplace; with the increase in their budgets, states are now hugely significant players in the market.

In general, there are two models of state support for the market. The first is indirect and involves building infrastructure, fostering human capital, providing security, establishing monetary policy, and governing honestly and transparently. The second advocates the formation of direct alliances with private-sector players. Other measures include the use of tariffs for the protection of infant industries, the creation of policies for the expansion of domestic products into foreign markets, and the dissemination of relevant state-generated research to private enterprise upon request. The state can also step in to provide certain functions that the market is unwilling to perform. In times of market failure, for example, interventions have ranged from deficit financing in the wake of the Great Depression to financing for institutions such as savings and loans agencies. Sometimes when a voluntary agreement cannot be reached, the state intervenes to bring together the parties concerned.

The creation of the territorial state has been a necessary precondition for the formation of the market. It opened up a space for one system of rules and the rule of law, in which movement between people and property is secure and the courts can arbitrate disputes in a predictable manner. The European absolutist state eliminated the plethora of rules for different groups and parts of territory that prevented the efficient passage of goods. Through aggressive expansionist policies, the territorial state expanded trade into a global system, first through conquest and empire building and subsequently through agreements for the formalization of the globalized economy. It has fallen to regional organizations, associations and agreements ranging from the European Union to the North American Free Trade Agreement (NAFTA) to reduce and ideally eliminate barriers to trade and commerce across national boundaries.

The relationship between the state and the market in industrialized countries has varied greatly over time. Capitalism is dominant today, but different institutional models for the regulation of relations between the state and the market persist. The core issues have been the protection of private property, the provision of a predictable set of rules for forming and expanding capital, and efforts to find the type of organization that will best achieve this. Nevertheless, the manner in which this has come about has varied greatly from the social market economy in Germany to massive wealth redistribution in Scandinavia to the primacy of the market in the United States.

Great Britain, the first industrial economy in the world, promoted a model that was referred to as the "cosmopolitical economy."[35] Germany explicitly adhered to the model of a national economy—or social market economy—promoted particularly by Ludwig Erhard after World War II. Japan and Germany were early developmental states in which the bureaucracy played a significant role in the stewardship of economic development. The east Asian economic growth after World War II also saw the heavy involvement of the bureaucracy guiding the economy, with South Korea and the Ministry of International Trade and Industry (MITI) in Japan blazing the trail, and others following suit. All in all, after the Great Depression in the industrialized world, the state became a partner of the market in order to contain market failure and to rescue, invest, and coordinate the larger economy through regulation.

The 1980s and 1990s saw both the reversal of this trend and the materialization of a new relationship between the state and the market. There was a radical shift in the market as the instrument for delivering an increasing range of services, particularly through outsourcing. The state was to play only a regulatory and ancillary role. Margaret Thatcher and Ronald Reagan both led the charge to remove the state from economic life, thereby opening up a range of industries to market competition. Underpinning this change were local government movements for public entrepreneurship. As we mention in chapter 5, the Washington Consensus outlined the state's key tasks as macromonetary and fiscal policy management, the establishment of an enabling environment for the market, the creation of secure property rights, and prioritization and discipline of public expenditure management. The collapse of Communism seemed to bear out the thesis that the state was ineffective as a medium for economic development.

Now, however, with several decades of experience behind us, the market does not seem all powerful; the private sector alone is not always the answer—sometimes the state can actually be more effective than business and is a precondition to effective market activity in today's complex world. Yet no matter whether the state delivers a service directly or subcontracts work, its role in setting standards for production and the delivery of public value remains its distinguishing characteristic. The question is not "state" or "market" but the allocation of functions and tasks between them and the establishment of a framework within which each actor can operate effectively and cooperate over the long term. Indeed, the market in advanced industrial countries does not have the same institutional structure from state to state. It has often been noted that a textbook on political economy written from within Germany's social economy would be unrecognizable in Anglo-Saxon countries. Indeed, the decisions of the Ministry of Trade and Industry in Japan and South Korea to support industry would make little sense in open-market economies. When dysfunctional states have tried to copy state intervention in the economy as it was carried out in east Asia, they have often failed and only created further obstacles to economic growth. The role of the state is highly context specific. But while the degree of regulation or deregulation in various sectors has varied historically in different countries, the general trend is toward deregulation, thereby ensuring that competition will remain a central concern for the state.

The creation of enabling mechanisms through which large segments of the population can participate in the market—such as mortgages or the stock market—greatly enhances the legitimacy of the market as a mechanism of social and economic mobility.[36] The establishment of functioning markets has led to the victory of capitalism over its competitors as a model of economic organization by harnessing the creative and entrepreneurial energies of large numbers of people as stakeholders in the market economy. Corporations, as well as small and medium-sized enterprises, are the main employers. This situation allows the state to focus on its major functional tasks, such as setting standards for the relations between state and corporation, rather than on providing employment. There are now empirical grounds for the proposition that wealth is boundless, thereby leading to a transition from an economic model that emphasizes wealth redistribution.

In a developed state, a relationship of creative tension exists between state and market in view of the fact that the market can fulfill certain functions better than the state, yet the state provides the architecture within which the market operates. In developing countries, this constellation does not exist. When weak states cannot enable the market to function or when they actually subvert its functioning, they block development and prosperity and fail to generate institutional linkages. This freezes capital, which cannot flow through the economy. Inadequate regulation leads to the informalization of transactions, and if property security is precarious and arbitration unpredictable, then capital is not attracted to a state but flees it instead. Similarly, if a ruling elite use its position for self-enrichment at the expense of creating broader opportunities, then disparity between rich and poor increases, and opportunities for wealth generation are lost. The very legitimacy of the order is called into question.

In a context where the economy and information diffusion are both global, yet in which politics remains largely national, a critical series of issues affects the relationship between the state and the marketplace. Nowadays a dysfunctional state faces a much weightier global market than before, one that reflects organizational experience and reinforcing ties behind it that it often does not fully understand, in contrast to the less wealthy, nationally confined firms of the past. As we have mentioned, it is the unattractive side of the global economy (i.e., extractive industries and technical assistance) that seeks rents from these countries, while the purported advisers to the dysfunctional states, the aid complex, can offer little advice on how to create a market, or they act to deliver the state's assets into the hands of predators through hastily organized, nontransparent privatizations.

Wealthy countries and global financial aid organizations keep preaching the virtues of the market to underdeveloped countries and seek to protect their intellectual property regimes, yet they prevent the global market in agriculture from functioning. Both Europe and the United States provide huge subsidies to economic sectors that are considered vital to their national economy or presumably have the potential to undermine social peace (hence the persistence of massive farm subsidies). The discussions in the Doha round of trade negotiations since 2001 have made it clear that both continents need to choose between subsidies to their agricultural producers and an open global trading regime. Both middle- and low-income countries are increasingly arguing that subsidies to agriculture constitute a major barrier to the development of competitive export industries.

In particular, food aid continues on a large scale despite its lack of suitability as an instrument for tackling the problems it purports to address. The food distribution system is highly inefficient: 50–70 percent of the cost of this aid goes toward transporting grain from the U.S. Midwest to East Africa and other countries facing famine. In many cases, local agricultural livelihoods are devastated when imported food is dumped on the market; if food distribution is required, then in most cases the provisions could be purchased from the domestic markets of the afflicted country or those of neighboring countries. Finally, it has been demonstrated that cash-for-work programs, which allow the beneficiaries to purchase food with the money they earn, are much more effective than free food distributions in tackling many situations of famine since the core issue is the marginalization of people from job opportunities. The status quo persists because a coalition of farming states and their politicians, shipping interests, NGOs, and international organizations such as World Food Program are the beneficiaries of this system and thus have a stake in its continued existence.

Rules of law that protect intellectual property have been the basis of the wealth generated by information technology, intellectual creativity, and scientific research in areas ranging from music, books, and software to films and pharmaceutical industries. An intellectual property regime transforms ideas into capital that rewards creativity and innovation with recognition and wealth. The tension here, however, as Lawrence Lessig has pointed out in a series of books, is the balance between the emergence of new forms of commons that provide the platform for further creativity on the one hand and incentives that encourage development on the other. The challenge for the state is to strike a balance between public benefit in the commons and private gain as an incentive to creativity. The development of a Creative Commons license and a limit on the number of years a patent is available are examples of imaginative responses to this issue. Whether rising economies will recognize the intellectual property of established economies remains an open question.

The established axiom that individual greed can spontaneously lead to collective order has come under renewed examination in developed countries, where it is reflected in a series of corporate scandals that involve accounting and auditing practices, collusion between state officials and big business, and outright corruption in dealings between legislators, lobbyists, and government officials. As a result, public dissatisfaction with corporate behavior is high, and governments have moved to increase accountability. The government of Canada, for example, has enacted new legislation on accountability that requires detailed public scrutiny of decision making. In the United States, the Sarbanes-Oxley legislation was a rapid and seemingly costly response to the same problem. With the move to provide huge, multiyear infrastructure projects (e.g., the Channel Tunnel or the Denmark bridge) through the private sector, vast sums of money will be allocated to schedules and for cost projections that will inevitably change over time. For businesses to engage in the long term, collaborative efforts are required to solve the problems of accountability, transparency, and cost effectiveness.

With the current volume and speed of global economic flows and the emergence of new centers of economic activity, our national and international mechanisms for monitoring and regulating these flows are struggling to keep up. The panic generated by the subprime crisis is generating an intense debate on regulation and the extent to which the public should be responsible for rescuing and rewarding risky behavior. Few people could have imagined the emergence and scale of today's hedge funds, state reserve funds, and sovereign wealth funds; no international organization currently has the authority to convene these funds or their managers to agree to rules of the game. Whereas the International Monetary Fund (IMF) might previously have stepped in, with the loss of trust in the IMF by east Asian and Latin American governments following its handling of the 1998 economic crisis, a major vacuum has developed. There is now no global arbiter to evaluate trends credibly and provide mechanisms of risk management (and rescue, if necessary).

MANAGEMENT OF PUBLIC ASSETS

The state's capital is not just made up of money but also a huge array of assets ranging from fixed assets—land, equipment, buildings, cultural heritage—to natural capital—forests, rivers, seas, minerals—to intangible assets such as licenses to operate services and manage the radio spectrum or to import and export goods. Even the image or brand of the country is an asset. While budgets have traditionally captured only revenues and expenditures, these assets have far more actual and potential value to citizens if appropriately mobilized. The way these assets are put to work for the collective good is a marker of the state's effectiveness.

Four clusters of activities are particularly significant: the management and allocation of rights to land and water, the sustainable use of natural capital, including extractive industries, the management and protection of the environment, including forests, and the licensing of industrial and commercial activities. The state provides a framework for land use; confers and enforces rights of private ownership; establishes user rights through mechanisms such as zoning; and acquires private property for public purposes. Water management, too, is a major matter for the state. Its regulation of navigation on rivers and oceans has had direct implications for market expansion. Another chief area of state activity has been the harnessing of rivers by means of dams and canals. In both urban and agricultural areas, regulations on alternative uses of water have been critical to long-term planning. Arbitration between domestic and international regions is crucial in determining riparian rights.

Mining provided the basis for the industrial age: For decades, quantities of coal and steel served as a measure of industrialization. The state has played a critical role in establishing and enforcing regimes of rights for natural resources, which have ranged from recognition of outright petroleum ownership to establishment of rules that declare all subsoil assets to be public property. Depending on the legal regime, the state's role has varied from taxing extractive industries to acting as direct partner or rent collector. Equally diverse is the extent to which the current generation uses rents from natural resources or reserves them for the future.

Despite the adverse impacts of extractive industries on the environment and the surrounding communities, developed countries were slow to recognize these harmful effects and legislate remedies for them. Rental and other fees from extractive industries have been both an asset and a liability: The economic syndrome called the "Dutch disease" acquired its name from the unfavorable consequences for manufacturing in the Netherlands that resulted from the discovery of natural gas there in the 1960s. Recognition of the rights of future generations can help to circumvent such situations in which one generation receives windfall profits without the capacity to spend; in these instances the savings can be harnessed to productive future uses that are carefully worked out.

Moreover, the range and magnitude of the environmental damage caused by human activity has brought about a social movement, bolstered by scientific analysis, that now recognizes the critical importance of sustainable development in safeguarding the interests of current and future generations. The environmental movement's agenda, which encompasses everything from air and water pollution to national park creation to species preservation to global warming, has generated landmark legislation at both the national and international levels.

Long before scientists understood the environmental dangers of carbon emissions, some far-sighted political leaders embarked on the creation of national parks. These spaces have become essential to the quality of life in urban and metropolitan areas because they preserve species and landscapes of great beauty and biological diversity. Few Americans have the opportunity to go to Alaska to get firsthand exposure to the fragility of permafrost, yet the environmental movement has succeeded in preserving this pristine beauty as a space for global well-being.

Places themselves become metaphors and carry enduring images that have either positive or negative associations. The image of the country itself can be an asset or a liability. Countries that have endured prolonged conflict have particular difficulty overcoming the legacy of negative associations with danger and criminality. The value of a brand is reflected by the extent to which illicit industries copy it—like fashion from Italy or a watch from Switzerland. For firms like Coke and Disney, one formula produces the bulk of their revenue. For countries, huge opportunities lie in promoting a particular attribute of their cultural heritage, landscape, or products. One of the positive effects of public asset management is that land ownership has been consolidated as a system of rights and obligations. Regulation of land has resulted in livable cities and national parks or reservations preserved for the needs of future generations. With the recognition of the adverse impact of extractive and other industries, a series of policies and projects to reverse them have been implemented, thereby demonstrating that cleaner water and air are achievable.

Each of the state functions described here is an asset that can be mobilized. Failing to utilize that asset ultimately reduces citizens' trust in their government. The negative outcome of the failure to manage public assets responsibly is unmistakable. For example, income from extractive industries has often been "off budget," subject to little scrutiny, and unavailable to the public at large. The exploitation of weak countries' natural resources has taken place with little regard to the environment or to the welfare of the workers employed by extractive industries. When licenses have been granted without a transparent competitive process, rental and lease fees have often been a fraction of the value such a process would have brought about, while the government and the public end up bearing the loss. The opaque processes in granting and perpetuating licenses are effectively patronage instruments that prevent the emergence of competitive markets, a vibrant domestic sector, and international investment. Likewise, in the absence of transparent processes for the acquisition of either land or private assets for the public interest, developmental projects have had tragic social effects that have sparked protests by the very populations (typically poor and indigenous) who were to have benefited from them.

Oil rents have emerged as a severe problem for those countries with significant oil reserves and unaccountable governments. Norway, which does have an accountable, responsive government, occupies a unique place among oil-producing countries, for it has managed both to avoid a negative impact on other sectors of the economy and to maintain a cohesive society. A key to Norway's ability to handle the economic windfall from its oil was the creation of a futures fund, in which the needs of future generations were allotted a weight equal to that of the current generation's needs, and revenue was distributed accordingly. This indicates that state stewardship can have a much longer-term horizon than the lifespan of its present citizens. Attempts to copy this model in Chad, however, ran up against the interests of the political elite. While in Norway the social consensus was generated through intense public discussion, in Chad the model was promoted by international organizations and the oil companies, who were eager to secure the imprimatur from those international groups. As our interviews with World Bank staff revealed, Chad's privileged citizens observed their commitments only as long as foreign aid was greater than the oil revenue. As soon as oil revenue exceeded foreign aid and the political elite realized that the companies were not about to stop pumping oil, their commitment evaporated.

Global interdependence is now giving rise to a new, twenty-first-century version of the commons. Accordingly, the definition of what constitutes a public or common asset needs to change with this new consensus. After 9/11 it is clear that security is a global public good because the security of the prosperous half of the world is inextricably linked with developments in poorer and less stable countries. The global climate and atmosphere have become our common resource (hence the enormous concern, debate, discussion, and public action for dealing with global warming and the threat posed by carbon emissions). With the information age, a significant debate about the extent to which spectrum licenses should be part of the global commons or allocated by government and market actors has begun in earnest; analysts Lawrence Lessig and John Thackara have described this well.[37] At the core of this debate is the role of regulation in either promoting or hampering innovation.

People, governments, and businesses can value and understand better what they can measure. For countries, the current framework for national accounts underestimates both the full potential of latent assets and the toll our activities take on natural capital. The most obvious difference between countries and companies is an attachment to cash accounts by the former versus accrual accounting by the latter. Companies routinely take account of their future commitments as liabilities on their books, while most governments operate on the basis of the cash that flows to the yearly budget, ignoring the cost of their medium to long-term commitments. A shift in the accounting perspective would significantly change the nature of both the public's and the governments' understanding of resources. But the issue is broader: What a state calculates and reports upon must be developed from its annual expenditure to take account of its use, misuse, or lack of use of the full range of its assets. At the same time, there is also a need to go beyond national accounting to global accounting of the planet's common assets, for only within regional and global accounting systems will we be able to appreciate the use of assets such as water, trade, and transport linkages.

EFFECTIVE PUBLIC BORROWING

Public borrowing, which is a basic foundation of the banking system, is critical to the operation of the financial sector. The state has always played a central role in the emergence of public lending institutions and the creation of instruments of public lending and borrowing, which initially grew out of the need to pay for wars. The Netherlands and Great Britain were the first countries to create central banks, which enabled their governments to finance relatively large military forces. This ability to raise money in turn enabled these states to acquire large colonial empires and create the publicly chartered companies that managed them.

Publicly floated bonds have been one means of transforming public savings into a capital asset for the state. Stock market regulation has encouraged the formation of large companies that shareholders from different segments of society own publicly. This expands the potential of the economy to create jobs, which in turn expands the state's tax base. Meanwhile, the sovereign guarantee helps to transform a legal concept into a field of productive financial and economic relations. In guaranteeing transactions on behalf of a private or a subsovereign entity, the state itself inevitably assumes a credit risk. Its capacity to assess the credit worthiness of these actors and its legal capability to fully understand the obligations that it undertakes are critical factors that underpin the sovereign guarantee.

Prior to the emergence of the Bretton Woods institutions, states had no form of concessional lending available to them. The International Bank for Reconstruction and Development—the core facility of the World Bank, which specializes in lending to middle-income countries—was initially designed for the reconstruction of Europe and made its first loans to the Netherlands. The massive financial flows from the Marshall Plan to Europe enabled the bank to focus on aiding other developing countries. Japan, South Korea, and Malaysia have been among those that have used large volumes of credit from the bank to transform their economies. Concessional lending in the form of international development assistance emerged in the 1960s, and outright grants have recently become part of the bank's arsenal for helping poor countries improve their economies.

In OECD countries, public borrowing constitutes a significant portion of the budget. In Canada, in 2004 and 2005, for instance, public borrowing constituted 38 percent of the GDP, and the country's goal set out in the 2006 budget was to reduce it to 25 percent of the GDP by 2013 or 2014. This means that twelve rather than sixteen cents of every dollar of revenue will to go to the payment of public debt. All European Union members now adhere to limits on public debt, which is set at 3 percent of GDP by the Stability and Growth Pact. The United States today is the largest debtor in the world, with $4.9 trillion in public debt. The U.S. bond market is the instrument that is used to attract capital from the rest of the world to finance this huge public debt. Effective borrowing has enabled the state to develop predictable payment mechanisms and thus the credibility to pay its service providers on the basis of its contracts. Public bonds enable the state to undertake large infrastructure projects, and because money is fungible, borrowing has enabled states in developed countries to fund human capital and citizenship programs, even in the face of large deficits. Thus the state's role as a major borrower has mobilized the public's savings into an instrument of public power and financial muscle to realize citizenship goals. More important still, when the market fails, a well-financed state is in a position to pick up the pieces and provide the seed money to rebuild.

With weak institutions, the negative consequences of public borrowing are equally clear. As a result of poor public borrowing decisions, some governments, such as those in Egypt and Iran, forfeited their independence and were transformed into colonies or near colonies. Others, such as the Ottoman Empire and Argentina, lost control or transferred the operations of their major revenue sources, such as customs imports, to their creditors' representatives. In other places throughout Latin America and Africa, financiers have designed and executed projects in unsustainable ways. The most significant impact of bad decisions on public borrowing has been the world debt crisis. In too many countries, resources devoted to servicing debt charges far exceed those allocated for human capital or infrastructure. In extreme cases, public borrowing has been a means for authoritarian leaders to enrich themselves by diverting funds out of the country in question.

With the assumption of the World Bank presidency by Robert McNamara in 1968, the use of sovereign guarantees became a key instrument in the bank's ability to borrow from the bond market.

All World Bank loans are guaranteed by the borrower government, and each loan has a maturation period. Payment of these loans takes priority over any other obligation of the borrower government. When payments are due and the government does not have available funds, the government will take out new loans to pay the installments that it owes. As a result, the World Bank has never cancelled a loan to its creditors, thereby guaranteeing its AAA rating in the bond market. In this way, the bank has made an income of $1 billion a year for the last fifteen years. As its website proclaims, "The World Bank is one of the most prudent and conservative financial institutions in the world."

Nonetheless, in the view of its critics, the World Bank has engaged in a vicious cycle of lending to poorly governed countries where future lending from the bank to the country became necessary in order to repay past loans. The borrower assumed all of the risks without the bank's incurring any losses in resources or reputation for poor project design and implementation. Risks of the projects were not assessed through market instruments; instead, risk assessments are drawn up by the project managers, who have an incentive in seeing their projects disbursed. If the loans had been subject to real market assessments, the Bank would most likely have lost a lot of money. This led to an organizational culture in which the emphasis was on design and approval of projects rather than ensuring good implementation and results on the ground, thereby inhibiting innovation. That is not to say that all World Bank–financed projects are worthless. However, its own internal evaluation documents have shown that a significant proportion of its loans are problematic. Equally, borrowers treat the bank's lending as an entitlement for which they have few accountabilities.

There is an assumption that the sovereign guarantee is essential to the continued operation of the aid system. But two organizations within the aid system that operate loans without sovereign guarantees—the International Finance Corporation (IFC) and the European Bank for Reconstruction and Development (EBRD)—demonstrate that multilateral institutions can be profitable without requiring sovereign guarantees. The IFC's lending has been confined to the private sector, but EBRD lending has expanded to a range of operations, both public and private, including the extending of loans to municipal governments in Russia. As a result, the EBRD wrote off only €145 million in loans between 2001 and 2006 out of a total asset portfolio of €28.4 billion by year-end 2005. In 2007 the EBRD announced profits of €2.4 billion. As a result of this policy (according to remarks made to us by the EBRD president, Jean Lemierre), it is clear that the EBRD takes due diligence on all of its projects extremely seriously, perhaps far more so than if it had access to the sovereign guarantee. One way to tackle the crisis of indebtedness would be for lenders such as the World Bank and others who are backed by the sovereign guarantee to share the risks with their borrowers. This mechanism might also put added pressure on those preparing the projects for the lenders to pay added attention to the quality of the projects. While the World Bank has designed some very good projects, it has also had a share of highly problematic ones.

Looking to the future, we note five key innovations that are necessary for effective public borrowing worldwide:

1. removal of the sovereign guarantee (or its transformation into a mechanism to share risk between lender and borrower) in order to ensure far more prudence and quality in lending
2. introduction of independent risk assessments of institutional capability and projects
3. independent estimates of costs and benefits of projects and programs
4. public disclosure and monitoring of the fulfillment of obligations, along with an increased focus on implementation, rather than just project design and approval
5. development of market-based instruments for mobilization of savings in the poorest countries.

THE SOVEREIGNTY DIVIDEND AND THE SOVEREIGNTY GAP

The performance of these ten functions produces a clustering effect. When a state performs all ten simultaneously, the synergy creates a virtuous circle in which decisions in the different domains reinforce enfranchisement and opportunity for the citizenry. This supports the legitimacy of the decision makers and their decisions, builds trust in the overall system, and thereby produces a "sovereignty dividend." Conversely, when one or several of the functions are not performed effectively, a vicious circle begins: Various centers of power vie for control, multiple decision-making processes confuse priorities, citizens lose trust in the government, institutions lose their legitimacy, and the populace is disenfranchised. In the most extreme cases, violence results. This negative cycle creates the sovereignty gap.

If we can agree on the list of the functions that sovereign states must perform, we could create a framework for measuring the sovereignty gap in a given state. Such a "sovereignty index" would show objectively a state's improvement or decline in performance of any combination of functions, which could be tracked over time. Once a quantitative framework is in place, we can assess proposed interventions on the extent to which they close or open the sovereignty gap. Each function depends on some or all of the other functions being performed. For example, an army requires a payment system to operate; a market economy requires an educated workforce; and rule of law must be carried out through an effective administrative system. States in the developed world carry out these functions in an integrated manner by establishing organizations with distinctive mandates, rules, and resources to undertake them. Each of these organizations acquires a distinctive culture that can become an asset or a liability. Coordination across functions is established through either the cabinet (in parliamentary systems) or the presidency (in presidential systems). Their alignment results from the programs and policies of the party in power, based on the mandate the party receives from the people. Viewed from the perspective of the international system, a state's ability to execute its functions coherently is what renders it truly sovereign.

The functions of the state are never completely fixed. While issues of security prior to September 11 were not uppermost in public concern in developed countries, the impact of that defining event has proven that functions once considered routine will change when a new challenge arises. The degree to which the performance of a particular function looms in an electoral program is usually a reflection of the wider public concern about that issue. Dissatisfaction among the people is likely to nurture public debate about the matter and how to remedy its defects. Regardless of the historical origin of each function, the issue today is how well a state carries it out. History makes it clear that the state's assumption of new functions has been central to its role as the provider and guarantor of public interest. What enables the performance of a sovereign-level function is an agreement among a significant body of citizens that it is in the public interest. Then a political process determines how best to create the capacity for fulfilling it. The state thus maintains its relevance, while acquiring—and enhancing—its legitimacy.

The state forms an integrated whole in which all of the functions are interlinked. Other analysts tend to focus on those aspects of the state that have been most salient to their own particular concerns.

Those that deal with weak or failing states, for example, are inclined to view security as the dominant state function, which pushes economic or political issues into the background. Similarly, those engaged with the developmental state have focused on the economy, thereby over-looking political and security matters, and those involved with European issues have looked more at juridical and political processes and less at security. Focusing on all of these issues simultaneously provides us with a much more holistic overview of the functions that the state must perform in our interdependent world if it is to have legitimacy as a sovereign state at home and play a responsible role as a constituent member of the international system.

Levels: Global, National, Local

An effective state does not equate with a centralized state. Effective-ness is derived from a delineation of governance processes that assigns decision rights to the appropriate level of government. When a lower level of government can handle a particular function, higher levels can stand back to monitor, plan, and set the agenda. In an effective state, flows of information, decision rights, and policies are aligned to ensure their effective performance. As we argue later, national programs del-egated to local governments should actually enhance their implemen-tation capability. The point of transferring decision-making power to a province or state, a capital, a specific city or municipality, a district, a county, or even a village is to ensure the accomplishment of certain policies. From an administrative perspective, those lower levels of gov-ernment must be embedded within two-way flows of rules, people, and resources that result in the creation of a stock of trust, respon-siveness, and credibility. With urbanization, devising the right form of governance for urban areas, ranging from neighborhoods to major cities, is another distinctive challenge for the sovereign state. And with globalization, there is clearly a need for regional and global planning for a range of activities from health to trade and transportation infra-structure, which can no longer take place within national boundaries alone. The functions are therefore fractal; attributes can be replicated at different levels of organizations and on different scales.

The centralization of the state, we should not forget, is based on both a military formation of governance—the modern standing army was first organized on the basis of strict hierarchy—and functional division of labor. In the preindustrial and industrial eras the cost of processing information was high. Widespread usage of the telephone, television, fax machine, and computer has taken place within the past fifty years or so. Global firms have already begun integrating information technology as part of their organizational strategies, based on the assumption of instantaneous communication of information around the globe. Governments, however, have yet to adapt to the full implications of modern information technology. The rapid decline in the cost of information and communication not only calls attention to the drawbacks of slow decision making and old hierarchies but also to the very necessity of hierarchical communication. When different levels of the government can communicate with one another without going through a central node and when modern technology enables increasing numbers of cities to interact with the government, the mechanisms of governance itself must be radically reenvisaged. Thus the modern, effective sovereign state can combine the participatory democracy of the Greek polis with the Roman notion of public law, in which engaged citizens can both participate in determining the government's agenda and monitor the implementation of the mandate that they have given to their leaders.

Agreement on state functions would assist all elements of the international development, security, and business communities to work with national partners in order to coproduce "sovereignty strategies" designed to build effective states and close the sovereignty gap. A key virtue of this kind of consensus is that it would provide a map for devising and managing critical tasks, produce timelines for those assignments, and measure their progress. Above all, consensus on what a sovereign state ought to do, function by function, offers a way to organize the full range of actors working on projects all over the world, whose activities all too frequently exacerbate division and confusion because they have not been pursued as part of a unified strategy.

PART THREE

A NEW AGENDA FOR STATE BUILDING

EIGHT

International Compacts

Sovereignty Strategies

T HE CRISIS OF the state in developing countries and the unintended impact of global aid in weakening those states have undermined their sovereignty. A stable world, as we have argued, requires functioning states to overcome the challenges that threaten the international political and economic system. If global security is dependent on the structural stability of functioning states, then the global system must, over the medium term, cohere around the goal of building sovereign states and make it a high priority. Transformation of states into organizations that provide human security and prosperity for their citizens and act as responsible members of the international community requires a new approach from both domestic and global leadership. We are proposing that in any context, instead of the many different interventions—humanitarian projects, security, development, trade—agreeing on a long-term, state-building strategy tailored to specific contexts and designed to achieve a fully functioning state should be an organizing principle for the international community. Above all, this requires harnessing collective energies and capital.

A vision that truly takes predominance over subordinate agendas can be pursued only through a conscious formulation of and adherence to a strategy. This idea is not new. For hundreds of years the military world has been structured around the use of strategy as the driver of organization and activities. Napoleon's practices provided the ground for Clausewitz's theorization of military strategy as a doctrine. First the

German military and then nearly all military organizations focused on cultivating their top officers' strategic capability. In times of peace, the highest-ranking officers spend their time refining strategy and "war gaming" different scenarios.

In business, too, strategy drives the decision making of the best corporations. Because the globalization of the economy has turned nearly all business assumptions on their head, there has been an explosion of discussions on strategic thinking, and businesses now pay hundreds of millions of dollars a year for "strategic advice." In the 1960s, the formulation of strategy was about choice and position as the competitive environment was well known and companies could benchmark one another. Increasingly, strategy is about managing in a world of increasing uncertainty, where the life cycle of a product might be only six months. Even in the most uncertain contexts, the business world is now finding ways for pathbreaking by constantly revising its assumptions and plans and checking them against context, using a range of techniques such as scenario planning and "future proofing." Unlike in the military, where strategy remains the purview of the leaders, in the business world, tactics are increasingly becoming networked. In both, success or failure is clearly marked—by an announcement in the company quarterly report or by victory or loss in conventional industrial warfare.

To date, the term "strategy" has been imported into the development and humanitarian worlds, but it has not become a general organizing principle. Instead, these organizations, which have often worked at cross-purposes, have developed what they call "strategy," but it demonstrates very few of the true qualities of strategy. Most important, different organizations apply various approaches to diverse areas, usually without any interaction. Consequently, multiple "strategies" coexist, which violate the core principles of unity of purpose and clarity of focus. A simple examination of the core principles of military tactics—efficient resource use, maintenance of momentum until the job is done, unity of command, and concentration of resources at the decisive moment—clearly shows that most development initiatives would not pass muster.

The state, like the global corporation, is a cluster of organizations. As such, its dynamism, stasis, or failure also depends on how its leaders utilize rules to organize its people, assets, and internal processes toward realistic yet inspiring common goals. A strategy cannot be formulated unless leaders have a correct reading of the external environment, an understanding of their organization's or country's internal strengths and weaknesses, and the imagination to articulate a distinctive model of development. As consumers have acquired voice and choice, companies have had to transform themselves in order to be responsive to their demands. Similarly, as state legitimacy rests on citizen trust, the citizens' perspective is the critical test of judging the internal effectiveness of a state and ultimately its capability to attain the external legitimacy that provides the basis for access to global systems of information, knowledge, and capital.

In this chapter we propose a definition of a sovereignty strategy. This description includes a number of components, each of which we examine in turn. We offer an integrated model for state or institution building, which we believe has practical relevance as a tool for both national leaders and the international community in their search for policy coherence. Most important, the model offers a common language for the different stakeholder groups who are currently pursuing different and fragmented agendas that undermine the wider goals of global stability and prosperity.

Before doing so, we must make it clear that putting sovereignty strategies into practice requires the involvement of a wide range of international actors, as well as the dedication and skills of leaders in the countries concerned. For member countries of the international system to become truly sovereign according to our definition, we must begin from the realization that a sovereignty deficit exists across many of the functions that a modern state should perform. For a particular country to acquire the capacity to perform a function, partnerships with a range of actors will be necessary, including universities, voluntary associations, scientific research groups, and the private sector, as well as the more traditional interlocutors of the development agencies. This in turn will require innovative forms of collaboration.

If sovereignty strategies are put into practice, then the current incentives and modalities of the aid system will need to change. A useful concept might be that of coproduction or conditional management, in which a country and its international partners agree to manage a particular function through shared responsibilities or explicit conditionalities, for which each party has agreed rights and responsibilities. Our approach to sovereignty strategies is not limited to countries in conflict. The point of departure for a sovereignty strategy can range from a country in actual conflict to one that is seemingly stable but is experiencing a crisis of governance, to one recovering from natural disasters, to one that seeks a different economic and political trajectory, as well as new opportunities.

Writing the history of the future is now an established practice. As Mahathir bin Mohamad, former prime minister of Malaysia, has pointed out, the choice of the year 2020 as a target year for the country was not accidental. He explains: "Malaysia entered year 2000, the first year of the 21st century and third millennium, determined to achieve its objective of becoming a fully developed country by the year 2020. Some have wondered why 2020 and not some other year. As a doctor I am attracted to the optometrist measurement of vision; 2020 indicates 100 percent good vision in both eyes. Our Vision 2020 for Malaysia implies this clear vision of where we want to go and what we want to be."[1]

Future planning has become a global trend, and corporations, universities, cities, and countries around the world now engage in this exercise. A number of U.S. cities that embarked on such activity received support from either citizens or the government. All of these cities now utilize task forces composed of both citizens and government officials to engage in intensive consultation on prioritization of future goals and analysis of the current conditions. On economic development, either the local chambers of commerce have articulated an agenda, or they have sought specialized advice from consulting firms. Budgeting in these cities acquires a medium-term perspective, and citizens carefully track and reflect on the results. Imagining the future forces people to deal with present constraints.

The city of Hamilton, Ohio, started its visioning exercise because a citizen watched a television program called "Back from the Brink," which discussed urban regeneration by the American Institute of Architects. Inspired by this story, in February 1998 the Hamilton city council launched an intensive cooperative process that involved both the city government and citizen volunteers. Its report describes how the "government's role and its relationship to citizens are being re-evaluated within the context of the modern world," recognizing that "complexity, diversity, and pace of change will characterize the business environment for the 21st century." It looked at the nature and role of governance in an age of "real time communication." The report also described citizens' increasing desire to provide input into those rules and regulations that affect their daily lives; in addition, it discussed the level of responsibility each citizen will have and how this responsibility might be carried out.

Newport, Oregon, has gone through two phases of visioning. The first was completed in the fall of 1999 and focused on infrastructure, image identity, and jobs. Having completed nearly all of its strategic goals by 2004, Newport began to articulate its vision for 2020. The core strategy is to bolster the city's long-standing assets in tourism, fine and performing arts, and the fishing industry by creating a strong, high-tech business base centered on the marine sciences. Described as the "coastal gem" of Oregon, Newport aims to integrate its natural beauty with urban design. Its vision comprises seven distinctive strategies, with specific benchmarks and allocations of responsibility.

As a city-state, Dubai has also focused relentlessly on the future. The driving force behind its vision has been Sheikh Mohammed bin Rashid Al Maktoum, the current ruler, who has demonstrated that an oil-driven economy can successfully diversify. The Dubai of today is not only a sea and air transport hub but also a center of global finance. Driven by foreign management and labor, the rhythm of construction in Dubai has resulted in a new term in the industry: "Dubai time," which means twenty-four hours of construction, seven days a week. While immigrant workers do not enjoy the rights of citizenship, countries throughout South and Southeast Asia are lining up to send their workers to Dubai, a place that in the 1970s hardly figured in their understanding of geography and politics. The initiatives are managed by companies, and their names indicate the scale of creativity and construction under way as Dubai positions itself as the nerve center of the region for finance, trade, and tourism: Dubailand, Dubai Healthcare City, Dubai Outsourcing Zone, the International Media Production Zone, Dubai Internet City, Dubai Media City, Dubai Humanitarian City, Dubai e-Hosting, Dubai Knowledge Village, Dubai Maritime City, Dubai Metals and Commodities Centre, Jebel Ali Free Zone, and Dubai International Financial Center. Dubai has been able to enter the international arena not only by means of its sovereign wealth but also through its management skills.

Regardless of where the initiative comes from, the process of "visioning" forces the participants to draw very clear contrasts between the future they want and the current realities they face. In the Indian state of Andhra Pradesh, visioning forced a sobering reading of conditions: corruption, inefficient use of state resources, short-term planning, and poor infrastructure. This reading of context enabled participants to embrace change and leaders to set a clear sense of direction. Visioning also forces participants to look at mechanisms for goal realization and the new alliances that will make these objectives possible. In the state of Gujarat, the city of Ahmadabad was able to forge connections with the financial markets to issue $25 million in bonds in 1998 (without a state guarantee) to finance partially a water supply and sewage system project. This is interesting because it represents the city's first step toward a fully market-based system of local governance finance.

Whether citizen driven or government driven, these more recent visioning projects differ fundamentally from the Soviet planning approach. Their aim is not some distant utopia but a concrete set of deliverables, a widening of prosperity that is felt by a range of social groups, a careful understanding of opportunities and constraints in the regional and global economy, and the formation of worldwide and local partnerships with both civic and market players. Inspired by these examples, we now turn to our definition of a sovereignty strategy and its core attributes.

WHAT IS A SOVEREIGNTY STRATEGY?

We define a sovereignty strategy as the alignment of internal and external stakeholders to the goals of a sovereign state through the joint formulation, calibration of, and adherence to the rules of the game. Citizens attain these goals by mandating their leaders and managers to mobilize sufficient resources, perform or allocate critical tasks, and ensure ongoing reflexive monitoring and adjustment of implementation. We discuss each segment of this definition in turn.

Alignment

A frequent complaint made about public sector organizations, whether governmental or intergovernmental, is that the whole is less than the sum of the parts. In the United States, this complaint concerns the government's major policy-making areas, which range from security to economic policy. At the World Bank, various divisions are continually vying with one another to secure resources. At the United Nations, the dissonance is between myriad autonomous agencies. In many aid organizations work is often carried out in "silos" and is therefore at cross-purposes. A clear example of such interventions is the poppy problem in Afghanistan: WFP dumps food aid, which may be encouraging farmers to switch to poppy growing; law enforcement agencies hire companies that spray the poppy fields, consequently angering the population; and insurgency results in more military deployment that diverts resources from the sort of investment that might provide jobs. Each agency thus ends up (by default, not design) working at cross-purposes. In the wake of a peace agreement, hundreds of people descend on the capital city from numerous agencies, each booking successive meetings on the same topics with the same people. This imposes a huge cost in time and results in multiple projects and plans with as many as fifty different "strategies" for the same country. Often not even the most basic coordination takes place, particularly with the military, as many groups are uncomfortable communicating with security forces despite the fact that the military brings significant resources and decision-making capability with them.

The syndromes of a misaligned organization are that the staff, resources, culture, and processes are not geared to serving a common objective. Among the many useful ideas on alignment in the business management literature, one stands out: in order to ensure ongoing success, a financial perspective alone is insufficient. Leaders must pay simultaneous attention to customer perspectives, internal perspectives, learning and growth, and the external environment through a balanced-scorecard approach. This method aims to balance internal and external, financial and nonfinancial, and past and future time frames to reposition an organization's strategy. It has been part of the trend of business thinking that stresses multiple perspectives and understanding of the drivers of success.[2] Applying these insights to state management, country leaders and managers must constantly reexamine rules, processes, organizations, tasks, and people to ensure that they are integrated to serve the goal at hand and not work at cross-purposes.

The same assets combined in various ways can produce very different outcomes. Assets can either bring stakeholders together behind a common purpose or drive them apart. When a system is aligned, it acquires a synergistic relationship between actors and levels to achieve its goals. When it is misaligned, chaos, division, and confusion ensue.

Internal and External Stakeholders

The global context today places the dynamics of state formation within the context of global organizations and networks, as well as regional systems and networks. Before 1945 the IMF, UN, and World Trade Organization (WTO) did not exist, nor did the hundreds of international agencies and tens of thousands of nongovernmental organizations that now operate around the world. The current set of organizations creates a context that is highly complex, which reduces room in which to maneuver. Developing countries face a bewildering range of external stakeholders whose actions have important domestic consequences for ordinary people. These range from international organizations in the aid, trade, security, and humanitarian spheres; states; global corporations, which range from companies that extract valuable natural resources to global construction firms and manufacturers of goods; and humanitarian and nongovernmental organizations such as Christian and Islamic networks and Doctors without Borders.

The degree of presence and significance of these players varies according to context. When a shift from conflict to peace occurs, the presence and activities of these stakeholders usually intensifies considerably, and dozens of agencies and hundreds of NGOs generally arrive in a particular place with their own funding sources. Often responsibilities and lines of authority are unclear, which creates competing agendas and overly complex sets of relationships. These stakeholders affect the state's ability to set rules, access resources (information, knowledge, trade systems, credit, aid), and determine the way its citizens are perceived from abroad. But the dynamics of the global economy are changing so rapidly that what are sound, accepted practices in one context may have little relevance in another; advice that was appropriate ten years ago may not be relevant now. These forces do not act in harmony with one another but provide different signals and require constant adaptation and calibration. Often they arrive with conflicting agendas and compete for resources and attention. Their prescriptions have multiple rules, which results in fragmented policies, and they tend to obstruct accountability. Only the national leadership can align these forces.

Domestic players, which are equally complex, range from businesses and government agencies to armed groups and youth organizations. They may be formed around an identity or interest (e.g., ethnic groups with grievances), or they may represent students, professionals, or commercial concerns. Governments themselves can be characterized as a series of organizations, each of which hopes to maximize its position; these agencies can choose to direct their energies toward public service, personal wealth creation, or the pursuit of ethnic or tribal agendas. Networks create cross-cutting connections between and among individual organizations that crystallize around particular issues. Entrepreneurs emerge at the hubs of these networks to mediate relations between those inside and outside the country. Because the legitimate monopoly on violence is rarely ensured, armed groups that rely on the threat of violence are often a feature of weak states.

The diversity of networks and organizations that both operate on the basis of different rules and incentives and respond to different national and international constituencies inside the country generally makes for a fragmented strategy. When there is a wide range of stakeholders uncommitted to any single goal, the results are contradictory pulls and pushes and both fragmentation and confusion. Each of these players commands and makes decisions over the allocation of significant resources, which allows them autonomy of action. There is no common forum for making decisions, pooling resources, sharing information, or tracking decisions on key policy initiatives. The pursuit of subordinate goals threatens the achievement of the overall target. A weak state results when internal and external actors prove themselves incapable of aligning around the goal of sovereignty. The first phases of a sovereignty strategy therefore place a heavy burden on international stakeholders to work with the domestic players on a unified strategy and secure the division of labor and mechanisms of accountability between them. An initial stocktaking and mapping of interest groups is essential to identify the forces that will resist the creation of a sustainable state.

One of the most important resources at the disposal of international organizations (e.g., the Bretton Woods institutions, as well as leaders of other nations and corporations) is symbolic: the extension of legitimacy to a domestic player by the international system. When international agents encounter war criminals, drugs dealers, and human rights violators, they can choose whether to make them partners or enemies. While particular circumstances might justify one course of action or another, these choices have an impact on the goal of building a sovereign state.

Aligning external and internal stakeholders requires consensus building, as stakeholders jointly define overarching goals, processes, and measurements of efficiency. This requires creation of common forums across existing stovepipes to agree on common objectives. Consensus building in practice is extremely difficult in view of the fact that each organization may have several different sources of authority, financing, and accountability. Leaders in countries emerging from conflict report spending a significant proportion of their time in "coordinating the donors"—that is, aligning the panoply of external agents to national priorities. The opportunity cost is in the time not spent on managing complex domestic issues and advancing the goal of institution building.

We have defined a sovereign state as one that earns legitimacy at home and abroad by performing its critical functions in an aligned manner. The strategic goal is a fully functioning and sovereign state that is more autonomous and less dependent than before. Critical to this is an understanding that to be fully sovereign and independent, a country must be able to generate revenue self-sufficiently and exercise its sovereign functions in a capable manner. While the goal of a sovereignty strategy is the creation of state institutions that fulfill all ten core functions, the point of departure and the method of prioritization are context specific. In each country, some dimensions of sovereignty are likely to be more critical than others to establishing the state's legitimacy and effectiveness. Within the overall theme of sovereignty, leaders must establish the key priorities in terms of the functions that need to be performed and set up specific timelines.

Elevating and assigning priority to some dimensions of sovereignty, we emphasize, is only a short-term measure. The overall goal of a sovereign state cannot be accomplished without addressing all ten dimensions within a medium-term framework. People attach priority to some dimensions initially: after conditions of war, security is naturally the immediate priority. But once the problem of security is settled, people's continued trust in the process requires other functions to be fulfilled: jobs, education, health services, trade, and the creation of a functioning bureaucracy.

Local populations often state that the "quick-impact projects" designed to win their hearts and minds are disappointing in their quality. People would rather take more time to build reliable water, power, and sanitation services—or even simply to establish the state's capacity to provide an environment in which all these functions can work. An interview with a woman in Mazar-e-Sharif in northern Afghanistan in February 2002 bore this out. Observing the large white Land Cruisers negotiating the muddy backstreets of Mazar to count houses for food distribution, she stated that she had heard President Karzai announce that he had been given more than $4.2 billion for the reconstruction of Afghanistan. She claimed that it would be a waste to spend it on the short-term distribution of food: "Take these wasteful NGOs away. We've been hungry for twenty years," she said, "but I want my children and their children to have a better life. And the only way for that to happen is for the money to be put in a trust fund and spent on building an accountable civil service that would be able to provide for their life chances." Legitimization is a dynamic process in which success breeds further expectations.

While it is the responsibility of the sovereign authorities to ensure that the functions are carried out, both the level of government at which decision rights are vested and the capacity for making those decisions are open to appropriate design. Different actors—whether the private sector, a government agency, citizen group, civil society organization, or individual—can be mandated or contracted to implement services. The state's role is to monitor and ensure the performance of those functions, not necessarily to implement them directly. This does not suggest a highly centralized state—only one that guarantees working services for its citizens.

Since visible progress is essential for establishing momentum and building a virtuous circle, it is critical that internal and external forces create shared understanding of both the problems and the mechanisms for solving them. Failing to establish a common understanding can lead to insecurity among critical stakeholders, thereby putting the entire process at risk. It can lead to stalled development, where actions do not follow up on initial discussions. Articulating a vision and agreeing on the overarching goal are also prerequisites for partnership and progress. When sectoral strategies or small projects are not embedded in a larger strategy, unintended consequences can emerge that undermine the overall objective of state building.

Rules of the Game: Formulation, Calibration, and Adherence

Even where sovereignty has become weak in effect, the state maintains responsibility for creating and enforcing rules. Given that any state operates across multiple functions and levels of government, rules follow a hierarchy that starts with constitutions and binding conventions and ends with primary and secondary legislation and administrative manuals. Examining administration manuals at the lowest level of government reveals the actual limitations of a governmental authority. Comparing this manual to the constitution is a useful indicator of the formal alignment of these rules. When the promulgation of new legislation is not accompanied by an organized process for annulling previous legislation or removing contradictions between laws, confusion and delays can result.

Unlike previous centuries, during which the legal practices of any country could be fairly autonomous from external influences, law making must now take account of an increasing consensus on a set of standards that are becoming global. Misalignment with these principles can prove costly in terms of direct private-sector investment. The corollary to this is that the state has less autonomy in choosing the laws it wishes to enact. There is a benefit, however. Today the opportunities for cross-country learning and collaboration are much greater; thus, the more common these standards are, the more regional and global trade, as well as economic integration and participation in global supply chains, can occur. The experience of European integration and accession are two examples of harmonization of laws and standards that promote economic growth. Given the fragmented nature of the international system, external actors need to recognize, acknowledge, and partner with the state to make sure that they reinforce, rather than undermine, coherent rule making.

Institutions are the "rules of the game," which structure and incentivize behavior. In practice, these rules remain imperfect, and, regardless of a country's degree of development, there is never a perfect fit between the formal rules (which exist on paper and in the statute books) and informal ones (which people follow on a daily basis).[3] Trust in a system, however, is dependent on the degree of fit between these formal and informal rules. As each of the ten functions is an institution, by necessity a series of "rules" defines the "game." They determine the resources, the boundaries between legitimate and illegitimate actions, the processes through which players can join the game, incentives for playing by the rules, and sanctions for violations. For any game to be played repeatedly there must be a process for closure—a mechanism for binding decision making on whether the participants have played and won by the rules.

In developed countries, most rules have been routinized over decades if not centuries, which is the reason the population often assumes them to be stable and unalterable. When rules have not been in play for a long period of time, stakeholders are more likely to contest them because they believe they can be altered. Since repetition of play generates trust, it can be useful to devise benchmarks and ensure their fulfillment; doing so reinforces the sense that rules are in fact being followed.

A country in active conflict is by definition a country without a consensus on the rules of the game. The first task in moving a country from conflict to stability is to formulate rules to ensure that stakeholders acknowledge each other's claims within a framework of politics rather than violence. Peace agreements often constitute the vehicle for securing such an agreement. Their content reveals the often-detailed nature of the central issues of contention in a society and mechanisms for their resolution. The degree to which the specific provisions of peace agreements are implemented constitutes a path toward either stability or renewed conflict.[4]

In Africa we have repeatedly seen the renewal of conflict despite peace agreements on paper, while in Central America peace agreements by and large have held. In Central America (El Salvador and Guatemala are the prime examples), ruling elites agreed to enter into genuine discussions with their armed opponents to end civil war. They accepted some painful restructurings of the security sector and allowed their armed opponents to turn into political parties that could compete in—and perhaps win—elections. Sufficient change took place to make people stakeholders in the new arrangements. The economic and social promises have not been realized, and inequality and crime are still significant problems, but the countries have avoided a resumption of civil wars.

In contrast, peace agreements in the 1990s in African countries such as Sierra Leone and Liberia essentially entailed the surrender of the state to armed militias, whose formal induction into the state did not result in a citizen-oriented process of movement toward stability. The peace agreement in Cambodia explicitly envisaged the creation of a democratic system, which the United Nations was to mediate through the assumption of special powers during a transitional period. In practice, however, corruption levels mushroomed, and the international community increasingly had to lower its goals and ultimately accept what has been widely interpreted as a coup d'état by Hun Sen.[5]

Time is a resource that can be divided into meaningful segments. Stakeholders have an incentive to wait for the next segment because they might then have an opportunity to alter the balance of forces in their favor. This encourages them to remain within the field of play. Should the time horizon be too long, it might create incentives for some of the stakeholders to play the spoiler. On the other hand, should the segments be too short, the players will focus on tactical maneuvering rather than on the goal of building capacity for performing functions that would move them toward the goal of sovereignty.

The Bonn Agreement in Afghanistan set the following two distinctive phases of transition. The first involved the transfer of power to an interim administration for six months. The second called for the election of an emergency grand council to choose a head of state and key positions in the transitional government; it further required the appointment of a constitutional commission to draft a constitution, the election of a constitutional convention to debate and adopt a constitution, direct presidential elections to elect a president, and parliamentary elections. At each stage the agreement provided citizens with means by which to assess, participate in, and monitor progress.

Making the rules of the game adhere necessarily means bringing in an ever-increasing number of stakeholders and opening up the possibility of new alliances among the existing stakeholders. If cross-cutting ties between stakeholder groups can develop, then incentives for playing by the rules become greater than the desire among factions to achieve short-term gains. Here the rules' fairness and inclusiveness are critical. Selection procedures for key leadership and management positions can ensure access to positions on an even-handed basis, which can increase the perception, as well as the fact, of state inclusiveness. Fair contracting processes, asset sales, and licenses are crucial for creating legitimate private-sector interest groups. Forums for discussion on key policy issues similarly offer opportunities to engage stakeholder groups and broaden the state's inclusiveness. As the next chapter explains, national programs provide a mechanism for involving ever-larger segments of the population in a collective endeavor.

Without interaction, people often assume that other groups have fixed interests and positions. People do not necessarily adhere to those attributed concerns; they cannot be assigned a rigid perception of their interest based only on their sociological category. By bringing stakeholder groups together through what we call "critical stakeholder inquiry" to examine the country's present condition and possible futures, individuals and groups can perceive their concerns in very different ways. In Nepal we facilitated intensive discussions with a wide cross-section of stakeholders in 2006 and 2007 and identified the key issues that the groups could agree upon. These talks revealed each group's willingness to reimagine its place in a new Nepal that would be more inclusive, democratic, and stable. As a result, representatives from different groups formed a national visioning team to begin to flesh out a common strategy for the country.

The need to calibrate the rules of the game usually arises when new stakeholders have emerged that do not have a place within the existing rules, when a disruption occurs in the balance of forces between stakeholders who had initially agreed on a set of rules, or when the informal rules depart radically from the formal ones and thereby make a mockery of the latter. There are many unhappy examples of this: Afghanistan in the 1990s, Liberia, Mexico during the Chiapas revolt, the Philippines during the Moro revolt, the Caucasus and southern Sudan before the Comprehensive Peace Agreement, and Darfur. In these situations, the possibility of violence looms large. A willingness to recalibrate rules is critical for avoiding conflict and restoring trust in the formal system. In contrast, the separation of the Czech Republic and Slovakia (often referred to as the "velvet divorce") stands as an impressive example of political leadership in resolving a disagreement.

Under these conditions a referee is clearly needed. Typically, the appointment of a special representative to a country by the Secretary General of the United Nations opens up an opportunity for international and domestic participants to alter the existing rules of the game. The effectiveness of the referee depends on both the degree of support from the major players in the international system and an acknowledgment of the time horizon necessary for reutilizing the rules of the game. Early disengagement and a quick declaration of victory have often resulted in resumed violence—hence the need to learn the lessons from those postconflict countries where initial enthusiasm gave way to despair and further hostilities. East Timor is a prime example of a relatively quick exit by the international community that has not resulted in sustained peace. In contrast, in Kosovo and Bosnia, the absence of an agreement on the future political settlement means that international forces that were initially deployed for a short time are still there a decade later.

While in many cases the mechanism for refereeing progress is allocated to the United Nations in the form of a special representative and specifically designed mission, the accession process of the European Union provides for an alternative type of refereeing. In this process, intensive monitoring missions take place in order to assess progress in the adoption and implementation of the body of rules that form the *acquis communautaire*. This is the set of laws, procedures, and practices a country must adopt in order to enter into negotiation with and ultimately join the European Union. An external referee may be essential for bringing the process to closure. For example, the referee can declare an electoral process either legitimate or illegitimate (the EU played this role in the Ukrainian elections of 2005). Once the rule of law takes hold, refereeing then becomes internal to the system and obviates the need for an external arbiter.

Mobilization of Resources

The mobilization of resources has largely been equated with the convening of a donor conference, where donors pledge to make financial resources available, usually for a short period of time. The emphasis is nearly always on financial capital, which is usually spent inefficiently through multiple contracting chains. External financial resources are sometimes necessary but never sufficient in themselves to catalyze sustainable development. The resources (or stocks) are much broader. Most countries that we perceive as poor possess impressive actual and potential resources. They usually have both existing domestic resources and, through the use of imagination and the regulatory power of government, the possibility of creating new ones.

Rarely do leaders take a comprehensive view of all of the available forms of capital. In every country a range of capitals can be put to work if appropriately harnessed. As we saw in chapter 2, states can generate an enhanced stock of capitals to transform their political and economic outlook. These include human capital, social capital (trust and goodwill), information, physical infrastructures, natural capital (e.g., forests, water, air, minerals, land), and social and institutional capital. Mobilizing resources effectively requires a coherent, multilevel approach; an understanding of the interdependence among resources; communication with the primary stakeholders—the people; and the maintenance of momentum by carefully managing and sequencing the use of assets.

An example of untapped domestic resources is the wealth possessed by expatriates—citizens who have been forced into exile in other countries. The challenge is to find ways to translate this money into active financial capital in their home countries through investment and financial management vehicles such as venture capital funds and risk guarantees. And it is not only Afghans in exile who are wealthy; in Afghanistan in 2003 we estimated that hundreds of millions of dollars in savings existed that people kept in their houses; if this wealth had been deposited in banks, it could have been recycled through the Afghan economy to create jobs. Instead of making the money work for Afghanistan, dozens of Afghans a day would fly to Dubai and queue up to put their money into storage there.

Other untapped domestic resources include the potential to develop tourism and cultural heritage industries or to nurture domestic markets and export industries. Domestic markets have often been viewed from the perspective of the obstacles to production within the country. Instead, were they to be seen from the perspective of global access and the value chain that makes that access possible, the untapped resources could be utilized both more effectively and sustainably. Removal of legal impediments to exports to rich countries is a necessary but not sufficient action. Active development of the value chains and marketing arrangements is essential to utilize the latent potential of the country's economy.

Transparent licensing of goods and services—for example, mobile phone licensing—offers a country an opportunity not only to provide services for poor people but also to raise revenue through significant license fees and taxes. In Afghanistan in 2002, while the UN advised that donors pay Ericsson tens of millions to provide phones and AT&T asked the government for $60 million in fees, a transparent licensing program resulted in revenues of more than $800 million for the government. At the same time, this arrangement has resulted in the provision of more than 2.5 million mobile phones and coverage of 70 percent of the country. The allocation of mobile phone licenses was designed to ensure the broadest geographic spread and accessibility to communications services. This policy resulted in the award of two licenses through a fair tender process in 2002 and was followed by the award of two more licenses in 2006. When this program began in 2002, there were only one hundred mobile phones (courtesy of the United Nations) in the country. At the beginning of 2006 the number of subscriptions had risen to 1.5 million, and telecommunication companies contributed a significant amount of domestic revenue. This program has resulted in more than $550 million in private-sector investment. Design of the spectrum and internet policy for the country followed suit.

A country's mineral wealth can also be put to work. Here again, the real issue is how to license the mineral extraction so that the royalties will benefit the population and not the ruling elite—for future as well as current generations. A transparent process for using geological surveys to assess a country's natural resources, as well as preparation of concessions for the extractive industry through transparent regulatory systems, will be critical. Adding value to the minerals in a country—for example through jewelry making, marble polishing, steel making—is another way to increase the value of a resource for the people of that country.

The common thread running through these examples is the value of organizational and institutional capital. When the power of rules is harnessed to the creation of resources and when these rules are enforced through credible organizational capacity, the public becomes the major beneficiary. While basic infrastructure is necessary, early and focused investment on the enhancement of organizational capability through the formation of local stakeholders in the process can have immense payoffs for stability. Human capital is the lifeblood of society. But how human capital can be used—or dissipated—can vary greatly depending on the educational and employment opportunities created. The same individuals might become surgeons or drivers or simply be left to their own devices. Judicious use of existing infrastructure and careful planning of new infrastructure that will create the right linkages and synergies can prevent costly mistakes. The same building can be a school, a community center, or a weapons depot for local warlords.

The world has at its disposal a far greater array of resources than development agencies realize when they commit taxpayers' money at a donors' conference. The stocks of knowledge that are contained in its universities and corporations, the knowledge of supply chain management (all the way to the stocking of its supermarket shelves), its risk guarantees and other financial instruments, and its ability to facilitate regional synergies and preferential trading access are examples of the other types of resources that a country can mobilize, ones that could bring exponentially more value than the aid packages that are presently the norm. For example, reform of the port at Karachi, where transit goods destined for Afghanistan were routinely delayed for up to six months, could have been worth hundreds of millions of dollars over a five-year period to Afghanistan in terms of price stability and predictability. Similarly, reform of the Port of Sudan in the north of Sudan could have significant impact on integrating the diverging economies of the north and south while reducing the costs of basic goods and services for the population. If Eritrea and Ethiopia could agree, Eritrea's port could become the major port for East Africa.

The most significant resource is the goodwill and trust of the people. The vicious circle of violence and corruption could be reversed if leaders systematically set about creating and enhancing social capital through a process of constant communication, popular participation in the establishment of priorities and understanding constraints, and delivering on progress. If this underlying trust between leadership and citizens is absent, then even though figures might indicate a mirage of progress—that is, the number of roads built and clinics constructed— the roads might be terrorized by gangs and the clinics might lie empty of medical staff and supplies, and the tectonic plates beneath might be colliding. Legitimacy, in these circumstances more than ever, is a process and not a one-time event derived from a day of elections. Maintaining the trust and optimism of a population takes hard and continuous work. Distrust can emerge very rapidly. Once lost, regaining momentum is both difficult and expensive.

Designation of Critical Tasks

A critical task is an activity that, if implemented, furthers the goal of the sovereignty strategy. It forms the mechanism for translating the goal into outcomes on the ground by mobilizing people and resources and implementing processes. Within an organization or a country, it requires specifying what must be delivered, to whom, when, how, and at what cost. A leader or manager must prioritize certain tasks as critical, to map these priorities and provide focus while using the same critical tasks to create further capacity. Typically (and especially in a crisis) everything is treated as an emergency. Leaders must instead decide what is actually critical to success and develop a process for moving forward. One of the highest priorities is to put management itself on a predictable course by ensuring orderly decision making. One could argue that a president, cabinet member, and other key leaders should devote as much as 50 percent of their time to these issues.

In an unstable context, the leadership's attention is usually consumed by reactions to emergencies. In Khartoum, the leaders complained that more than 70 percent of their time was spent in crisis management. Similarly, when we met John Garang in Cairo in 2005, just before he became president of South Sudan, he admitted to being overwhelmed by the thousands of decisions that had to be made on a weekly basis. Instead of focusing on two thousand small decisions, focusing on six major decisions—or critical tasks—could break this logjam. As we write, the entire attention of Nepal's political leadership is centered on questions of political settlement rather than on reaching agreement on fundamental issues: restructuring the state, making development inclusive, and facilitating the market. Leadership may have good reason to focus on issues of the legal foundations for a long-term settlement. But the population will have no confidence in the leaders if they do not show credible signs of moving toward implementation of some of their promises. This has been made abundantly clear by the renewed violence of the Madhesi movement—the ongoing challenge to the Nepalese peace settlement from the residents of the Terai plains, who are widely considered to be Indian immigrants.

The hierarchical, bureaucratic model that we have inherited from earlier times is fundamentally unsuited to the current context in general and the state-building agenda in particular. Faced with constant revolutions in the business context, companies have reacted to the need for flexible and responsive organizations by increasingly empowering individuals and developing mechanisms to enhance cooperation and collective problem solving around critical tasks. The private sector has thus taken the lead in rethinking the nature of power through models of participation, cooperation, and collaboration. Such lessons can and should be applied to the state-building agenda, which desperately needs to build institutions that can foster stability and growth in their own specific context. Institutions are needed that can recognize and overcome the constraints that their own procedures and routines create.[6]

A famous example of this trend in the private sector is the Toyota production system. Toyota produced a leaner production system by testing existing processes in order to identify weaknesses and then apply "root cause analysis" to eliminate them. This process, designed to relax constraints on production on a continuous basis, departs from traditional production methods. Workers and managers cooperate to understand and improve processes and create overall synergies rather than remaining confined to fixed spheres in which they do not comprehend each other's work. A culture of teamwork across both functional areas and the lines of hierarchy is the essence of the organization's philosophy.

The process of learning to identify constraints produces solutions that in themselves engender new standards and therefore collective learning. The process of "bootstrapping" in this way remains underutilized in the field of development in general and state and institution building in particular.

The experience of Fundación Chile provides some intimation of the possibilities that flow from approaching an economy in terms of a theory of relaxing constraints. The foundation was created as a nonprofit corporation by the Chilean government in 1976 and initially, as a result of poor leadership and undefined priorities, provided only limited social services—school lunches, nutrition for infants—and then telecommunications equipment and other foodstuffs, for which the markets were incipient. However, the economic shock of 1982 created favorable conditions for domestic investment, and Fundación Chile noticed a niche in the salmon farming industry. Through intelligent mobilization of its resources, it supported what is now a $600 million per annum export business. Subsequently, the foundation began to co-venture with outside partners, increase the technological complexity of its projects (and thereby create networks among external associates), and ensure that the project selection mechanism generally became more competitive. Fundación Chile adopted a process of careful, continuous comparison against the best performers in the field to identify winning start-ups.

To ensure maximum inputs, fledgling businesses were advised on how to remove obstacles to creating clusters. As each new enterprise grew, greater synergy was generated, through removing constraints to the success of the whole, than would have been produced by isolated investments. And as each start-up is reinforced by success in other parts of the chain, the risk of failure is substantially reduced.[7]

The idea that the state-building agenda entails easing constraints on state institutions implies an approach that would see a variety of factors, including current wisdom on how to promote growth, as potential restrictions on the production of effective institutions. Rather than adhering to a model of state building that stipulates a priori both the institutions and the mechanisms for their creation, this approach encourages piecemeal, context-specific innovations and seeks to apply successes in this area to other problems. George Marshall, Lee Kwan Yew, the Irish leadership in the 1990s, and governors in the United States did not have all of the steps worked out when they embarked on the process of transformation; they had a general vision of their desired destination and then learned by trial and error.

This line of reasoning also suggests that the hierarchical concept of bureaucracy, which views individuals as automatons is out of synch with a conception of state building in the current context. The private sector has taken the lead in rethinking the nature of participation, cooperation, and the exercise of power by increasing individual empowerment and finding mechanisms that enhance collective problem solving.

The constraint-relaxing model we describe employs root cause analysis, a method of isolating problems in an existing system, identifying their causes, and proposing alternative strategies for overcoming them. The process of detecting difficulties is vital to reconfiguring the institution so that it systematically identifies and remedies other obstacles. All of this requires performance measures. In the case of the state-building agenda, these performance measures derive from using state functions to measure the sovereignty gap and tracking the critical tasks that must be accomplished for each function to be performed effectively.

Mandating Leaders and Managers

The kind of leadership and management needed for the state-building project in the contemporary world requires capabilities that are different from those historically associated with the classic state builders in the modern period. That model's features included strict hierarchical command and control, concentration of decision making in one person, refusal to enter into cooperative relationships, the monopolization of information, and secrecy. Today leaders must demonstrate that they can forge and maintain international partnerships for generating legitimacy in the international system and opportunity in the economy, understand and navigate the opportunities and constraints of globalization, and maintain the trust and loyalty of citizens at home by generating a belief that the state can enhance their lives and capabilities. They must be able to conceive of an architecture of change that operates across functions on global, national, and local levels. They must show their citizens that they can participate in the world as respected global leaders, as well as representatives of distinctive cultural identities.

Leadership in this context is a double task that involves inspiring and rallying people around a vision and mobilizing their latent energies and capabilities for the common good. Leaders must set goals that both government organizations and broader society can identify with; to be truly viable, the public must participate in the project of state building. With information technology, the public at large can join in both setting goals and monitoring their progress, thereby avoiding the expensive technical processes of monitoring. This also empowers ordinary people to become judges of and participants in the process of implementation.

Leaders must allocate decision rights and responsibilities for critical tasks with great care. The charge of management is then to design processes that implement these duties transparently, effectively, and accountably and to assure the public that this is the case. The indicators of transparency and effectiveness must therefore be straightforward enough to engage the public's attention. Management's invisible assignment, which involves preparation, planning, securing of resources, and setting of priorities, will remain hidden from the public's view, so there must be sufficient delivery on the ground to establish trust (or at least communication) with the public to ensure appreciation for their unseen work.

The literature on business administration contains lessons for the project of state building.[8] The most important of these are that a goal set by principals must be desirable, feasible, and credible and that leaders must be attuned to the discipline of implementation by continuously identifying and removing constraints. A leadership and management team must share the same objective and trust each other sufficiently to be able to improvise solutions for unexpected outcomes.

Designing processes to identify, motivate, and ensure the quality of other leaders is essential, and early wins are critical to achieving a sense of momentum.

When we spoke to Ed Breen, CEO of Tyco International, we noted striking similarities between his job in rebuilding trust in Tyco after a massive management scandal had damaged its share price and the task of the leadership of Sudan, Nepal, and Afghanistan in building or restoring citizens' trust in their leadership. Breen stated that his priority was to reinstate confidence among stakeholder groups—shareholders, employees, suppliers, customers, the public—in Tyco's credibility. He focused first on recruiting a top team of leaders and an intermediate team of managers and established a sense of trust both internally and externally before resuming business as usual.

A time horizon for transforming grand visions into more concrete deliverables is essential if ideas are not to remain pipe dreams or become nightmares. Attention to the discipline of detail in implementation is particularly important for this reason. Leaders cannot delegate implementation and remain satisfied with simply being strategists of the grand vision. Rather, they must monitor the detail to ensure that the overall plan is on course. Credibility is established by results. A results-based culture of management evolves and becomes routinized only when leaders focus on a delimited number of accomplishments on the ground.[9]

A simple test of this is the follow-up a government makes on its promises. In China, the leadership ensured the systematic accomplishment of projects with the World Bank through careful documentation, management, and follow-up. One of the country's largest dams on the Yellow River was finished two years ahead of schedule and several hundred million dollars under cost. Hundreds of officials attended major briefings on the project, and dozens of administrators from provincial governments went to Washington, D.C., to become familiar with World Bank procedures. As a result of this intense scrutiny, officials in meetings were able to refer to clauses agreed upon years before, and officials from capital to county had a full understanding of their responsibilities and took pride in their fulfillment.

In Rwanda, President Paul Kigame's leadership has acquired a reputation for follow-up throughout the various levels of government. Consequently, as a visitor from the United States recently told us, when Kigame makes an agreement, all the relevant ministers are informed of the decision and understand their responsibilities for fulfillment of those promises. By contrast, in some other countries, every minister gives a different story, and officials rarely bother to follow up on promises; as a result, speeches by leaders mean nothing in practice.

Reflexive Monitoring of the Implementation Process

Institutions are not machines composed of mechanical parts but ongoing human relationships in which unintended consequences of action may occur. Also, when a context changes, the understanding of it has to alter as well because approaches designed for one context are likely to be ineffective in another. We are clearly living in an era of rapid change. People have an inherent capacity for critical reflection and to draw lessons from experience so that they do not repeat mistakes or misjudgments. Therefore, building reflexive monitoring mechanisms to allow for a calibration of policies through constant evaluation is critical to ensuring progress toward the goal of building an increasingly sovereign—and functional—state.

Because the citizens of a country are the most important judges and juries in deciding whether the rules are legitimate, it is essential to report to them on a regular basis on progress toward the overall vision and subordinate goals. It is also necessary to find ways to obtain citizen feedback in order to calibrate the strategy and enhance the citizens' trust. Recognizing and providing voice to legitimate interest groups are two of the most effective ways of ensuring feedback loops and detecting general patterns and moods early on. The Ottawa 2020 Talent Plan builds in an annual report card to measure indicators such as "reduction of the employment gap between internationally trained professionals and Canadian born and trained professionals" as a measure of "a caring and inclusive city" and a reduction in "the gap between the highest and lowest 10% of household income" as a measure of "an innovative city where prosperity is shared by all."

The Double Compact in Practice

Two problems lie at the heart of relations between developing countries and developmental institutions. The capacity of governments to represent their people has diminished significantly and has weakened or even severed the bond between the citizen and the state. Formally, the governments of developing countries are given the legitimacy and voice to speak on behalf of their people. Substantively, however, the relationship has not been one of principals and agents but of rulers and ruled or even predatory agents preying on their people. This in turn is the basis of the second problem: the absence of an effective partnership between governments and global organizations for the creation of functioning state and market institutions that are oriented toward increasing citizens' economic and political enfranchisement. In practice, developmental bodies have too often depended upon strategies that attempt to drive reforms that, although designed to create strong associations, have failed because they have not been part of an integrated architecture of institutional change.

The conception of strategy that we have outlined repositions the international system as a catalyst and genuine partner in a process of enhancing state capabilities rather than as a competitor or a mechanism through which to substitute for state services. This conception of strategy draws inspiration from the best examples of collective arrangements and the idea of shared sovereignty to argue for a model of co-production of public value by citizens, nations, and international organizations. That is to say, a multistakeholder compact of sorts is necessary. Within the broad categories of citizen, nation-state, and international organization exists a wide array of different groupings that must, at a fundamental level, agree to work together through common rules and processes.

One way to approach the idea of this multistakeholder agreement is to employ the concept of a "double compact," which allows us to think about the intricate relationships among all of the stakeholders in any given country in simple, linear terms. Viewing sovereignty broadly as a set of both rights and obligations between citizens and their government, as well as between a government and the international community, the double compact expresses the web of rights and obligations that defines the functioning state. Beginning with a functioning state and market as a goal, such an approach would identify the constraints that prevent the attainment of an objective and then prepare and launch specific programs to overcome or change the restrictions. Instead of isolated projects or imposed adjustment programs, the focus of such a method would be upon systemwide coherence and the production of synergies that would make the whole greater than the sum of the parts.

In the case of Afghanistan, we proposed this mechanism in the design of the Bonn Agreement and then the National Development Framework and "Securing Afghanistan's Future." These not only envisaged a long-term program of public investments by the international community but also obliged the Afghan government to adhere to certain standards through the implementation of a series of national programs.

This compact was endorsed by sixty-two foreign and finance ministers in Berlin in 2004 and was the basis of the design of the London Compact, which was endorsed in 2006. From 2001 to 2004 leaders from Afghanistan and the international community, in partnership with citizens, focused relentlessly on meeting the political benchmarks agreed and conceiving and putting into operation national programs that would bring visible benefits to citizens while encouraging their participation. At the same time, much invisible work focused on the preparation of future plans and recruiting, training, and nurturing new leaders and managers. Recently, despite difficulties with completion and a loss of momentum, sober reflections on the way forward by both the Afghan government and the international community have brought about a renewed emphasis on the double compact and the national programs (described in the next chapter) as vehicles that provide a path to peace and stability. Significantly, the exercise has become a model for a number of other subsequent initiatives around the world.

Implementation of a double compact requires clear decisions on sequencing. As certain actions are prerequisites to others, the interrelationship between tasks needs to be determined. Early focus on developing capabilities in accountability and policy formulation are crucial to success in areas such as service delivery or infrastructure provision. For example, provision of payment and monitoring systems are prerequisites for every government service. Thus, under such a strategy, some of the social functions could initially be contracted out to non-state providers until the government acquires the capability to provide the service efficiently.

Reporting on achievements will facilitate learning from successes and failures and provide a basis for moving forward on other necessary actions. Reporting must become a learning activity that allows for innovation and experimentation with new paths; the strategy cannot be fully worked out from the beginning. The process of reporting enhances government leaders' credibility with both citizens and their international partners and thereby allows the officials to take more adventurous steps as time goes on.

This compact would delineate a series of roles for international actors in support of the strategy. They could shift their focus from managing parallel systems that substitute for state functions to becoming coproducers, catalysts, and referees of local systems, with a focus on building the state. Initially, the effective performance of functions will require active partnership and coproduction and would therefore call for skills in strategic governance. The roles can range from catalyst and adviser to referee and monitor and will depend both on context and on which function is primary. Honing such strategic skills require a constant exchange of experience between international and national civil servants and the creation of professional networks of interaction. Global foundations could become partners for this enterprise by creating forums for recognizing innovation and promoting investments in public-sector leadership.

The compacts could also explain where the international system might in some cases serve as a substitute provider for certain state services and functions. However, they would demarcate the specific duration and scope of responsibilities for substitution and provide a clear exit plan whereby the state would progressively take over responsibility for the substituted function. For example, in states where domestic law-and-order institutions are being established, peacekeepers might be deployed until certain standards have been met within the state's own police and security forces. External financial management and procurement agents might be contracted to manage a country's finances in the short term, provided that the agents receive significant incentives to build domestic capacity and hand over functions to a state-operated ministry of finance. Education and health services might be organized through the nongovernmental sector, UN agencies, or private contracts, but those services should be governed by and performed within the framework of national health and education policy.

People all over the world are demanding both effectiveness and efficiency in the use of public resources, but this cannot come about without a coherent double compact to align interests and allow for coproduction. For the agreement to work, the budget must be the mechanism that underpins all policy making. And it has become clear that weak public financial management is the key constraint to the effective expenditure of either government or donor financing and thus a major barrier to the development of such compacts.[10]

Our reviews of dysfunctional countries reveal a number of pathologies that require urgent attention if public or private investment is to improve living standards. Studies in many sub-Saharan African countries indicate that up to 90 percent of public investment does not reach its intended targets.[11] The gap exists not only in practice but is also inherent in support for policy making among bilateral and multilateral donors, NGOs, and the consulting industry. Requests between 2001 and 2005 from the Afghan Ministry of Finance to each of these entities did not yield practical, holistic policy advice. Moreover, our investigation of experiences in the field indicates that actionable, systemic "how to" guides or analysis on public finance functions do not exist either in whole or in part. Much better expenditure mechanisms are necessary for governments to spend revenues effectively and equitably. These must be based on the following six components that we call "National Accountability System":

1. Treasury. The key problem in a treasury system is the lack of predictability, transparency, and timeliness in the settlement of payments for civil service wages, goods, and services. In many countries, sizeable amounts of state funds are siphoned off for illegitimate purposes, and many thousands of separate accounts are maintained.

2. Budget. In most developing countries, the budget is not the central tool of policy making; it is neither aligned to the citizens' interests on paper nor implemented in practice. Investment, operations, and maintenance are not aligned, and in practice much of the budget disappears in the travel costs of senior politicians. The challenge is to make the budget function as the chief instrument of policy making, goal setting, and monitoring of results.

3. Procurement. Procurement is often viewed as a backroom function, yet this subfunction is at the heart of corruption. The way in which goods and services are procured and contracts are written and monitored may allow for significant monies to be siphoned off and contractors not to complete their projects. International organizations such as the World Bank have attempted to import their own rules to countries without taking into account their capabilities and legal contexts.

4. Accounting and auditing. Accounting and auditing provide a basis for compliance monitoring. Neither, however, has developed standardized methods that reflect the realities of often informal systems, and international organizations tend to turn again and again to the same three international firms, which do not necessarily offer value for money or adapt to the realities of local context. The challenge is to create auditing and accounting conventions and practices that can act as accountability mechanisms for domestic expenditure.

5. Preparation and management of programs and projects. In developing countries, the management of both programs and projects is currently riddled with problems in the quality of preparation and implementation. The world is now awash with money, yet at the same time, an insufficient number of

programs and projects are prepared to an adequate standard; the developing world is therefore littered with failed and half-completed projects. Projects may look good on paper, but, unless they translate into successful implementation, they will not reduce poverty.

6. Oversight and accountabilities. The controls on expenditure cannot be generated only from within an administration. Parliamentary and international oversight, as well as citizen monitoring of the budget, must all play an important part. In the age of rapid advances in information technology, such an approach is not only desirable but also feasible.

Progress is not possible if implementation is not the most important concern of key stakeholders. A strategy without implementation as its centerpiece is merely a pipe dream. The often-made distinction between strategy as the focus for leaders and implementation as that for subordinates is not only false but dangerous as well. An obvious and tragic example is the failure to put a governance agenda into operation in Iraq after the 2003 invasion. A striking contrast exists between military success and the failure to sustain the legitimacy of order or to build up other state functions following the destruction of a dictatorial regime. The result has been massive loss of life, worsened living conditions, and the flight of millions of refugees in search of security. These sorts of problems are not confined to the developing world, either: witness the dysfunctional government response to Hurricane Katrina in the United States. When we spoke with people from Louisiana, their description of the patterns of waste and the state's failure to help affected communities suggested that the aid complex in Afghanistan and the "rebuilding complex" in New Orleans suffer from very similar flaws.

Simply put, implementation is a discipline that translates a vision into a goal, then turns that goal into achievable subordinate targets, and finally converts these objectives into the critical tasks necessary to achieve the original vision. Strategy making inherently balances rational planning and improvisation. Unless implementation becomes the leaders' business and strategy the concern of everybody within either an organization or a nation, the gap between plan and implementation is likely to grow only larger.[12]

National Programs

The Challenge of Implementation

C ITIZEN TRUST IN the state-building process requires increasing public confidence in the government's capacity to manage the challenges faced by society. Once actors reach consensus on a contextualized state-building strategy, they must focus on finding realistic and innovative delivery mechanisms that create a steady momentum toward the goal of a functioning state. Currently, attempts at state building falter because they fail to link intentions to these delivery systems. There is a pervasive attitude that once a policy decision is made, policy makers can shift their attention to a different topic; in fact, the real work lies in implementation. In practice, we have found that national programs provide a useful instrument for marshalling energies to translate the vision and mission for each function into credible outcomes.

ATTRIBUTES OF NATIONAL PROGRAMS

The goal of a national program is to enable a government to perform a state function throughout its territory in an effective and transparent manner by mobilizing relevant forces—government, the private sector, and/or civil society—to execute critical tasks. The process has to deliver results and build domestic capability to carry out the function in the medium to long term. National programs have the following attributes:

A Unified Set of Rules

First and foremost, they possess a unified set of rules that are promulgated, modified, and enforced by the state. Rules are thereby constitutive of an order that provides a nested hierarchy of clear decision rights that in turn provide clear allocations of roles, rights, responsibilities, and career paths for people and pathways for flows of money and information.[1] Rules become the resources that create stakeholders and determine their relations with one another. Through repeated interactions, stakeholders thereby become legitimate interest groups with rights and obligations. Heightened trust is a by-product. Rules promulgated by the state define the contours of each program's existence and duration. They allocate clear decision rights and obligations, thereby making accountabilities and sanctions possible. By establishing a predictable order bound by the rule of law, they render the system legitimate.

While tailoring to specific local conditions may be possible, to reinforce a sense of national cohesion, rules and policies in general must be national in scope and address the totality or a category of the population through a particular program or an issue that is critical to systemwide functioning. In pluralistic or divided societies (and especially given the low levels of trust that follow conflict), it is essential that people see the fairness of the process. Even when the results are fair in an objective sense, if the process itself is not considered just, more rather than less tension may arise.

Mobilized and Harnessed Assets

Tailoring to context is a key attribute of national programs. In our developmental work in countries such as Russia, Sudan, China, and Nepal we have found that the issue of capacity is not necessarily whether states can create it from scratch but whether they can mobilize existing capabilities that are dispersed and fragmented. Therefore, a key to success in the development of national programs is to identify the types of capabilities that exist among different groups and organizations in a particular place and then to create partnerships and organizational designs that can network them into collective assets. The rules establish a field of cooperation between otherwise seemingly disparate groups and, by defining new roles, functions, and responsibilities for each of them, direct their energies toward a common goal. Rules and financing flows become the mechanisms for establishing clear vehicles of accountability among these groups. As a result of clear, measurable deliverables, comparison and benchmarking become possible, and performance can be successfully ratcheted up through learning from experience.[2]

Sound Management Systems

As previously dispersed nodes of decision making are now embedded within a defined set of relationships, sound management at each level becomes crucial to the success of the whole. To begin with, the decision rights and obligations at each level must be clearly defined, and flows of resources and information must become predictable. An open system of access to information (rather than systems based on maintaining bottlenecks on information at the upper echelons) is an important criterion for the successful design and implementation of national programs. The regularity of these flows, however, depends on putting in place clear systems for budgeting, allocation, procurement, accounting, reporting, and auditing. Therefore, the human development aspect of national programs must ensure investment in the creation of skills in each of these areas through clusters of universities, businesses, and the news media with specialist knowledge. Underlying a sound management system is an effective supply chain management to ensure that goods are provided in a timely, cost-effective, and predictable way, thereby simultaneously nurturing the domestic industry. Where markets are initially either ineffective or controlled by small groups, the market must be broadened and deepened.

Social and Institutional Capital

State building has had a reputation for a legacy of elitism, in which leadership has been defined at the strategic heights and other nodes in the system have been viewed as subordinate wheels in a vast machine. Such a hierarchical notion undermines national programs, for their success depends on the creation of multiple nodes of creative leadership to solve collective problems. In this alternative view, development becomes a collective national endeavor that calls upon each citizen to participate in organized and voluntary activities in their local surroundings. Success depends on their involvement.

This approach simultaneously allows for established methods of management and leadership within a society—which typically remain hidden from the view of developmental institutions and others at the global level—and provides mechanisms for bringing new leaders to the fore. One of the desired outcomes of these programs is an established process for fostering leadership from the lowest to the highest levels of government and creating transparent career paths to which any citizen can aspire. It also allows for institutional capital, which requires systematic accountability mechanisms, to be joined with social capital, which requires trust in cooperative endeavors. The Irish spatial planning system involves setting up hubs and gateways that connect communities to the center, as well as to each other and to the global market. At the same time it carefully allocates money to each area on the basis of fair criteria; this is an example of the balance between cooperation and accountability. Finally, this approach proposes concrete methods for the transfer of decision rights involving resources that result in increasing trust in (and therefore the legitimacy of) the social and political order. This rule-bound order draws citizens into a web of mutually reinforcing rights and obligations, which is the essence of the relationship between citizens and a functioning state.

Careful Sequencing

Sequencing is the critical link between idealism and pragmatism. From conception to implementation, building a national program is a time-consuming activity that requires both the attention and the cooperation of a number of people at the highest levels of government and among international partners. Rushing to decisions before the methods of implementation and cooperation are worked out can result in unintended consequences that can undermine the program's promise or effectiveness. In our experience, the design of each of these programs requires a minimum of six to twelve months. Therefore, during this period, resisting the pressures for quick delivery requires both political courage and sound communication skills. As a result, the number of programs planned within difficult institutional environments should be limited initially and developed gradually but systematically. Catalytic mechanisms can be a useful device; external stimuli can initiate a process that then becomes sustainable over the longer term without the need for the catalyst.

Calibration over Time

Because national programs are designed to overcome both institutional and social constraints, they will require calibration over time. The more they succeed, the more their goals and their critical tasks will need to change. For example, technical assistance or external funding may be required at the beginning of a program but, with revenue enhancement and the development of human and institutional capital in the country, will become increasingly redundant. Therefore, national programs require both program- and system-level monitoring by the cabinet or presidency to ensure that the rules do not become rigid; that legitimate interest groups do not metamorphose into entrenched interests; that there is a balance between creation and redistribution of wealth; that people at lower levels of government increasingly assume responsibilities; and that officials do not assert decision rights in order to escape accountability. To direct redistributive programs to the most vulnerable, programs that reallocate resources should evolve clear procedures for targeting individuals and groups that suffer from systematic exclusion.

National Programs Need Not Mirror Government Structures

It is important to ensure that the organization of the state at the central level—its agencies and autonomous departments—is not uncritically replicated at other levels. If a plan such as Afghanistan's National Solidarity Program (NSP) exists at the local level, there is no necessary reason, for instance, for separate health, education, and extension systems to exist at the village level also.

The creation of the Internet has brought renewed attention to the role of networks as sources of innovation and value. From trading diasporas to monastic orders, networks have been a social phenomenon for millennia. As a powerful, hierarchical organization that claims the loyalties of its people, the nation-state was intended to break transnational networks and make subjects of the people. National programs are a glue—of flows of information, rules, money, and decisions—that can combine the spontaneous ingenuity of networks with the hierarchical form of priority setting and resource mobilization to harness and balance energies in relationships of mutual accountability. In national programs, citizens are not inert objects to be acted upon or delivered to but are active agents with capabilities and ideas for collective action. National programs, therefore, become a vehicle for channeling energies toward problem solving and priority setting. In this context, instead of experiencing the government as a distant phenomenon that may or may not respond to them, people take responsibility for their own life paths and discover that the chief means of solving problems lies in their own hands.

National Programs as Instruments of Transformation

Recent history bears witness to the transformative effect of national programs on people, societies, and economies. National programs have generally originated in response to an urgent, society-wide challenge and have been triggered by the vision, drive, and experience of a person or a group at a node of decision making. National programs have provided the implementation vehicles that align vision, rules, resources, and participants to achieve a common goal.

Having personally experienced the enormous barriers to movement caused by lack of infrastructure in the United States, President Dwight Eisenhower spearheaded the development of the interstate highway system in the mid-1950s. In 1919 it took him sixty-two days to cross the country, negotiating its trails and rivers as part of the U.S. Army's first transcontinental motor convoy from Washington, D.C., to San Francisco. Later Eisenhower confronted large-scale logistical issues during his tenure as supreme commander of the Allied Forces in Europe and came to appreciate the German autobahn network when the allies finally fought their way into Germany. "The old convoy," he said, "had started me thinking about good, two-lane highways, but Germany had made me see the wisdom of broader ribbons across the land."[3] As president, he dedicated himself to providing the United States with a modern infrastructure of interstate highways that would serve far more than national security purposes (in case troops had to be transported across the country quickly and efficiently).

The 1956 Federal-Aid Highway Act, the largest public works project in U.S. history to that date, provided $34 billion for the construction of a vast highway network, which now includes forty-six thousand miles of highway, fifty-five thousand bridges, and eighty-two tunnels. The transformative effect of the interstate network on the national economy, polity, and culture earned it a nickname: "the conveyor belt of society." When the highways were completed, the journey that had taken Eisenhower more than two months was cut to just two weeks. Similarly coherent visions for infrastructure have been implemented on a national scale in both Asia and Europe. In the 1960s, Japan invested heavily in the bullet train, and South Korea spent great sums on ports and highways. China is currently engaged in a massive upgrading of highways, airports, and seaports. Moreover, India requires an estimated $350 billion in infrastructure in the next decade if it is to maintain its current 8 percent growth rate.

In the United States, the 1944 GI Bill of Rights was one of the most inventive examples of investing in the human capital of a generation that had endured enormous sacrifices. This program offered grants and loans for home ownership, health care, and business creation.[4] Its greatest impact, however, was in education. Previously accessible only to a relatively small number of elites, higher education became an instrument of upward social mobility to comfortable, middle-class status and an engine for innovation. At the same time, the United Kingdom undertook a massive investment in the welfare of its citizens along the lines described in the Beveridge Report of 1942 and put into practice between 1944 and 1949.

Canada has also used national programs as an instrument for territorial integration and the creation of citizenship to overcome social, geographic, and ethnic differences. In Canada, what Keith Banting calls "national social programs" created a network of linkages between the central government and citizens across the country that reinforced people's sense of national identity while also enhancing their trust in the state.[5] Programs originated from the central government, thereby creating loyalty to the state as a whole and mediating regional tensions. Banting argues that had the programs been controlled by other levels of administration, it is likely that the same programs would have created centrifugal rather than centripetal forces and thus exacerbated differences between groups.

Addressing the nature of the spatial divide has been the focus of European social policy through distinctive programs called structural and cohesion funds. The key lesson here is that programs need not bring about permanent entitlements for individuals but may focus on lifting key constraints and inequalities between regions. The programs set rules at the level of the European Union and provide criteria for allocation, releasing funds for activities ranging from rural development and infrastructure to telecommunications and skills training. Citizens, organizations, and local governments apply for this funding through bottom-up processes. The explicit aims of these programs are to address inequalities and promote solidarity among regions, as well as to integrate regional transportation infrastructures. The process of accession to the European Union itself can be seen as a vehicle for aligning the members of the union, where acceptance of the rules of Europe—the *acquis communautaire*—leads to the reorganization of an entire corpus of political, social, and cultural relationships within each country. The European authorities then explicitly negotiate, agree upon, referee, and monitor these relationships.

Ireland was able to effect rapid social and economic transformation in the 1990s. Beginning in 1991, it set up a series of imaginative programs called area-based partnerships to strengthen relationships between the Structural and Cohesion funds of the European Union, the Irish government, and local communities, administrations, and businesses.[6] Their primary aim was not only to generate employment but also to set up processes whereby this activity would promote administrative reform and improve the connections between administrators and local communities.

After the Asian financial crisis of 1997, the World Bank partnered with the government of Indonesia to put in place a nationwide community-empowerment program, the Kecamatan Development Program (KDP), designed not only to bring benefits rapidly and directly to the population but also to enfranchise them in a new relationship to the state. The program quickly covered twenty thousand villages that were selected for inclusion according to criteria of poverty and exclusion, which were applied without exception by means of a computer program. The plan released block grants to the villages, each of which agreed to three simple rules: The village would elect a council, hold a sufficiently participatory meeting, and publish its accounts in a public place. The program has adapted over time to link the villages to other levels of governance; it is also moving to catalyze market mechanisms to create assets and incorporate distributed, alternative-energy production, both of which will occur at the village level.

These experiences provide grounds for optimism toward institutional change. Theorists such as Douglass North and Robert Putnam have argued that institutional change requires centuries of civil engagement to create trust in institutions and solidarity among citizens.[7] The examples of national programs that we have cited, by contrast, indicate that fundamental institutional change can occur within relatively short periods of time if the political and social imagination of leaders and the public rises to the challenge. These examples underline the importance of designing implementation and delivery mechanisms that position stakeholders around formal rules, from which they benefit and to which they thereafter adhere.

These examples took place in contexts in which quite sophisticated systems of government were already firmly in place. Afghanistan illustrates the other extreme. At the end of 2001, the Karzai administration, composed of what even the peace agreement itself recognized as an unrepresentative group of people, faced the task of establishing a legitimate center. We designed national programs as the key instrument for fostering citizen trust in its capacity to govern. President Hamid Karzai, in his address to the Tokyo conference of donors in January 2002 (and simultaneously in his address to the nation), stated that national programs would be the vehicle for realizing his vision. Their primary focus would be to "revive and build the State apparatus, a system of democratic governance with active participation of the citizenry."[8]

This plan envisioned successive refinements through the National Development Framework, the budget, and the development of six national-priority subprograms. The latter focused on six key areas: community empowerment; job generation; creation of an integrated transportation and communications network; health care and education services; reform of the public finance system; and development of a network of dedicated public servants. In the spring of 2004, the vision was further outlined within a comprehensive document called "Securing Afghanistan's Future," which was presented in Berlin to a group of sixty-two finance and foreign ministers from around the world. The Afghan economic team, in partnership with a group of creative international agents, focused relentlessly on implementation of this series of programs.

One of these was the National Solidarity Program, designed to empower communities to manage their own reconstruction process. The government provided block grants of between $20,000 and $60,000 to every village in the country as long as they agreed to abide by requirements that the village elect its leadership council by secret ballot, hold participatory meetings to design its own recovery plan and projects, and post its accounts in a public place. While the government set the rules and managed the finances, it contracted NGOs to manage the personnel, facilitate and support the program, organize elections at the local level, and appoint an international firm to provide management and oversight services. Thus the government provided a legal framework and finances that empowered a range of actors that included communities, international agencies, businesses, and NGOs. Four years later, the program has seen more than twelve thousand village development councils elected and more than nineteen thousand project plans approved.

The intent of the National Solidarity Program was to address the process of democratization from the ground level up, in parallel to the process of constitution making and rule writing at the center, which culminated in the first direct presidential election in Afghanistan's history. The program aimed to break the vicious cycle of relations between the government and citizens, in which successive regimes had preyed on villages and used factionalism as a mechanism to entrench a type of authoritarianism. The secret-ballot election became a vehicle for empowering men and women to elect their village councils directly and hold them accountable by means of transparent processes of decision making. It also shared the responsibility for managing and supervising the block grants.

Villages that were once the sites of neglect or predatory behavior by lower-level government functionaries were turned into the building blocks of a democratic process. Developing capable states with substantive institutional reform and democratic decision making rather than by concentrating efforts on rewriting the formal rules of democracy as embodied in elections and constitutions actually consolidates the formal institution of democracy. This focus on clearly delineated state functions and achievable, assessable outcomes may thus avert the danger of promoting flawed democratic structures without substantive democratization of government institutions and processes.

Villagers themselves have articulated the change best, calling the National Solidarity Program the "national school of reconciliation and common endeavor," the "national tablecloth," and the "national learning school." Many representatives maintain that as a result of this program they—for the first time in their lives—feel like citizens of a state, they have rights, and they are not just people who are subject to the whims of a distant authority. As the program regularly brings the village representatives together both at the provincial and national levels to exchange views and learn from one another's experiences, awareness of common problems and innovative responses have both improved immeasurably. In the process, the village councils have become the first legitimate, lobbying interest groups in the country. In their meetings with various ministers and ministry officials, the councils have pointedly judged ministerial performance against the benchmark of the National Solidarity Program. In November 2007, community delegates gathered in Kabul for a "National Convention of Communities" to share ideas with each other and the government for innovation and peace building.

Having gathered the necessary institutional and social capital and demonstrated its usefulness in the creation of infrastructure and services, the program is now ready to become the platform for a more ambitious series of undertakings at the village level. It could, for instance, easily supervise the construction of schools, clinics, and small dams, undertake agricultural extension services, or become a mechanism for the registration and formalization of property rights and dispute resolution at the village level. At a later phase, the program could become a vehicle for wealth creation by supporting village enterprises, and the program's network could disseminate knowledge to and among the villages on how to grow higher-value crops, how to market them, and when and where to sell them to the farmers' best advantage. The program could also become the basis for distributing new types of technology, including wind, microhydro, and solar mechanisms that will provide distributed-energy solutions to the villages and enable them to benefit from electricity, sanitation, and communications infrastructures without connection to physical grids. Inspired by the Rocky Mountain Institute's work, the Institute for State Effectiveness and the Clinton Global Initiative have established a joint venture to determine whether this can become a reality for a number of countries.

The National Solidarity Program was an integral component of an integrated architecture of programs to create the capability for good governance and development at various levels of government. Other programs followed suit, including the National Emergency Employment Program, which was designed to provide cash for work on rural roads and irrigation, and the National Transportation Program, whose first priority was to complete a highway and its connecting spurs to the borders, which would transform Afghanistan into a "land bridge" for central Asia, south Asia, and the Gulf. As a landlocked country, Afghanistan could use this program to become a hub for the broader region in efforts to speed up trade and transit. Upon completion of this program, the capitals of Afghanistan's central Asian neighbors would be no more than a thirty-two-hour drive from the Gulf.

A national health program focused on preventive medicine, which entailed restructuring the ministry of health to fulfill the role of regulator and enlisting NGOs for service provision. As a result, the plan was able to provide immunization to all children throughout the country. Reduction of infant, under-five, and maternal mortality rates became its key goals. In addition, a national education program resulted in a massive increase in school enrolment. This took place in a country that had, in the five years before 2001, been subject to gender apartheid: girls had been denied all access to an education.

The National Accountability and Transparency Program involved the complete transformation of the public finance system. The program began with one of the fastest-ever changes in currency. In 2001 at least three different currencies were in circulation; they were printed in different centers, only one of which was under central government control. Although virtually identical in appearance, each traded for a different value, and only the money changers could ascertain the difference between them. Furthermore, each note was virtually worthless, and several bundles of currency were required to buy basic goods. The IMF warned that the exchange would take years, and the UN advised that it would require eight thousand bureaucrats. Through careful management, however, the process of replacing the currency took only four months. The secret was to identify the strengths in the existing society. A network of *hawala* dealers (Afghan money traders), whose reach spread across the countryside, already existed. When asked to help on behalf of the nation, they rapidly organized the collection and then burned and replaced the old money.

This reform was followed by others. By overhauling the budget process (through which the budget became the central policy instrument), execution could be measured against priorities, and a single treasury account could provide budget support. The treasury management system was strengthened by the use of computerized check issuance, which allowed for real-time reporting of all expenditures. Additionally, revenue collection was improved through custom reforms such as simplified tariff regimes, and a focus on compliance and enforcement (particularly for the largest tax-paying entities) was instituted. Finally, support for the banking system was established by enacting a modern legal framework for a two-tier banking system and by restructuring the central bank.

These changes were driven by delivering timely and detailed reports on revenue and expenditure—backed by improvements in the accounting and auditing systems—to the cabinet, the national delegates at the constitutional *loya jirgas* (grand councils), the news media, and the public.[9] The reports explained that technical assistance was no substitute for domestic leadership and that underpinning each of these reforms was a team of Afghan reformers who were recruited through a merit-based process and carefully nurtured and supported. In turn, they learned how to design and implement reforms by studying the experiences of their near and far neighbors in South Africa, Iran, and Singapore.

In terms of levels of government, Afghanistan is organized by district, province, municipality, and capital. To build the government's legitimacy as a whole, gaining the citizens' loyalty was an absolute requirement, and it would inevitably be determined by their interaction with the lowest government functionaries. Recognizing that this level of government could be either the weakest or the strongest link in the chain, the Afghanistan Stabilization Program provided sound governance at both the district and the provincial levels. The program provided an integrated complex of government buildings and modern communications infrastructures that allowed the local offices to communicate with the center and with one another; it also facilitated the recruitment and training—on the basis of transparent criteria—of civilian administrators and police officials. Progress on this program was uneven at first because the aid system had declined to fund the program. The World Bank refused to finance it under the Afghanistan Reconstruction Trust Fund because some of the areas in which it might operate could prove to be too dangerous for World Bank staff. Other donors refused because the funding of government buildings did not fit their criteria of poverty-reducing programs. As a result, the then minister of the interior chose not to promote the program.

A number of other programs, designed to bring transparent and effective management to Afghanistan's governance system and to address vocational training, civil aviation, private-sector development, transparent licensing, supply-chain management, and urban management, were also not advanced because a new leadership team—put in place in early 2005—decided to drop the concept of national programs in favor of letting the aid complex control the reconstruction process.

Each of the programs was designed to create a network of relationships and stakeholders with a vested interest in Afghanistan's movement toward prosperity and stability and simultaneously to demonstrate to the citizens that the government was incrementally—but coherently—addressing their needs. Combined, the programs were beginning to create a network of rights and obligations between citizens and government, citizens and firms, and firms and the government that would give the country a real chance to create internally generated development. Despite the tolerance of warlords and abuses of authority by people who had helped overthrow the Taliban, the country was able to create a momentum that resulted in massive popular participation in the first presidential election in the country's history. In December 2004 there was domestic and international consensus that Afghanistan was moving forward. Yet, despite this, the implementation of certain national programs was subverted by interest groups, or perhaps they failed to gain momentum because of lack of Afghan ownership and leadership or insufficient knowledge and understanding on the part of one or more international organizations.

Neither the Afghan government and people nor the international community alone could have managed this process. The programs, however, broke significant new ground on a model of partnership that changed the mold of aid effectiveness. They engaged a number of actors, ranging from international program managers, Afghan officials, NGOs, the private sector, and Afghan stakeholders, who formed various alliances, partnerships, and coalitions. Surprisingly, a group that made an immense contribution to the design and implementation of the national programs was the Canadian military. The Canadian officers' strategic planning capabilities and facilitation skills enabled them to think outside the conventions of aid and humanitarian industries, to reason backward from a goal of a stable Afghanistan to the realities on the ground, and to partner with the Afghan team.

Such initiatives require a model of co-production and cooperation. In case our description of programs in Afghanistan or the key requisites of national programs conveys an image of a preconceived order or a dogmatic view that was arrived at through abstract reasoning, we emphasize that the endeavor required not only intense discussion and negotiation but also agreement and cooperation among people from very diverse perspectives and backgrounds. These same people were motivated by a desire to render service to the citizens of a country that had been devastated by foreign invasion, civil war, and severe natural disasters. The key participants not only drew on their collective review of successful programs and projects at the World Bank and other developmental institutions but also engaged in systematic consultation exercises with villagers, civil society, and other people from across the country.[10]

NATIONAL PROGRAMS VERSUS OTHER APPROACHES

National programs work because they support sovereignty, enhance government capacity to perform functions, balance priorities, and are accountable to the people. The distinctiveness of national programs can best be illustrated by comparing them with four other types of humanitarian interventions: large-scale humanitarian involvement; quick-impact projects in the wake of an intervention; developmental projects; and sectoral approaches.

LARGE-SCALE HUMANITARIAN PROGRAMS

Large-scale humanitarian programs are of two types. The first is largely associated with the UN's refugee agency, the UN High Commissioner for Refugees (UNHCR), and involves transferring refugees from one location to another. This approach has now assumed the characteristics of a technology. The programs establish rules through negotiations or treaties to enshrine the right of return and protection from forced eviction, define entitlements to assistance, and make transportation arrangements. They deploy increasingly sophisticated technology to ensure accurate counting of people and benefits and have created a community of practice that can administer the programs. Problems arise because the programs leave the difficulties of the returnees' integration to either their countries of origin or to local villages (to which they might be returning after decades), as international agencies' efforts often do not cover the whole country, and indeed it would be prohibitive in cost for them to do so. The demobilization of excombatants has acquired similarly routinized features, with the problem of reintegration remaining unaddressed. Each of these programs performs an essential set of services but does not deal with the underlying causes of conflict through a clear strategy for inclusion.

If a national program were the basis for managing these problems, it would focus on the root causes and design measures that would address the short-, medium-, and long-term needs and aspirations of those groups that have been marginalized through conflict. Instead of perpetuating refugee camps, a national program would draw attention to reintegrating individuals and families within villages. Failure to address the needs of refugees, internally displaced people, and excombatants has been a factor in the perpetuation of criminality and ongoing conflict; better mechanisms to provide integration and inclusion could thus have an immense payoff.

The World Food Program (WFP) illustrates the second type of large-scale humanitarian program. The WFP is a vehicle for transferring the surplus food production of the developed world (largely wheat) for distribution to some of the poorest countries in the world through either free distribution or food-for-work systems. The cost of transporting the food constitutes a very significant part of the overall price of the program, and there is a network of interests ranging from subsidized farmers, politicians, shipping interests, and NGOs that benefit from and defend this activity. Even WFP officials admit that, in most contexts, cash-for-work plans or the purchase of food in national and regional markets are more effective mechanisms, but they acknowledge that they are unable to change the rules.[11] Andrew Natsios, the former director of USAID, tried to address this problem directly but met opposition from this network of interests and was unable to effect change.[12] In a positive step in August 2007, CARE

International took the unprecedented step of announcing that it would cease to accept federal funds for food aid, given its problematic effects on the ground.

The impact of these programs can vary. A top-down system of distribution, which entails WFP's delegating more decision rights on distribution to contracted agents tends to be the result since in most difficult environments WFP does not itself have the capacity for direct delivery. In terms of both the targeting and fairness of distribution, significant complaints have been made. There have also been allegations of fraud in food aid, as well as in broader UN agency programs. Speaking of the UN as a whole, Kofi Annan has stated that a "separate review conducted late in 2005 by external experts found major weaknesses in culture, management oversight and controls, including outdated procurement processes...a poor governance structure and lack of sufficient resources." He spoke of "isolated silos"—the specialized agencies that do not coordinate (or sometimes even communicate) with each other—and "a damaged culture which is seen as limiting creativity, enterprise, innovation and indeed leadership itself."[13]

If, as Annan has suggested, the extensive evidence gathered by the Volcker Commission on oil for food is emblematic of a wider trend, then collusion between companies and governmental and nongovernmental entities is a serious problem.[14] In researching this book, we have come across numerous examples of evidence of UN agencies' failure to meet basic standards of accountability—ranging from the oil-for-food program to Liberia to the tsunami funds. Time does not allow for a full investigation at this point, but it is sobering to realize that, when we have suggested to senior officials of European countries that audits should be conducted, they have rejected the proposal, maintaining that, if such audits came to light, democratic support for funding UN agencies might be undermined.

Recipients of aid become participants in a system of implicit entitlements that are not established through a national policy that is accountable to the population. Regardless of the ease or difficulty of handing out the goods concerned on the ground, the extent of distribution depends on decisions made prior to the actual allocation— sometimes many months in advance. Consequently, they miscalculate both the availability and the volume of potential assistance, as well as its timing, method of delivery, or the predictability of distribution, let alone the population's needs at the time of distribution. From a country perspective, the unintended consequences can be extremely severe.

In Afghanistan, weather conditions changed significantly in 2002 and 2003, marking the end of a long cycle of drought. Millions of refugees also returned to the country and provided a huge boost to agriculture. The extra labor and money available for investment helped rehabilitate the country's irrigation systems as well. At that time, the market as an institution in Afghanistan was able to ensure that food was available where there was purchasing power. Afghan officials therefore argued that maximum attention should be given both to the timing of the harvests (in view of the fact that the difference between the first and last harvests could be as much as four months) and to ensuring that farmers were provided with incentives to produce wheat and other basic commodities.

These officials emphasized two sets of imperatives—first, the need to avoid a surge in opium production, and second, the need to ensure that the majority of people who made their livelihoods from agriculture would benefit from the urban renewal and growth in investment. Instead, massive food distribution continued despite a lack of coordination with the government. When President Karzai and his cabinet officials questioned the policy and asked for a balance between the short-, medium-, and long-term needs of Afghanistan's poor people, they were labeled as anti-poor by WFP officials, who mobilized their considerable public relations operations in European and U.S. capitals to dispute Karzai's misgivings.

The end of 2003 witnessed a bumper harvest of wheat, but many farmers found that its market price was so depressed that the cost of harvesting was not warranted. Consequently, the wheat was left to rot. This event is unprecedented in the history of Afghanistan. On the basis of lessons learned from other countries and IMF/World Bank policy, the Afghan government did not wish to subsidize farmers, nor (given its very low domestic revenue) could it have done so even if it had so wished. The result was that the farmers, in order to survive, had to draw their own conclusions as to how best to earn a living by growing crops that could earn them the maximum revenue regardless of state or Islamic law, which both clearly forbid growing opium.

Were a national program to address the balance of interests over the short, medium, and long term of Afghanistan's hungry citizens, its farmers, its urban population, the country as a whole, the region, and the world, a coherent framework of trade-offs could be devised. This would allow the state to direct investments to address the root causes of hunger, the challenges of agricultural production, and the cultivation of opium poppies.

QUICK-IMPACT PROJECTS

The aim of quick-impact projects is to provide relief at moments of massive humanitarian need, such as in the wake of natural disasters or hostilities. In postconflict environments, the desire is to demonstrate a much-needed "peace dividend" to the affected population. Forgotten long-term conflicts, such as Afghanistan prior to September 11, 2001, are by definition not in the orbit of major development institutions and donors and are therefore taken off the front burner. In most cases, given the lack of attention, there are generally no coherent plans or programs in place that can be initiated upon the abrupt availability of large amounts of cash that the "CNN window" of renewed attention makes available. As donors then make financing available to respond to the emergency at hand, an array of organizations rush to the scene and quickly put together proposals for projects that can be delivered rapidly.

This type of aid, instead of being a catalyst for the creation of institutional capacity, can become an instrument for division, resentment, and corruption. While the UN often tries to ensure equality, the apparent randomness of allocations creates a sense of unfairness among citizens and thus feeds divisions and jealousies between regions and groups. The distributive schemes create a sense of entitlement without legal foundation, as they are not rooted in legal and policy frameworks. Unintended consequences can also be severe. For example, digging hundreds of wells without a coherent examination or understanding of the basic geology risks depletion of the water table and reduction in the availability of water, while increasing the likelihood of drought. The inefficiencies of staffing hundreds of project units result in redundant, inefficient management in overseeing costly projects. Rather, states and NGOs should focus on working through larger, more integrated programs.

Both the government and citizens are completely bypassed, and the government loses the capability to respond to its citizens' complaints. Because the aid agencies managing the projects are based in capitals far away, beyond the reach of domestic citizens and with no direct legal responsibilities to beneficiaries, disappointed citizens have no official recourse. Similarly, citizens of the aid agencies' countries are too remote from the actual facts to hold those agencies answerable. Any bonds of accountability are therefore absent.

In Afghanistan, with the help of a team of international economists, we reviewed more than four hundred projects in early 2002 that had been proposed to the donors by UN agencies as part of the UN appeal. In dialogue with the sponsoring agencies of the United Nations, we established that the absolute majority of these projects had not been prepared on any sound criteria of economic viability, financial feasibility, or sustainability. While each individual project might have had a desirable outcome, the cost-effectiveness and feasibility of each project, as well as the sum total of projects, raised serious questions. The projects were prepared without consideration of any spatial or social fairness criteria: some districts had many planned projects with which an NGO or agency had previously been involved, whereas other districts had no projects designed for them at all. While the actual reason for the disparity in allocation was not intentional discrimination but rather the practice of project-based aid, this would—we rightly feared—lead to increased tensions between groups throughout Afghanistan who would allege that aid had been allocated according to discriminatory policies.

Exhausted UN officials in Kabul had actually prepared the projects over a ten-day period at the end of December 2001. This took place in the UN agencies' rush to ensure that they—and not the World Bank— garnered the bulk of the aid resources that the donors were about to pledge at the Tokyo conference in January 2002. Facing a financing crisis, UN agencies needed to meet their headquarters' overheads and saw every appeal as an opportunity to do so. While these efforts to raise finances are understandable, they are not necessarily productive for the countries that the agencies set out to help.

When we mapped proposed projects against WFP's own assessment of vulnerability in districts, there was little fit. Projected costs, as well as some of the projects themselves, had little or no justification. Some involved the construction of bridges or medium-sized investments in a particular location that bore no relationship to the national program on transportation infrastructure that the Afghan government was developing. While the brochures describing the overall appeal were written in engaging language and invoked all of the currently fashionable development vocabulary, the glue holding them together was nothing more than a random series of projects put together in response to the available $1.8 billion that the aid system had allocated to the United Nations.[15]

The UN agencies shared project documents for the $1.8 billion worth of projects when prodded to do so, but, in practice, obfuscation and opaqueness continued. After billions of dollars in UN expenditure, no systematic audit of UN agency operations in Afghanistan has yet been carried out that we are aware of. Popular resentment with the apparent waste and ineffectiveness of UN agency and NGO expenditure now (regrettably but inevitably) runs very deep and provides a platform for demagogic politicians to demand draconian measures against the international presence.

The Afghan team was acutely aware of the need for a peace dividend. Programs such as the National Emergency Employment Program (NEEP) and NSP provided visible projects across the country and displayed the signs of partnership between government and people to help enhance popular trust in government. Because the government was the proper entity for making critical decisions about Afghanistan's future and because it had to balance the complete spectrum of competing agendas and priorities, it was the sole body with the requisite legitimacy and breadth of vision to develop a comprehensive strategic framework. Yet the national programs that it devised to implement its strategic objectives were actively impeded and subverted by those who lacked both the legitimacy and the necessary vision to determine sound policy.

DEVELOPMENTAL PROJECTS

The developmental project is a third type of intervention. In contrast to quick-impact projects, developmental projects require both a series of well-designed steps in their preparation, ranging from prefeasibility to full feasibility studies, and, ideally, exploration of alternatives that maximize environmental and social benefits and minimize adverse impacts on people and the environment. Problems arise from a lack of integration with broader sectoral and national policies; creation of parallel management systems and structures; proliferation of reporting arrangements; lack of subsequent attention to operation and maintenance; and rising costs due to delays. When donors do not have independent quality-control departments that monitor the projects during implementation and after completion, the quality of these plans suffers even more. Further, senior management time that could be devoted to lifting constraints in the overall system is used up in micromanaging projects.

For example, in Afghanistan, all of the partners agreed that completion of the ring road—the road that would connect the major cities of Herat, Mazar, Kabul, and Kandahar in a loop—would have maximum impact for economic development, social integration, political stability, and service delivery. However, the donors divided the ring road into segments, each of which was managed as a separate project. The reason for this timeline was that each year the World Bank would finance only one segment, and under the bank's rules, the Afghan government could not make a commitment to contractors or prepare for the project prior to the approval of each discrete venture by the Asian Development Bank.

While adherence to organizational rules is understandable, the result has been that the overall project remains unfinished five years later. Standards for different components of the ring road also differ from each other, and there are major variations in costs. There was no systematic program of vocational training for construction or maintenance, no program to promote the emergence of a domestic construction industry, and no attempt to provide supply-chain management arrangements that could have ensured cost-effective and timely delivery of critical components. During the process, different donors contracted one major U.S. firm to implement two different segments. As one donor assigned priority to the southern link, the firm delayed completion of the northern link by months, thereby fuelling tensions between different areas of the country. Furthermore, contracting mostly with Western companies prevented the regional cooperation that could have occurred. For example, enlisting Uzbekistan's substantial engineering and construction capacity or signing long-term contracts with Iran for asphalt were plausible options. These are mistakes that were made in a very difficult context—but they are mistakes we can rectify in similar situations in the future.

SECTOR APPROACHES

Attempts to improve the quality of projects on the one hand and macroeconomic crises in a number of countries in the 1980s and 1990s on the other focused the attention of development institutions on sectors as the point of linkage between policy and projects. They sensibly understood that without a proper policy environment, the impact of developmental projects would remain limited. Simultaneously, policy reform, unless carried out by means of developmental projects, would remain unfulfilled. The World Bank and other developmental institutions therefore designed specific instruments for sectoral reform and made them part of their adjustment programs, which were renamed "development policy lending."

When properly carried out, sectoral approaches can come close to the benefits of a national program. But in most cases several problems develop. First, the reform is externally driven and not tailored to context. Second, the timelines have often been unrealistic in expecting major reforms to take hold within just a few months. As a result, developmental institutions have repeatedly lent sums of money for the same reform measures. Third, integration of projects and programs has proven difficult as most donors have continued to establish discrete projects while paying lip service to their integration within a sectoral strategy. In some instances the same set of UN agency projects is repackaged as a "program" even though they are unrelated projects. Fourth, existing government bureaucracies are assumed, without consideration of the overlapping jurisdictions or diffused mandates that hamper coordination and effective implementation. Fifth, there have been few systematic attempts to put together domestic coalitions of legitimate interests that would become stakeholders and advocates for fundamental and lasting change. Little attention has focused on building the necessary capacity in policy ministries that would have the detailed knowledge of the sectors necessary for coordination, supervision, and facilitation.

Despite its good intentions, the "aid system" evidently suffers from an inherent resistance to transparency and accountability and often cannot provide coherent advice and solutions to national governments. For example, a World Bank conference on what the Afghan ministry of finance should do yielded some practical advice but did not lead to any definitive solutions. After a multimillion-dollar study, BearingPoint, the technical assistance provider on contract by USAID, concluded that it would probably not be possible to pay civil servants. Indeed, U.S. contractors (as documented by the U.S. Government Accountability Office) either would or could provide but little information on their programs to the people of the United States and Afghanistan. Instead of supporting efforts to bring transparency to public expenditure, UN agencies also initially refused to provide any details on its $1.8-billion suite of projects to the Afghan president and his cabinet and two years later refused to account for their expenditure to the people of Afghanistan at the constitutional loya jirga.

The national programs model could have contributed to much more significant accomplishments had all partners been willing to adhere to it and adopt a more harmonized approach. However, the fragmentary rules and practices of large development agencies resulted in parallel initiatives.[16] There were real obstacles in the approaches of many of the humanitarian aid industry professionals regarding both understanding of and participation in the national programs as they preferred instead to promote their own methods. Now, after seeing the results of the programs, the same individuals who were the most vocal opponents of the system are some of the national programs' biggest supporters.

Conclusion

Collective Power

THE DAWNING OF our interdependence offers the possibility of a new, global open moment. If our unprecedented worldwide prosperity is to expand, it has to become inclusive. Security will not be guaranteed by the use of force, though military intervention might be called upon from time to time. Security will come through the creation of functioning states, whereby the failure of politics and aid is overcome by a double compact that binds citizens, their governments, and international players in webs of rights and obligations.

Networks have been with us for centuries, and the world of the twenty-first century is one of increasing connections. Networks have become webs of mutual dependence, and the relationship between markets, states, and people has fundamentally changed. Networks now provide the source of our prosperity and also pose significant dangers to it. As a result, we need to find mechanisms to harness and expand these webs of creativity and value and to minimize systems of criminality and violence. The framework we have outlined here provides an approach to building such mechanisms.

From the perspective of the mid-twentieth century it would be hard to imagine either the affluence and knowledge that are now available or the scale and interdependence of challenges that are confronting us. In 1947 it was unclear that markets were to be the principal mechanism for organization of the economy or that democracy was to be the principal means for organization of the state. The Great Depression had made people distrustful of the market. Millions of people were looking to the Soviet Union as a successful model for development. Information was tightly managed and controlled: In 1930 the cost of a three-minute trans-Atlantic call was the equivalent of $250 today. Moreover, the world was consumed with the fear of atomic destruction.

Since then, half of the world has succeeded in finding a balance between the market, the state, and the citizenry. Europe, the site of two world wars, has developed a formula to overcome its differences and is now democratic, prosperous, and relatively secure. China's transformation since 1978 and India's since 1990 have enabled these two giants to join the web of global flows and lift millions out of poverty. In the United States, investment in innovation has unleashed stunning technological progress. With the decline of alternative organizational models for the state and the economy—communism, corporatism, and authoritarianism—the consensus on democracy and the market seemed inevitable.

The pendulum has now swung to pessimism, however. The global failure to provide answers for Russia in the 1990s, the lack of attention to the detritus of the Cold War, the rise of new networks of criminality and terror, and the persistence of poverty and conflict in sub-Saharan Africa have challenged our complacency. The liberation of dynamic new political, social, and economic forces has not only created limitless possibilities for wealth and knowledge but also has left close to half of the world's population out of this process, mired in fear, poverty, and insecurity. With the globalization of communication, images of life in the West are available for all to see, and as a result, citizens everywhere want inclusion in the global system of prosperity—not exclusion from it.

We have a choice in how to deal with this problem: either we turn poor and excluded people into stakeholders in a global system, or we leave them to their own devices, or, worse, we declare a clash of civilizations, which would only become a self-fulfilling prophecy. We have argued that exclusion is the result of the sovereignty gap. A global compact to make the world whole through the creation of legitimate states fit for the twenty-first century will be key to solving problems of disorder, poverty, and exclusion. We have argued that there is enough accumulated wisdom, money, and practical experience in the world to achieve this goal.

Dysfunctional states are the breeding grounds of networks of criminality and terror. Formal government positions are subordinated to them rather than oriented toward the provision of services to citizens. It is the predatory character of these states that is producing the crisis of legitimacy for the global order. Throughout history, hierarchical organizations endowed with legitimacy by their people have been an instrument for containing networks of disorder. With the changed character of war, creating states that can earn the trust and therefore command the loyalty of their people is necessary to preempt a long war in the poorest parts of the world. Given the nature of networks and globalization, citizens cannot be secure while their armies are fighting elsewhere: boundaries to the battlefield no longer exist.

The hierarchy today is not that of the past. Today it must enable and partner with market forces and be responsive to the changing needs of citizens and entrepreneurial networks. Furthermore, hierarchy can no longer be defined by its traditional organizational boundaries: in a new global context it has to cope with speed, coordination, and collaboration within and between organizations, businesses, and countries. It can no longer monitor others while hiding from the observation of citizens or consumers—the hierarchy now operates under citizens' constant scrutiny.

It is in this context that the world needs to craft an agenda to catalyze functioning states that enjoy legitimacy in the eyes of their citizens and the international community. We have demonstrated that states in today's world are best viewed as performing a series of essential functions. This concept stands in sharp contrast to the imposition of force that characterized the creation of nation-states from the sixteenth century to the twentieth. Functioning states today are flexible, dynamic, and able to coordinate and collaborate across boundaries. State functionality is based upon the smooth interface between the polity, the economy, and the citizens—an arrangement that creates a compact for effective governance by means of reinforcing and self-perpetuating loops. It is also based on people as citizens, consumers, and producers of the public good.

In order to understand today's state we have put forth a new framework for state functionality based not just on state theory but more importantly on state practice. There is no essence to the state, as states are instruments of collective power and are subject to processes of revisiting, reimagining, and reordering. As Dewey argued, "A public articulated and operating through representative officers is the state; there is no state without a government, but also there is none without the public." Focusing on state functions is hardly a functionalist argument: in fact, the assumption of these functions by the state changes its structure and character. Because the state cannot exist without the public, assuming or shedding functions can come only through a process of public discussion, debate, and consensus.

In the past, states have been organized like pyramids, with lower levels subordinate to higher ones. Rules that constitute the states have also varied in their assignment of rights to specific functions and levels. On closer examination, the pyramid reveals a web of cross-cutting ties and relationships with regard to levels and functions. Over time, decentralized units can become more centralized, and centralized units can become more decentralized. The federal government of the United States, for instance, initially had minimal powers because the states insisted on their rights. Particularly in response to war, the economy, and social obligations, the federal government has assumed distinctive powers. The Chinese state, heavily centralized until 1978, at first delegated substantial decision rights to provinces, counties, and cities in the southern coastal region and is now strongly engaged in setting norms and standards for a range of activities across the country. Europe completely reinvented a set of mechanisms for rule making, cooperation, and the coordination of its constituent units. The architecture of the state is far more flexible than we might sometimes imagine.

States become the source of stability for the market and their citizens through predictable rule making. The use of force that Weber isolated as the definition of the modern state becomes legitimized when it is governed by legal status (see chapter 6). Rule of law is not only about the subordination of government to rules but also about the ability of stakeholders to change outmoded laws and to acquire and maintain legal status. An order is consolidated and legitimized when social tensions are resolved through law. The challenge is to strike the right balance between the predictability necessary for the market and the citizenry and the flexibility to respond to rapid changes in context. The reputation of a state depends on its adherence to its legal obligations, from public borrowing to protection of property to human rights conventions. We have argued that it is the imposition of legal limits on power paired with what we call collective power that increases a state's legitimacy. Whereas arbitrary power is weak, power that is limited by rules and enjoys the consent and participation of multiple stakeholders becomes stable.

The key demand around the world is for inclusion in the globalizing economy, so that the lives of future generations will be better than those of the present. And the obstacles to these aspirations, as we have seen, are dysfunctional governments. Billions of poor and disenfranchised people around the world are not interested in going to war with the West. But we declare "war" on terror, poverty, and AIDS.

Markets and civil and entrepreneurial networks might be much more able to contain global threats than armies trained in conventional warfare. Charity can win temporary acknowledgement, but it will never be the source of sustained gratitude. The accomplishments of the past teach us that we need to embark on the creation of an inclusive global order that makes poor and excluded people genuine stakeholders in stability.

The need for effective, dynamic international organizations has never been greater. Both the scale of the challenges and the rise of new centers of power require forums for discussion and consensus on multilateral approaches and their implementation. International action requires global legitimacy. Recently, multilateral actions have proven far more legitimate than unilateral ones. The disenchantment with international organizations has come from the gap between their promises and their performance. Renewal of international organizations will require that they become catalysts in a process of state building. By definition, a catalyst leaves the scene when its action has taken place.

If we are right in thinking that the poverty of the aid complex arises from its design, then it is the design of the system that we need to revisit. State architecture has shown that it can be flexible and dynamic: the architecture of international organizations has been rigid, bureaucratic, and at times downright dysfunctional. All successful cases of development have depended on a design based on partnership and real empowerment. As catalysts, international organizations would provide national partners with knowledge and access to networks to perform specific state functions and depart as soon as possible. The key to an exit strategy in turn lies in ensuring that the state can perform its functions as rapidly as possible. Instead of best practice, the heart of strategy making will involve stitching together local capabilities and resources and tailoring tactics to context. Beginning with the premise of a double compact, the major task would be to create and enhance systems of national accountability, as well as national programs that can harness citizen energies toward the task of state building. A strong case can be made for re-examining the use of the sovereign guarantee.

If implementing sovereignty strategies is to become the central objective of these organizations, their incentives and mental models must undergo a radical transformation to enable staff to devote their energies to the achievement of medium- and long-term goals rather than only the short-term disbursement of funds. Most of the staff members in these organizations have not been trained to work across the political, security, and economic issues that now confront weak states. The dominant approach to training has been through specializations that explicitly avoid the development of skills for state-building endeavors or multidisciplinary teamwork that would facilitate, co-produce, and allow partnership with national actors on the basis of mutual accountabilities. Investment in training to prepare personnel to work as catalytic agents for the implementation of sovereignty strategies is essential if we are to avoid the mistakes of the past.

Facilitation of such a unified framework requires that specialists from the security, developmental, and political domains engage in the type of collaboration and exchange of views that makes them fully aware of the implications of their recommendations and actions for the overall goal of state building. International teams that share a common vision and a willingness to learn from one another and are empowered and supported by leaders in their organizations can play an invaluable role in bringing focus and unity to the task.

Aid will still be required, but the leaders and people of developing countries must commit themselves to wealth-generating strategies that can allow them to underwrite their social contracts. Employees in both the public and private sectors are adept at embracing new slogans without changing their practices. In like manner, officials in international organizations face a high degree of personal insecurity, for the longer they stay in these organizations, the slimmer their chances of finding equally high-paying jobs elsewhere. A buyout program for some staff members in international organizations might be a valuable investment in the future of these organizations. Business practices—skills, incentives, locations, instruments, and time horizons—required for the new challenges could then be put in place.

Historically, social scientists have been poor at predicting the future trajectories of countries. Gunnar Myrdal, the eminent authority on Asia and the American South, predicted in the 1960s that Singapore would explode. World Bank economists were confident that Burma and the Philippines would be the development stars of east Asia yet insisted that South Korea and Taiwan had few prospects for growth. Our certainties about the prospects for the world's poorest countries must be tempered by the weight of history.

Backwardness can actually offer some advantages. The kingdom of Tonga, for instance, has become the site of one of the boldest experiments in bandwidth communications. An American innovator named Dewayne Hendricks, frustrated with regulatory regimes in the United

States, set out, at the invitation of Tonga's Crown Prince Tupouto'a, to demonstrate that, in an open regulatory regime, the airwaves could be used for cheap and effective communication across the island. Japanese development in the 1950s and 1960s provides another example. John Foster Dulles, Eisenhower's secretary of state, advised the Japanese that they should look to Asia to export their cars, as they would never be able to produce the type of vehicles that American consumers would want. Now that Toyota has replaced General Motors as the world's largest producer of cars, significant numbers of business schools are rewriting their casebooks. Innovation and entrepreneurship, combined with perseverance, can make the difference. It is not primarily the aid system but also innovators from institutes, universities, and businesses that can supply this new advice. The very fact that significant parts of the world lack modern infrastructure could present the best experimental grounds for innovative design and reliance on alternative sources of energy rather than replication of the unsustainable industrial path that many people are advising them to follow. The rapid pace of institutional change in some of the recent accession countries in Europe should serve as a cautionary note for assertions that the creation of institutions requires many years.

Sustained change in international organizations will not take place without the active engagement of G8 and G20 leaders. Although G8 communiqués consistently refer to the significant problems of our times, there is hardly any systematic follow-up to their meetings. As global panels and commissions are reaching consensus on the need for effective states as the answer to many of the world's most significant challenges, it is time for G20 leaders to act in the world's collective interest. Because state functions are performed by ministries at the national level, it is time to establish networks between and among such institutions rather than to mediate through a dysfunctional aid system. Experience and wisdom lie within the functioning institutions of developing countries, and these should be networked into open-source, peer-to-peer, global learning organizations that focus on specific tasks. Entrenched interests—within both the aid bureaucracies and the multibillion-dollar technical assistance industry—will try to block this, but we must persevere.

Aid may alleviate poverty, but it will not bring about sustainable development. The history of the last sixty years is clear: functioning markets will be the engine of sustained prosperity. Some of the greatest resources are the global flows of information, knowledge, and money, but they are mostly locked within the corporate world. With new instruments and a greater level of social engagement, the private sector could become an agent of stability. The role of corporations in promoting peace and global prosperity should go beyond corporate social responsibility, however. If worldwide insecurity is a threat to international prosperity and to the future of globalization, then businesses should have an inherent interest in creating the market conditions for a level playing field and doing what they do best—generating jobs and opportunities.

It is ironic that instruments of risk management are expanding and thriving in the most advanced economies but are hardly being used in places that need them the most, namely the forty to sixty countries where crumbling states are turning the market into a corrupt playing field. If the widespread criminalization of economies is to be avoided, then global corporations should find it in their interest to promote a citizenship-based, state-building model that strengthens the state's capability for the rule of law and for regulation of the country's invisible assets. The Extractive Industries Transparency Initiative (EITI) is the first step in this process. Fields ranging from telecommunications to carbon trading to intellectual rights in biodiversity provide immense scope for innovation, risk management, and the creation of value chains that would create domestic constituencies for global engagement and national transformation. In the minds of many citizens in failing countries, the corporation represents primarily technical assistance and unbridled resource extraction. Nonetheless, the opportunity exists to demonstrate the liberating potential of a new phase of capital investment.

All of these organizations need to come to terms with the instantaneous nature of global communication. With the traditional boundaries of local, national, and international entities collapsing along with censorship under the weight of the demand for (and availability of) information, organizations that are trying to build stable states must face the challenge of communicating effectively with an informed global citizenry. Under such circumstances, developmental processes must not only deliver their intended results but also be seen as fair by an informed citizenry. The right to information is not a luxury or a dispensation to be granted periodically by rulers or international bureaucracies. It is now a necessity for forging coalitions and maintaining the momentum for systemic transformation.

Civil society is a manifestation of a public organized for debate and collective action. A renewed spirit of volunteerism seems to be emerging. The commitment to open communications that spurred the invention of the World Wide Web in the first place, the open source movement, and global civic campaigns are just three manifestations of public-spiritedness. Online communities are emerging as mechanisms for collective problem solving for significant numbers of people around the world. If we can harness this momentum to an agenda for global cooperation for open-source innovation on how each state function should be performed and monitored, we will have taken a tremendous step forward. Transparency is technically within our reach; it is agreement on standards and disclosure of information that could make it into a social process. Our global problems are not going to be solved through slogans alone but through relentless technical work and collaboration on mechanisms of governance.

Reaching consensus on an index of state functions could facilitate accountability. Issuing a report card on each function in the global media and at the UN and World Bank annual meetings could help us to focus attention on issues of governance. A judgment of the effectiveness of each state according to each of its ten functions and in terms of the overall effectiveness and the extent of change, in relation to its own past performance and to other states, could prove effective in promoting a path toward global transparency and stability.

Such an index could in turn embody the notion of a double compact. As we have argued, one component of this agreement is between citizens and their government according to the citizenship-based model for state building. The other involves a government and the international community, international organizations, global civil society, the news media, and businesses. Agreement on a consistent framework of functions to be performed, as well as comparative measurement of effectiveness in performing these functions, would provide grounds for mobilization and allocation of resources. The aid system would become more efficient and ultimately redundant as institutional transformation, the revenue compact, and wealth creation transform a country's prospects and progressively diminish the need for aid and development assistance, except in cases of natural disasters and other catastrophes. The public could thereby converge around such a compact measured according to the index. Progress along the index indicators would reinforce a new international community of practice united around a common vision and equipped with the discipline of detail. In 2005 we created a global Sovereignty Index that could serve as a model.

Our webs of interconnection require new capabilities and styles of leadership. Management today is about dealing with complexity and understanding the interface of hierarchy, markets, and networks. It is about convening power (rather than command and control) and the ability to listen to others and reach agreement on rules that groups of stakeholders can adhere to. Leadership is about reframing perspectives, reorienting assets, and working out details through constant diligence, pragmatism, and imagination. It is a team effort and must be subordinated to the rule of law. Cultivation of this style of leadership will help make statecraft both principled and pragmatic.

Leadership needs to be nurtured at all levels of society—in government and businesses, from the village to the presidency, the workshop to the boardroom. When citizens have been entrusted with decision rights through national programs, they have shown remarkable capability for management and problem solving. Mechanisms like these would enable the public to acquire voice, hold their governments accountable, and provide an exit from a technical assistance system that has proved inadequate after sixty years. There is no worse indictment of a system than the fact that after several decades it still claims that it is required to assist the government with the performance of elementary tasks.

Companies facing restructuring can draw on an entire body of knowledge about the matter. Political leaders who are facing similar challenges, however, have no comparable body of pragmatic knowledge to guide them. They must either muddle their way through, using abstract principles, or act on the recommendations of international experts who are relying on "best practice," which may be unsuitable for the context. A systematic body of knowledge on each state function, the variety of ways in which specific political leaders have managed to perform these functions, and the appropriateness of various mechanisms in specific contexts could become the basis for a community of practice. The best source of technical assistance can actually come from the open-source, government-to-government, leader-to-leader, manager-to-manager networks we have described, which would make much technical assistance redundant.

The framework that we are offering is fractal: it can operate at many levels. Actions can begin at many points—from village to country to regional and global levels—to create the initial trust for taking longer and longer horizons into account. While the map of the functions is general, application to each context will depend on pre-existing conditions, assets, and capabilities. The heart of the strategy will come from networking of like-minded people. It is not best-practice but path-breaking approaches that are going to generate momentum. Earning citizen trust requires constant monitoring and the creation of credible mechanisms of feedback and interaction. Leaders cannot simply trust their instincts. They must also subject themselves to public scrutiny and engagement.

There are rare open moments in history, when a challenge forces the world to revise its assumptions. The emergence of world religions, the nation-state, the industrial revolution, the Great Depression, the end of World War II, the end of Communism, and the emergence of the Internet all marked a rupture between one era and the next. Each of these have set in motion long chains of events and changed the way people understand, interrelate, organize, and carry on business with one another.

Our world today is at just such an open moment. The confluence of emerging trends presents us with a challenge that has outstripped our established ways of understanding and acting. How we frame the problems and their solutions will determine whether we collaborate productively or make the clash of civilizations a self-fulfilling prophecy. An inclusive global order is within our grasp. Our actions could also provoke a further descent into disorder, uncertainty, and violence.

Open moments are most productive when leaders who see the future in the present seize opportunities. Today there is a clear opportunity to create a map for the future and to initiate a wide-ranging global public discussion on the common destiny of our fragmented world. We believe that the world now possesses assets—in the form of not only trillions of dollars but also a range of capitals (e.g., social, institutional, and human)—to make this vision realistic. With imagination, leadership, and appropriate management, globalization can be harnessed to create effective states, which will serve as vehicles for prosperity and security rather than poverty and instability.

Notes

Chapter 1

1. The sense of insecurity that is pervasive across great sections of the globe is captured in Gabriel García Márquez's *News of a Kidnapping* (Translated by Edith Grossman, Knopf, New York, 1997).
2. Hernando de Soto, *The Mystery of Capital: Why Capitalism Triumphs in the West and Fails Everywhere Else* (London: Black Swan, 2001).
3. Paul Collier has conducted the seminal study in this area.
4. From Wolfowitz speech, cited in "Why Wolfowitz Should Stay," Nuhu Ribadu, *New York Times*, May 1, 2007.
5. *Bringing the State Back In*, ed. Peter Evans, Dietrich Rueschemeyer, and Theda Skocpol (New York: Cambridge University Press, 1985).
6. See http://www.commissionforafrica.org/english/report/introduction.html (accessed August 10 2007).
7. *A More Secure World: Our Shared Responsibility; Report on the Secretary-general's High-level Panel on Threats, Challenges, and Change* (New York: United Nations Foundation, 2004). Section II D.1 (paragraph 34) and Section II C (paragraph 30).
8. *Bringing the State Back In.*
9. Rupert Smith, *The Utility of Force: The Art of War in the Modern World* (New York: Knopf, 2007).

Chapter 2

1. Interview, Radio 4, Today Program, June 20, 2007.
2. Meredith Hindley, "How the Marshall Plan Came About," *Humanities* 19(6) (November/December 1998): 22–27.
3. John Maynard Keynes, *The Economic Consequences of the Peace* (New York: Harcourt Brace New York, 1920).
4. Dean Acheson, *Present at the Creation: My Years in the State Department* (New York: Norton, 1969).

5. Lee Kwan Yew, *From Third World to First: The Singapore Story: 1965–2000* (New York: HarperCollins, 2000).

6. Ibid.

7. Ibid.

8. Ibid.

9. http://www.transparency.org/policy_research/surveys_indices/cpi/2006 (accessed Oct. 15, 2007).

10. PSA International Pte Ltd., annual report, 2006, p. 5; http://www.internationalpsa .com/about/pdf/AR2006/PSA_AR06.pdf (accessed August 14, 2007).

11. S. Simon (C. Tay, ed.), *A Mandarin and the Making of Public Policy: Reflections by Ngiam Tong Dow* (Singapore: NUS Press, 2006).

12. Yew, *From Third World to First,* 72–73.

13. Ibid., 73.

14. Ibid.

15. Ibid.

16. W. K. Cho, "Socio-Economic and Psychological Attributes of Rural Poverty in Mississippi," research bulletin no. 17.

17. From Michael J. Klarman, *"Brown v. Board:* 50 Years Later," *Humanities* 25(2) (March/April 2004).

18. Milken Institute, "Best Performing Cities 2005: Where America's Jobs Are Created and Sustained," February 2006; http://www.milkeninstitute.org/ publications/publications.taf?function=detail&ID=478&cat=ResRep (accessed Oct. 15, 2007).

19. Gov. Bob Riley, 2007, state of the state address; http://www.stateline.org/live/ details/speech?contentId=187177 (accessed Oct. 15, 2007).

20. Gov. Jim Gilmore, 2000, state of the commonwealth speech; http://www.stateline .org/live/details/speech?contentId=16018 (accessed Oct. 15, 2007).

21. Gov. Mike Easley, 2007, state of the state address; http://www.stateline.org/ live/details/speech?contentId=182266 (accessed Oct. 15, 2007).

22. Gov. Kathleen Blanco, 2007, state of the state address; http://www.stateline .org/live/printable/speech?contentId=203931 (accessed Oct. 15, 2007).

23. "A Special Report on the American South," *Economist* (Mar. 3, 2007).

24. Gov. Roy Barnes, 2001, state of the state address; http://www.stateline.org/ live/details/speech?contentId=16091 (accessed Oct. 15, 2007).

25. Governor Easley, 2001, state of the state address; http://www.stateline.org/ live/details/speech?contentId=16092 (accessed Oct. 15, 2007).

26. Gov. Sonny Perdue, 2006, state of the state address; http://www.stateline.org/ live/details/speech?contentId=80376 (accessed Oct. 15, 2007).

27. http://www.rtp.org.

28. See note 19.

29. Governor Perdue, 2007, state of the state address; http://www.stateline.org/ live/details/speech?contentId=169993 (accessed Oct. 15, 2007).

30. Governor Easley, 2003, state of the state address; http://www.stateline.org/ live/details/speech?contentId=16176 (accessed Oct. 15, 2007).

31. Governor Blanco, 2004, state of the state address; http://www.stateline.org/live/details/speech?contentId=16221 (accessed Oct. 15, 2007).

32. See note 26.

33. See note 22.

34. Gov. Mark Warner, 2002, state of the commonwealth address; http://www.stateline.org/live/printable/speech?contentId=16105 (accessed Oct. 15, 2007).

35. Governor Perdue, 2004, state of the state address; http://www.stateline.org/live/details/speech?contentId=16194 (accessed Oct. 15, 2007).

36. See note 27.

37. See note 26.

38. See note 17.

39. See note 27.

40. Statistics taken from Central Statistics Office Ireland 1901–1990; http://www.cso.ie/statistics/Population1901–2006.htm; L. M. Cullen, *Economic History of Ireland since 1660*, 2d ed. (London: Batsford); and CAIN (Conflict Archive on the Internet) Web Service.

41. "Engels to Marx in London," Manchester, May 23, 1856; http://www.marxists.org/archive/marx/works/1856/letters/56_05_23.htm (accessed Oct. 15, 2007).

42. Economist Intelligence Unit. Regardless of EU expansion, which has lowered the average GDP, this is still a highly impressive record of economic growth. If compares favorably to that of both Germany (115 percent) and Japan (122 percent), for example.

43. http://www.ndp.ie/docs/NDP_Homepage/1131.htm.

44. Using purchasing power parity.

45. http://www.heritage.org/index/.

46. http://www.economist.com/media/pdf/QUALITY_OF_LIFE.pdf.

47. http://www.cso.ie/releasespublications/documents/statisticalyearbook/2006/Chapter%202%20Labour%20Market%20and%20Social%20Inclusion.pdf.

48. http://www.cato.org/dailys/04–21–03.html.

49. Remarks by Bruton after being presented with the Schuman medal by the European People's Party and European Democrats in the European Parliament, September 9, 1998; http://www.epp-ed.eu/Activities/pspeech/spe06_en.asp (accessed Oct. 16, 2007).

50. http://www.ndp.ie/docs/NDP_2007–2013_-_All_sections_downloadable_by_chapter/1900.htm.

51. Irish National Spatial Strategy; http://www.irishspatialstrate.

Chapter 3

1. This is the total number of passengers that was forecast to pass through the world's 725 biggest airports in 2007. Air4casts Online; http://www.air4casts.com/newsletter/nls_tot.php.

2. Blacklist of Unsafe Airlines, 2006; http://www.newssafety.com/stories/insi/air.htm. The original list included ninety-two airlines, based mainly in Africa.

In June 2006 the EU added a further three airlines (one based in Suriname and two in Kyrgyzstan) and removed an airline based in Libya.

3. World merchandise exports, 2005, cited in "Recent Trade Developments and Selected Trends in Trade" (WTO, 2005), p. 6; http://www.wto.org/English/res_e/booksp_e/anrep_e/wtro6–1a_e.pdf.

4. Parliamentary Papers no. 11, Great Britain, 1884, 456.

5. *Encyclopedia Britannica*, 1911, 822–823; *Encyclopedia of the Social Sciences*, 1934, 76.

6. Between 1873 and 1910 world shipping tonnage increased by almost two and a half times. *Encyclopedia Britannica*, 1911, 873.

7. IMF staff papers, vol. 50, "Comment on Security Transactions, Taxes, and Financial Markets" (2003), 183; http://www.imf.org/external/pubs/ft/staffp/2002/00–00/pdf/Forbes.pdf.

8. This figure includes world merchandise exports and commercial services for 2005 as cited in "Recent Trade Developments and Selected Trends in Trade" (WTO, 2005), 6; http://www.wto.org/English/res_e/booksp_e/anrep_e/wtro6–1a_e.pdf.

9. Lester Salamon, "The Rise of the Non-profit Sector," *Foreign Affairs* (July/August 1994).

10. http://www.worldpress.org/Americas/2864.cfm.

11. http://www.un.org/geninfo/ir/index.asp?id=150. Approximately half of this amount comes from voluntary contributions from member states; the rest from mandatory assessments on those states.

12. Ibid.

13. http://www.nacubo.org/documents/research/2006NES_Listing.pdf. The New York City Board of Education budget—not counting pensions and debt-servicing costs—is around $12.4 billion per annum. The top twenty U.S. universities have combined endowments of $153.9 billion.

14. http://www.forbes.com/lists/2007/18/biz_07forbes2000_The-Global-2000_Rank.html and http://money.cnn.com/2006/01/11/markets/job_bonuses/index.htm.

Chapter 4

1. The National Pact (al Mithaq al Watani), an unwritten agreement, came into being in the summer of 1943 as the result of numerous meetings between Bishara al-Khuri (a Maronite), Lebanon's first president, and the first prime minister, Riyad al-Sulh (also cited as Solh), a Sunni.

Chapter 5

1. Dean Acheson, *Present at the Creation: My Years in the State Department* (New York: Norton, 1969).

2. Herbert A. Simon, *Sciences of the Artificial*, 3d ed. (Cambridge, Mass.: MIT Press, 1996).

3. http://www.iic-offp.org/.

4. http://www.gao.gov/new.items/d07597.pdf.

5. http://www.un.org/reform/investinginun/report.shtml.

6. www.usunnewyork.usmission.gov/.../OIOS%20REPORTS%20JAN%2007 %20-%20MARCH%2007/A-61-264(Part%20II).pdf

7. www.centerforunreform.org/system/files/Report+of+the+Office+of+Internal+ Oversight+Services.pdf

8. Kuan Lew Yee, *From Third World to First: The Singapore Story, 1965–2000* (New York: HarperCollins, 2000), 50.

9. http://www.commissionforafrica.org/english/report/introduction.html.

10. http://www.publicintegrity.org/wow/bio.aspx?act=pro&ddlC=8.

11. "Delays Hurting U.S. Rebuilding in Afghanistan," David Rohde and Carlotta Gall, *New York Times* (Nov. 7, 2005), A1.

Chapter 6

1. See Sabine's ideas on the state in the *Encyclopedia of Social Sciences*, vol. 14, 1934, pp. 328–332 (New York: Macmillan, 1934).

2. See, for example, M. Weber, *Economy and Society*, ed. Guenther Roth and Claus Wittich (New York: Bedminister Press, 1968).

3. See for example, M. Mann, *The Sources of Social Power*, Volumes I and II (Cambridge: Cambridge University Press, 1986 and 1993).

4. Weber, of course, was describing the functions performed by the German state between 1870 and 1916, where the marriage of state and capital produced a distinctive form of the German national economy and industrialization.

5. John Stuart Mill, *Principles of Political* Economy (London: Longmans, 1926).

6. Ibid., pp. 796, 797, 801.

7. William Pitt the Younger first devised the income tax in preparation for the Napoleonic Wars. At that time the tax raised revenues of slightly more than £6 million.

8. William Gladstone, budget speech, 1853.

9. http://www.hmrc.gov.uk/history/taxhis2.htm. Income tax is still a "temporary" tax in the United Kingdom; it expires each year on April 5, and Parliament has to reapply it by an annual finance act.

10. http://www.hm-treasury.gov.uk/budget/budget_1998/bud98_speech.cfm.

11. http://www.hm-treasury.gov.uk/budget/budget_1998/budget1998_budget_ report/bud98_budmeas_annexc.cfm.

12. http://www.hm-treasury.gov.uk/budget/budget_07/bud_bud07_speech.cfm.

13. Ibid.

14. http://www.libertynet.org/edcivic/fdr.html.

15. See, for example, one of the many versions of Cicero's *Treatise on the Laws* (51 BC).

16. Franklin Delano Roosevelt, Annual Message to Congress, 1941 (Washington, D.C., January 6).

Chapter 7

1. See Hernando de Soto, *The Mystery of Capital: Why Capitalism Triumphs in the West and Fails Everywhere Else* (New York: Basic Books, 2000).

2. Lee Kwan Yew, *From Third World to First: The Singapore Story: 1965–2000* (New York: HarperCollins, 2000).

3. http://www.sipri.org/contents/milap/milex/mex_trends.html.

4. John W. Cole and Eric R. Wolf, *The Hidden Frontier: Ecology and Ethnicity in an Alpine Valley* (Berkeley: University of California Press, 1999).

5. Global Network on Local Governance, http://gnlg.org/global-network-local-governance-1.asp?sub_id=103&sub_menu=PROFILE percent20F percent-20LOCAL percent20GOVERNMENTS&id=1.

6. Paula Tiihonen, "From Telework to New Forms of Work in the Information Society," international symposium, Quebec, May 15–16, 2001; http://arkisto .tieke.fi/online/jtiedotteet.nsf/38e4483ea7238da4c225650f004a738d/20fec21d3 80f6b6fc2256bce0, 5.

7. http://www.oecdobserver.org/news/get_file.php3/id/25/file/OECDInFigures 2006–2007.pdf.

8. David Osborne and Ted Gaebler, *Reinventing Government: How the Entrepreneurial Spirit Is Transforming the Public Sector* (Reading, Mass.: Addison-Wesley, 1992).

9. Mark Moore *Creating Public Value: Strategic Management in Government* (Boston, Mass.: Harvard University Press, 1995).

10. http://www.cabinetoffice.gov.uk/upload/assets/www.cabinetoffice.gov.uk/ strategy/public_value2.pdf

11. Cited in S. Simon (C. Tay, ed.), *A Mandarin and the Making of Public Policy: Reflections by Ngiam Tong Dow* (Singapore: NUS Press, 2006), 34.

12. F. H. Cardoso, *The Accidental President of Brazil: A Memoir* (Public Affairs, 2006)

13. Democracy Now! http://www.democracynow.org/article.pl?sid=04/06/30/1514255.

14. Konard H. Jarausch, "The Social Transformation of the University: The Case of Prussia, 1865–1914," *Journal of Social History* 12(4) 1979: 609–636.

15. U.S. Department of Education, National Center for Education Statistics, *Digest of Education Statistics 1988* (Washington, D.C.: GPO), table 114, 132.

16. OECD Rates Australian Education Spending as World Class; http://www .dest.gov.au/ministers/nelson/sept03/n462_160903.htm.

17. http://news.bbc.co.uk/2/hi/uk_news/education/6474789.stm.

18. http://www.uis.unesco.org/ev_en.php?ID=5029_201&ID2=DO_TOPIC.

19. Figures for 2003. "Effects of Healthcare Spending on the U.S. Economy"; http://aspe.hhs.gov/health/costgrowth/report.pdf.

20. "Carolina Announces $245 Million Public-private Investment in Genomics"; http://www.unc.edu/news/archives/feb01/geneo22201.htm.

21. http://unstats.un.org/unsd/Demographic/products/socind/health.htm.

22. http://www.actionaid.org/docs/real-aid-findings-summary.pdf.

23. Statement of David Walker, comptroller general of the United States, testimony before the House Committee on Armed Services: Securing, Stabilizing, and Rebuilding Iraq, GAO Audit Approach and Findings, Jan. 18, 2007; http://www.gao.gov/new.items/d07385t.pdf.

24. M. Castells, *The Rise of the Network Society* (Oxford: Blackwell, 1996).

25. Beveridge Report, November 1942; http://www.fordham.edu/halsall/mod/1942beveridge.html.

26. http://stats.oecd.org/glossary/detail.asp?ID=2485.

27. "Money Go-round," *Economist* (July 26, 2007).

28. Trends in Public Spending on Transportation and Water Infrastructure, 1956–2004. Congressional Budget Office.

29. http://www.hq.usace.army.mil/history/Vignettes/Vignette_88.htm.

30. "Infrastructure Spending Gets a Push" (Jan. 9, 2006); http://www.projectsmonitor.com.

31. http://humandevelopment.bu.edu/dev_indicators/start.cfm?header_id=16.

32. http://www.strategy-business.com/export/export.php?article_id=23502998.

33. A. Chandler, Jr., *The Visible Hand: The Managerial Revolution in American Business* (Cambridge, Mass.: Harvard Belknap, 1977).

34. See Paul Hawken, Amory Lovins, and L. Hunter Lovins, *Natural Capitalism: Creating the Next Industrial Revolution* (New York: Back Bay Books, 2000).

35. The term "cosmopolitical economy" was used by Frederick List, who was cited in an article by John Austin in the *Edinburgh Review* 75 (1842).

36. *The Mystery of Capital* by de Soto, a compelling work on the genesis of the market, describes the transformation of property from a "dead asset" to a form of living capital by means of a mortgage.

37. See J. Thakara, *In the Bubble: Designing in a Complex World* (Cambridge, Mass.: MIT Press, 2005) and L. Lessig, *The Future of Ideas: The Fate of the Commons in a Connected World* (New York: Random House, 2001).

Chapter 8

1. http://unpan1.un.org/intradoc/groups/public/documents/apcity/unpan003222.pdf.

2. The balanced-scorecard approach, which was developed by Robert Kaplan and David Norton, is designed to generate a more complete picture of a company's prospects, strengths, and weaknesses by supplementing financial measurements with three other criteria—learning and growth, business processes, and customer perspectives—to help companies achieve their broader strategic vision and ensure future value. The scorecard provides not merely a measurement but also a management system.

3. Douglass C. North takes "institutions" to mean three things: "(1) the formal rules of the game that are defined in legal terms, (2) the informal norms of behavior that supplement and complement and modify institutions, and (3) the effectiveness of enforcement mechanisms." See North's speech titled "Dealing with a Non-ergodic World: Institutional Economics, Property Rights, and the Global Environment."

4. See Paul Collier's research on conflict at http://users.ox.ac.uk/~econpco/research/conflict.htm.

5. For a comprehensive overview of every intrastate war settlement between 1980 and 1998 in which international actors played a key role see Stephen J. Stedman,

Donald Rothchild, and Elizabeth M. Cousens, *Ending Civil Wars: The Implementation of Peace Agreements* (Boulder, Colo.: Lynne Rienner, 2002).

6. See Charles F. Sabel, "Bootstrapping Development: Rethinking the Problem of Public Intervention in Promoting Growth," paper presented at the Protestant Ethic and Spirit of Capitalism conference, Cornell University, Ithaca, N.Y., Oct. 8–10, 2004.

7. Ibid., 30.

8. See, for example, Eliyahu M. Goldratt and Jeff Cox, *The Goal: A Process of Ongoing Improvement* (New York: North River Press, 1984); Robert S. Kaplan and David P. Norton, *The Balanced Scorecard: Translating Strategy into Action* (Boston: Harvard Business School Press, 1996) and *Alignment: Using the Balanced Scorecard to Create Corporate Synergies* (Boston, Mass.: Harvard Business School Press, 2006); Michael L. Tushman and Charles A. O'Reilly III, *Winning through Innovation: A Practical Guide to Leading Organizational Change and Renewal*, rev. ed. (Boston, Mass.: Harvard Business School Press, 2002).

9. John P. Kotter, *The Leadership Factor* (New York: Free Press, 1990); Edgar Schein, "Three Cultures of Management: The Key to Organizational Learning," *MIT Sloan Management Review*, *38* (1), pp. 9–20; Carl E. Larson and David D. Chrislip, "Setting the Stage for Success," in *Collaborative Leadership: How Citizens and Civic Leaders Can Make a Difference*, ed. Carl E. Larson and David D. Chrislip, pp. 55–75 (San Francisco: Jossey-Bass, 1994).

10. See, for example, General Hillier's analysis as commander of the International Security Assistance Force (ISAF) in Afghanistan, which points to "credible institutions" and specifically a "public finance system" as the key drivers of stability and prosperity in the country. Institute for State Effectiveness reports on Sudan, Lebanon, and Nepal corroborate the same findings; http://www.effectivestate.org.

11. See Paul Collier, *The Bottom Billion: Why the Poorest Countries Are Failing and What Can Be Done about It* (New York: Oxford University Press, 2007).

12. Larry Bossidy and Ram Charan, with Charles Buck (ed., Clare Smith), *Execution: The Discipline of Getting Things Done* (New York: Random House Business Books, 2002).

Chapter 9

1. See Charles Sabel's discussion of constitutional orders, bootstrapping, and rule making in "Constitutional Orders: Trust Building and Response to Change," in *Contemporary Capitalism: The Embeddedness of Institutions*, ed. J. R. Hollingsworth and R. Boyer (New York: Cambridge University Press, 1997), 154–188.

2. Susan Helper, John Paul MacDuffie, and Charles Sabel, "Pragmatic Collaborations: Advancing Knowledge while Controlling Opportunism" in *Industrial and Corporate Change*, Volume 9, Number 3 (Oxford University Press, 2000), 443–448.

3. Dwight D. Eisenhower, *At Ease: Stories I Tell to Friends* (Garden City, N.Y.: Doubleday, 1967).

4. Theda Skocpol, *Social Policy in the United States: Future Possibilities in Historical Perspective* (Princeton, N.J.: Princeton University Press, 1995).

5. See Keith Banting, "The Welfare State as Statecraft: Territorial Politics and Canadian Social Policy," in *European Social Policy: Between Fragmentation and Integration*, ed. Stephan Leibfried and Paul Pierson (Washington, D.C.: Brookings Institution, 1995).

6. Charles Sabel, "Local Development in Ireland: Partnership, Innovation, and Social Justice." OECD report, 1996.

7. Douglass C. North, *Institutions, Institutional Change, and Economic Performance* (New York: Cambridge University Press, 1990); Robert D. Putnam, with Robert Leonardi and Raffaella Y. Nanetti, *Making Democracy Work: Civic Traditions in Modern Italy* (Princeton, N.J.: Princeton University Press, 1994).

8. Hamid Karzai, chair of the interim administration of Afghanistan, "A Vision for Afghanistan," speech given at the Tokyo conference of donors, January 2002.

9. For details on these reforms see, for example, "Securing Afghanistan's Future: Accomplishments and the Strategic Path Forward," government/international agency report, Mar. 17, 2004, http://www.adb.org/Documents/Reports/Afghanistan/securing-afghanistan-future-final.pdf.

10. These programs included "Learning from Our Successes" and the quality assurance group; reviews of structural adjustment; country assistance strategies, a review of a very large literature on social policy in Europe and globally that we were drawing on to define a social development agenda; and an in-depth analysis of three national programs—the Kecamatan Development Program, Columbia Medio, and the Russia Coal Sectoral Adjustment Program.

11. We held discussions with several WFP officials throughout the 2001–2004 period, in which such admissions were frequently made.

12. Andrew S. Natsios, "Food through Force: Humanitarian Intervention and U.S. Policy," *Washington Quarterly* 17(1) (1994): 129–144.

13. "Investing in the United Nations for a Stronger Organization Worldwide," Report of the Secretary-General, section IV.B, para 67.

14. The Independent Inquiry Committee into the United Nations Oil-for-Food Program (the Volcker Commission) website address is http://iic-offp.org/index.html.

15. It was reported to us that officials representing the United Nations Development Group, a body representing UN agencies in New York, formed an agreement with the U.S. government and the World Bank that the UN agencies would receive all of the money from the first two and a half years of donor contributions to Afghanistan after 9/11.

16. See Ashraf Ghani, Michael Carnahan, and Clare Lockhart, "Stability, State Building, and Development Assistance: An Outside Perspective," Princeton Security Project Working Paper; http://www.wws.princeton.edu/ppns/papers/ghani.pdf.

Index

Engineering Africa, 143
entitlement, 138, 204
    quick-impact projects and, 215
    recipients of aid and, 213
entrepreneurship, 152, 227
environment
    global issues, 24
    impact of extractive industries, 157
    impact of projects, 97
    stewardship of, 44
environmental movement, 157
equality, 144. *See also* inequality
Erhard, Ludwig, 152
Eritrea, port reform, 186
Ethiopia, 186
ethnic cleansing, 130, 146
Europe, 222. *See also* European Union
    education spending, 141
    post-World War II recovery, 34–35, 87
European Bank for Reconstruction and
    Development, 162
European Cooperation Administration, 87
European Steel and Coal Community, 35
European Union, 35
    accession of Ireland, 46–47
    accession process, 30, 183, 204
    agricultural subsidies, 154
    banning of airlines, 56
    consensus on citizenship rights, 146
    elimination of trade barriers, 151
    gross domestic product, 234n
    investment in poor regions, 145
    limits on public debt, 161
    mechanisms for coordination, 180, 204, 224
    tax revenues, 136
everyday life, role of state, 54–55
exclusion, 66, 222
    as catalyst for violence, 73–75, 133
    due to lack of infrastructure, 148
    of local businesses from contracts, 98–99
    in social policies, 145–146
excombatants, demobilization of, 212
expatriates, wealth of, 184
expenditure mechanisms, recommendations, 196–197
exploitation, in aid system, 86
exports
    barriers to, 154, 184
    policies, 151
external environment, importance of
    understanding, 170
extractive industries, 57, 185
    disclosure of contracts, 20, 228
    revenues from, 158
    in Sudan, 72
    taxation of, 157
Extractive Industries Transparency Initiative, 228

facilities funding, 89, 95
fair trade, 49
farm subsidies. *See* agricultural subsidies
Federal-Aid Highway Act, 203
federal employees. *See also* civil service
    unnecessary, 136–137
feedback loops, 192
financial capital, 86
financial control, 9
financial flows
    in aid system, 91–95
    illegal, 23–24
financial management, 195. *See also* public finance
    as essential state function, 135–139
    failure of, 139
financial system, 239n
    global transactions, 58
    in Lebanon, 69–70
    in Nepal, 74
fingerprinting, drawbacks of, 78
Finland, use of information technology, 134
flexibility
    balance with predictability, 224
    in government processes, 126
floods, 65
food aid
    cost of transporting, 212
    effect on agricultural markets, 154–155, 214
    fraud in, 213
    targeting and distribution problems, 154, 213
    types of, 212
food-for-work systems, 212
force. *See* military; use of force
foreign investment, quality of administration and, 133
foreign policy
    as foundation for state support, 67
    oil driven, 57
forestry, in Nepal, 74
foundations, expenditures of, 62
France, development of uniformity, 132
freedom of action, 59
freedom of movement, 129–130
frontiers, administrative practices in, 132
Fundación Chile, 188–189
future planning, 172. *See also* visioning
futures funds, 158–159

Gaebler, Ted, 136
G8 and G20 leaders, importance of engaging, 227
gangs, in refugee camps, 106
Garang, John, 71, 72, 187
gender inequality, 146
    in Afghanistan, 208
General Motors, 227
genocide, 68, 130, 146
geological surveys, 185
Georgia, 41, 42, 43
Germany, social market economy, 152
GI Bill of Rights, 140–141, 204
Gilmore, Jim, 42, 45
Gladstone, William, 118
global climate, 159
global communication, 228. *See also* information
    technology
Global Fund to Fight AIDS, TB, and Malaria, 94
global infrastructure index, 149
globalization, 51, 151
    compatibility of rules, 128
    demand for inclusion, 224
    dependence on extractive industries, 57
    factors in failing to adapt to, 133
    Keynes's response to, 62
    obstacles to participation, 58
    participation of Dubai, 173
    ramifications for state building, 9–10, 120
    rents and, 154
    response of Ireland, 47

personal responsibility, fostering, 202
pessimism, 222
philanthropic foundations, assets of, 62
Phillipines, 81–82, 226
Pitt the Younger, William, 236n
Plato, 121
police, in United Kingdom, 129
policy. *See also* social policy
  formulating, 194
  forums for discussing, 182
  importance of budget, 195
  linkage to projects, 218
  recipient countries as drivers of, 87
  relationship with politics and poverty, 82
  role in everyday transactions, 54
  scope of, 199
  value creation and, 60
political elites, 127, 200
  in Afghanistan, 76
  in Chad, 159
  importance of discussions with, 181
  in Nepal, 73, 74
  self-enrichment, 153
political resettlement, in Nepal, 187
politics
  failed, 80, 81
  militarization of, 130
  processes, 165
  relationship with poverty, 82
poppy growing, in Afghanistan, 174, 214
populist movements, catalysts for, 25
post-war reconstruction, 34, 87, 152
poverty, 53, 65–66
  in American South, 40
  attitudes toward, 145
  context of, 68
  entrenchment and social policies, 146
  international responses to, 5
  investment in human capital and, 142
  money and, 82
Poverty Reduction Strategy Paper, 91
power
  arbitrary, 10
  centralization of, 130
  concepts of, 116, 188
  legal limits on, 224
  transfer of, 81, 165, 181
Prachanda, Chairman (Pushpa Kamal Dahal), 75
predictability, 59
  of rules, 224
  trust and, 132–133
press, role in accountability, 133
preventive deployment, 105
preventive health, 141
prioritization, 187
  community as focus for, 134
  need for, 178
private gain, as incentive, 155
private property. *See* property
private-public partnerships, 47–50, 52
  in Afghanistan, 206
private sector
  as agent of stability, 228
  development, 210
  disadvantage of local, 98
  growth of associations, 62
  versus public sector, 49

regulation of, 149–150
  role for competitive, 90
privitization, 154
problem solving
  collective, 188, 189
  as focus of education, 141
  in online communities, 144, 229
procurement, 95. *See also* contracts
  corruption in, 196
  potential positive effects, 100
  procedures, 99, 133
  waste in, 108
production, 188
  automobile, 57, 227
  standards for, 152
product quality, 58
professional networks, 195
professions, emergence of, 140
projects
  addressing human capital and infrastructure, 90
  developmental, 112, 217–218
  estimates of costs and benefits, 163
  implementation, 96, 109
  integration with programs, 219
  linkage to policy, 218
  management, 95–101
  quality, 96, 178
  quick-impact, 106–107, 178
  redundant, 175
  segmentation of, 218
  social impact, 97
  supervision by donors, 96
  sustainability, 97, 107
promises, implementation of, 187
property
  legality of, 21
  rights, 150, 151, 156
  security of, 130
prosecution, immunity of officials from, 79
prosperity, 239n. *See also* wealth creation
  generation of, 6
  inclusiveness of, 174, 221
  intellectual property and, 140
  markets and, 227
  role of private sector, 228
  role of rights, 144
protection. *See* security
Prussia
  administrative reforms, 133
  compulsory education, 140
PSA International, 38
public asset management, as essential state function, 156–160
public borrowing
  as an essential state function, 160–163
  effects of poor decisions, 161
public debt, 118, 139, 161
public finance
  analysis of functions, 196
  rights and obligations and, 120–121
  transformation of, 208–209
public health
  immunization, 208
  investment in, 89, 141
  relation to infrastructure, 148
public opinion, 192, 230
  accountability and, 83

public relations, of aid organizations, 107
public sector
    complaints about, 174
    private sector versus, 49
public value, 122, 136–137, 152
    creation, 133, 193
    networks as source of, 202
purchase of goods, role of trust, 58
Putnam, Robert, 205

quality of life, national parks and, 157
quality-of-life index, 46
quick-impact projects, 106–107, 178
    national programs versus, 215–217
    soundness and quality, 216

race, 146
racism, in American South, 41
railways, 56, 132
Reagan, Ronald, 152
reconstruction. *See also* infrastructure
    community management of, 206
    post-war, 34, 87, 152
recruitment
    of leaders, 191, 200–201
    transparency in, 127, 132, 210
redistribution, 75, 118, 153
referees, effectiveness of, 183
reform, 126, 136–137, 219
    of seaports, 186
refugees, 23, 106, 211–212
    establishing identification, 21
    return to Afghanistan, 214
regulations
    haphazard, 21, 58
    inadequate and market health, 153
    role in everyday life, 55
    role in innovation, 159
reintegration, of refugees, 212
reinventing government, 136–137
rent, 57, 82, 154, 158
reporting, 192, 194, 209
Research Triangle Park, North Carolina, 43–44, 143
resentment
    over project waste, 217
    populist movements and, 25
resources. *See also* natural resources
    diversion in Nepal, 74
    effect of war on public, 23
    mobilization of, 183–186
results-based culture, 191
revenue. *See also* taxation
    collection, 130, 209
    destiny of, 30
    from extractive industries, 158
    generation, 117, 178, 185
    in OECD countries, 136
revolutionary movements, contrasted to civil
    disobedience, 125
rights and obligations, 7–8, 52, 118, 221
    allocation of, 190, 199
    clearly defined, 126, 200
    double compact and, 193
    effect of aid system on, 108
    fostering in Afghanistan, 210

land ownership and, 158
public finances and, 120–121
rule and order and, 129, 201
social policy and, 137–138, 145
Riley, Bob, 41
riparian rights, 156
risk assessment, 162, 163
risk guarantees, 184
risk management, 57, 163, 228
rivers, harnessing, 156
roads. *See also* highways; infrastructure
    in Afghanistan, 75
Rocky Mountain Institute, 208
Roosevelt, Franklin D., 121, 122, 127
root cause analysis, 188
rule of law, 224. *See also* laws
    as essential state function, 121, 122, 125–128
    fragmentation, 100
    generating demand for, 89
    insubordination of military to, 130
    stability and, 126, 180
    as vehicle for dispute resolution, 129
rules
    calibrating, 180, 182–183
    enforcement of, 52, 127
    fairness and inclusiveness, 182
    for forming and expanding captial, 151
    hierarchy of, 179
    legitimacy of, 192
    predictability of, 132–133, 224
    unified, 132, 199
Russia, municipal loans, 162
Russia Coal Sectoral Adjustment Program, 240n
Rwanda, 191

salmon farming industry, in Chile, 188–189
Sarbanes-Oxley Act, 155
savings
    mandatory, 38
    mobilization of, 163
    personal, 20
schools. *See also* education
    management by parents, 74
Schuman, Robert, 35, 87
seaports
    development of, 148
    reform, 186
sector approaches, 218–220
"Securing Afghanistan's Future," 206
security, 129, 130, 221
    achieving sense of, 59
    citizen anxiety, 20
    of commodity production sites, 25
    common understanding and, 179
    costs, 25
    effect on capital, 153
    institutions as managerial systems, 129
    obstacles to global, 14
    -political nexus, 105
    as state function, 59, 165
security firms, 106
segregation, in the American South, 40–41
sequencing, 194, 201
service delivery, role of market, 152
sewage systems, 148
shipping interests, role in food aid, 212

Printed in Great Britain
by Amazon